"In the coming years, one of the most significant private-sector divides will be between companies that embrace collaboration, bridge-building, and collective action to help them thrive and those that remain limited by siloed thinking and poor partnership skills. Gardner and Matviak will help your business ensure it is on the right side of that line."

—**PAUL POLMAN**, former CEO, Unilever; business leader; campaigner; coauthor, *Net Positive*

"The authors' deep grasp of the business world combines with expertise in the psychology underpinning our human foibles. The result is actionable advice for implementing smarter collaboration to capture its financial and human benefits."

—**AMY C. EDMONDSON**, professor, Harvard Business School; author, *The Fearless Organization*

"Gardner and Matviak provide leaders with a clear guide to making smarter collaboration happen. It's full of tips on today's most pressing topics, including hybrid working, inclusion, diversity and equity, and the role of technology and analytics. This is a must-read for any business leader."

—**NHLAMU DLOMU**, Global Head of People, KPMG International

"An organization's culture determines its destiny. *Smarter Collaboration* does an excellent job of showing you how to get a great one."

—**RAY DALIO**, founder, Bridgewater Associates; author, *Principles*

"Everyone talks about collaboration, but relatively few people actually know how to do it effectively. Gardner and Matviak have written the go-to guide for doing collaboration right. Their use cases for smarter collaboration will resonate deeply with any business leader who's seeking to rev up innovation, profitability, and employee engagement."

—**GUNJAN KEDIA**, Vice Chairman, U.S. Bank

"With the scale and complexity of challenges facing business and society today, knowing how to collaborate—how to *really* collaborate—is one of the most important skills of our time. Through pragmatic insight and engaging examples, Gardner and Matviak illuminate a path for leaders that begins with truly valuing the wisdom people bring, and results in innovations beyond what any one group could create alone."

—**SANDY SPEICHER**, former CEO, IDEO

"*Smarter Collaboration* gives a practical blueprint for how leaders can systematically embed collaboration within and across organizational boundaries to achieve more meaningful, purpose-driven outcomes."

—**RANJAY GULATI**, professor, Harvard Business School; author, *Deep Purpose*

"Research-backed, full of case studies and practical advice, this book lays out a realistic road map for leaders who want to implement smarter collaboration and reap the benefits. *Smarter Collaboration* is highly readable and thought provoking."

—**NEIL DHAR**, Vice Chair and Chief Clients Officer, PwC United States

# SMARTER
## COLLABORATION

# SMARTER
# COLLABORATION

## A New Approach to Breaking Down Barriers and Transforming Work

## HEIDI K. GARDNER
## IVAN A. MATVIAK

Harvard Business Review Press

Boston, Massachusetts

Printed in the United States of America

10 9 8 7 6 5 4 3 2 1

Library of Congress Cataloging-in-Publication Data

Names: Gardner, Heidi K., author. | Matviak, Ivan A., author.
Title: Smarter collaboration : a new approach to breaking down barriers
    and transforming work / Heidi K Gardner, Ivan A Matviak.
Description: Boston, Massachusetts : Harvard Business Review Press, [2022] |
    Includes index.
Identifiers: LCCN 2022016717 (print) | LCCN 2022016718 (ebook) |
    ISBN 9781647822743 (hardcover) | ISBN 9781647822750 (epub)
Subjects: LCSH: Cooperation. | Professional corporations. | Success in business. |
    Cooperativeness.
Classification: LCC HD2963 .G37 2022 (print) | LCC HD2963 (ebook) |
    DDC 334—dc23/eng/20220708
LC record available at https://lccn.loc.gov/2022016717
LC ebook record available at https://lccn.loc.gov/2022016718

ISBN: 978-1-64782-274-3
eISBN: 978-1-64782-275-0

The paper used in this publication meets the requirements of the American National Standard for Permanence of Paper for Publications and Documents in Libraries and Archives Z39.48-1992.

*To our daughters Anya and Zoe, and their whole generation
of upcoming smart collaborators.
You are our hope and our future. Remember,
If you want to go fast, go alone;
if you want to go far, go together.*

# CONTENTS

# PREFACE

# The Origins of Smarter Collaboration

This book is an example of smarter collaboration in action. A half decade ago, Harvard Business Review Press published my first book, *Smart Collaboration*. As my thinking evolved and my work with organizations expanded, I came to see both the tremendous untapped opportunities related to smart collaboration and the limits of my own experiences and knowledge base in pursuing those opportunities. So as I explain later, I took my own advice and joined forces with a smart collaborator—Ivan Matviak. You'll hear from him in a moment.

*Smart Collaboration* drew on my somewhat eclectic experiences over the previous two decades or so, in both the academic and professional worlds. I had earned graduate degrees in organizational behavior from the London School of Economics and London Business School, and I had spent five years working as a consultant for McKinsey & Company. The result—as I can now see in retrospect—was a perspective that was both data driven and strategy oriented.

I subsequently broadened that perspective through a decade of teaching and research at Harvard's business and law schools, both institutions with a keen interest in the intersection of theory and practice. My research at that time focused on the economics and working practices of large, complex professional service firms (PSFs): law firms, accountancies, consulting and engineering firms, and so on. Several of those PSFs granted me extraordinary and unprecedented access to their financials, for which I will always be grateful. I learned a lot from them, and with them.

*Smart Collaboration* focused on a challenge confronting those leading PSFs. Their clients increasingly needed them to tackle the kinds of VUCA problems—volatile, uncertain, complex, and ambiguous—that only multidisciplinary, cross-functional teams of experts could address effectively. But PSFs had historically organized themselves into narrowly defined and highly specialized practice areas—an organizational structure that tended to make intrafirm collaboration messy, risky, and expensive.

My decade of research revealed an important insight: *Firms that figured out how to collaborate across silos, building teams of experts with complementary expertise, gained a major competitive edge over those that did not.* That edge took many forms. For example, collaborative firms tended to move into higher-margin work, gain more satisfied clients, improve their lateral hiring, decrease enterprise risk, innovate faster, engage their employees more fully, and strengthen their bottom-line results.

Highly collaborative individuals benefited as well. Practitioners who thrived successfully built networks across boundaries within the firm and then invoked those networks to deliver higher-value work to clients.

And this turned out to be a virtuous circle. Solving one complex client problem collaboratively—in a realm like cybersecurity, or mergers and acquisitions, or cross-border trade—earned those collaboration-oriented practitioners the opportunity to get involved in bigger (and more lucrative) challenges down the road. The individuals, their firm, and ultimately their clients all benefited.

I came to call this virtuous circle *smart collaboration*, which became the focus and title of that first book. *Smart Collaboration* caused a bit of a stir. It became a *Washington Post* bestseller and was recognized among PSFs as the go-to resource on collaboration. I continued to advocate for the book's main prescriptions, advising PSF leaders and speaking to tens of thousands of people at hundreds of events around the world. Through that advocacy, I noticed a surprising phenomenon: whereas my initial clients and audiences tended to consist mainly of representatives from PSFs, over time, more and more private-sector and not-for-profit leaders reached out to me. My research and client work increasingly focused on corporations, government agencies, and nongovernmental organizations. The marketplace, I realized, was confirming that smart collaboration had implications far beyond the world of PSFs. Drawing on this broader framework, I wrote multiple collaboration-oriented *Harvard Business Review* articles, including "The Overcommitted Organization" (2017, with Mark Mortensen) that laid the foundations for Chapter 12 in this book and "Collaboration in a Crisis" (2020).

My coauthor on that second article was Ivan A. Matviak. I'll turn it over to him now.

. . .

Over the years, Heidi and I talked about how the concepts of smart collaboration were evolving. During the Covid-19 pandemic, we worked together on a couple of articles published in *Harvard Business Review.*

Those articles were well-received, and the two of us—who happen to be married—decided to collaborate on a new book. While she was writing the first book, I had served as a real-world sounding board, and early on we discussed applying the ideas beyond PSFs to various industries I've worked in. My own experiences working around the world and across several industries—for example, as president of a software company, in executive roles at a major global bank, as a consultant at Bain & Company, and as an adviser to private equity firms—added new dimensions to the research and ideas in this book.

. . .

From that point on, we've been working as a pair of smart collaborators—bringing different expertise, experiences, and perspectives to bear on a complex problem. The "I" narrative voice of *Smart*

*Collaboration* turned into the "we" of *Smarter Collaboration*. In that spirit, we welcome you to the broader horizons of smarter collaboration.

—Heidi K. Gardner and
Ivan Matviak

# Get Smarter about Collaboration

R ight now, the stakes for effective collaboration could not be higher. A fly-on-the-wall visit to a Bay Area fintech company we'll call ModFin provides a typical business example.

Oren Weiss runs a key division at ModFin, and he knows that his team and the larger company are in trouble. For the past few years, competitors have been faster to market with new products, and ModFin has lost several important clients. Meanwhile, the challenges faced by the entire fintech sector have been mounting steadily—for example, meeting ever-greater demands for complex data and analytics, enhancing the user experience through personalized services, and complying with regulations. Weiss knows that only companies that address these challenges will survive.

ModFin has hardly been coasting. Like many of its competitors, it took advantage of remote working to hire new developers and salespeople in Edinburgh, Boston, Austin, Mumbai, and Miami—all while growing in double digits.

But Weiss is pretty sure it's not all rosy. To him, it feels like ModFin's culture, formerly a strong suit, is declining. His team members seem to have lost the sense of pride, ownership, and excitement they felt in the fintech's startup days.

Weiss decides that broad-based collaboration on a big, meaningful project might help revive that sense of purpose. Toward that end, he pulls together a cross-functional, company-wide team to rethink their product road map: What new functionalities should they develop, and how can they get there *faster*?

Using a combination of in-person meetings and remote teaming platforms, the group spends two days brainstorming ideas. While the sessions seem reasonably productive, several things give him pause:

- Most in-person attendees are members of Weiss's long-standing core team, who have worked together for years. Left to their own devices, they are likely to regroup on their own after the sessions to decide what's *really* going to happen.

- Meanwhile, the people participating through the company's video platform are mostly new to ModFin, aren't familiar with other participants' roles, and struggle to contribute to the sessions.

- A product manager from another division says, "OK, but I don't really see how my products fit in."

- Several of his senior engineers roll their eyes whenever one of the younger digital marketing managers puts an idea on the table.

- One of the new hot-shot developers seems to be tuning out during much of the conversation. Over lunch, Weiss asks her what's going on. "Sorry," the developer replies. "But this is the seventh project I've been asked to work on this month. I'm tapped out."

Overall, Weiss's instincts are on target. ModFin does indeed have problems, external and internal, and fixing those problems will require new kinds of input. And this is the same conclusion that many savvy business leaders today are reaching: success going forward will *absolutely demand* multifaceted inputs, necessitating more and better collaboration both within their organizations and with outside partners.

And by the way, this same challenge faces all kinds of complex organizations. Yes, for-profits need to find ways to get ahead of their business challenges, to serve their customers better, or to more consistently engage in more profitable work. At the same time, though, nonprofits also want to carry out their missions more effectively.

So collaboration has become a hot topic. Across many sectors and industries, organizations are realizing that they have to get better at collaboration, and many are plunging in. But it's easy to get implementation wrong and fall into what might be called "collaboration traps."

For example, some leaders treat collaboration as a magic cure-all, as if all they need to do is form a team and their challenges will go away. Others consider collaboration an "initiative" that can be "implemented" and then left to fend for itself. Some organizations focus on collaboration as a goal in and of itself. In those cases, collaboration becomes an explicit "organizational value." This *sounds* good, but in practice, it often means that people aren't shown how specific collaborative behaviors will help realize the company's strategic goals. Some managers wind up throwing teams at every problem, which commits valuable employees to too many different projects and thus stretches good people too thin. Some leaders instruct people to collaborate on X, Y, or Z without equipping them with the skills or technology to do it well. Some go the exact opposite route, showering people with teamworking technologies on the assumption that getting people "wired up right" will lead naturally to great outcomes. Some companies develop strong implementation plans but backtrack in the face of a crisis or retrench when they don't get the quick payback they are hoping for. Many leaders fail to realize how badly managed collaboration can undermine their already complicated diversity, equity, and inclusion initiatives.

This is a sobering list of collaborative traps, myths, and missteps, and the danger is real. But what about the upside? What about *smart* collaboration? Done right, collaboration *works*, and it amply rewards those organizations that embrace it. In the half-decade since the publication of *Smart Collaboration*, we have seen many organizations deeply transformed through their embrace of the concepts we laid out in that book. They have accelerated innovation, improved service, and enhanced employee engagement. In the process, they also generated higher revenues and profits, gained market share, and accelerated growth. Nonprofits have experienced similar gratifying results from effective collaboration, advancing their strategies in new and compelling ways.

This past half-decade has given us the opportunity to research how these diverse organizations have rolled out their collaboration initiatives, and to assess their results. Based on solid implementations of collaboration in an ever-broader range of sectors, we've continued to refine our understanding of its basic tenets. Organizations ranging from the Dana-Farber Cancer Institute to Bridgewater Associates to PwC to the US CyberSpace Solarium Commission have worked with us, pushed our thinking, and helped us make real contributions to the field.[1] Through this iterative process, our definition of *smart collaboration* has gotten broader and deeper.

Now it's time to take these ideas to the next level. We need to consolidate learnings about best practices and provide a road map for execution. Looking forward, it's the right juncture to help new people, teams, and companies get into *smarter* collaboration—and thereby reap the benefits of a uniquely powerful approach to organizing, deploying, and retaining some of their most important talent. That's what this book is about.

## The Whys, Whos, and Hows of Smarter Collaboration

*Smart Collaboration* focused primarily on the *why*. It stressed that the benefits of cross-functional collaboration are real and can be measured: outcomes like revenues, profits, customer loyalty, diversity, and employee attraction, retention, and engagement. In other words, smart collaboration is far from a "soft" topic or a "nice to have." Instead, it's at the very heart of how savvy organizations operate today.

Over the past half-decade, we've conducted more than four hundred in-depth interviews with senior corporate leaders. Based in part on that input, we've launched collaboration pilot projects with some of the world's leading companies, applying the concepts of smarter collaboration to address real-world obstacles and drive successes.

Building on these foundations, *Smarter Collaboration* continues to make the *why* case—now expanded to reflect our work in such diverse industries as financial services, health care, biotech and pharma, consumer products, automotive, technology, telecoms and media, energy, government, and higher education. But *Smarter Collaboration* goes much further, with a new emphasis on the *who* and *how*.

For example, when it comes to *who*, we now recommend a focus on *who thinks differently from me,* as well as *who knows something different from me.* In the past half-decade, diversity, equity, and inclusion issues have come to the fore in a wide range of organizational settings. *Diversity* means an appropriate mix of function-related talents that must contribute to solving the problem at hand, such as marketing, product, finance, and technology. But it also means a purposeful mix of educational, geographic, and economic backgrounds, as well as genders and ethnicities, especially if the problem extends beyond the purely technical.

Reflecting another new dimension of *who*, we also explore third-party collaboration, which has become significantly more important since the publication of the previous book. Just as professionals must increasingly specialize in their domain to develop deep expertise, so too must organizations focus their talent and resources to differentiate themselves from the competition. This means they need to collaborate with experts outside their own boundaries.

By design, this book asks and answers practical questions. What are the barriers to smart collaboration? How are they overcome? And those answers, again, come directly from the front lines. For example, we worked with one very large company for more than three years across forty-five countries, starting from scratch and continuing through the codevelopment, testing, and rolling out of tailored solutions around the world. These real-world collaborators consistently pushed us to focus on implementation: *why, who,* and *how.*

Today, we continue to work with a growing list of complex institutions to refine these practical solutions. Collectively, these experiences help anchor our narrative in up-to-the-minute organizational realities. For example, how do corporations break down internal silos to generate innovative solutions to customers' most complex problems and thereby drive profitable growth? How do companies use technology, data, and analytics to facilitate, analyze, and continually improve collaboration—especially given the realities of hybrid working? How do organizations work across government, corporate, and nongovernmental organization boundaries to address some of society's biggest challenges like climate change? The rich examples in this book will show vividly how smart collaboration goes well beyond classic teaming.

## THE FUNDAMENTALS OF SMARTER COLLABORATION

Throughout this book, we'll use three lenses to explore smarter collaboration:

### The WHY

- Hyperintentional to tackle truly complex issues
- Aimed at achieving breakthrough insights, innovation, and transformational change
- Focused on a sense of purpose

### The WHO

- The *right* number of team members
- Expanding beyond the boundaries of the "usual suspects"
- Diverse in expertise, perspectives, and other aspects

### The HOW

- Inclusive: not just having people on the team, but truly engaging them
- Tech- and tool-based to facilitate communication, support hybrid working, analyze performance, and increase efficiency
- Measured: both collaboration and the related outcomes
- Developmental: creating real-time learning environments to increase collaborative capabilities

# The Road Map

*Smarter Collaboration* consists of four parts. Part 1, *The Case for Smarter Collaboration*, lays out the competitive arguments in favor of collaboration (Chapter 1: The Business Case) and moves on to the talent case—that is, why embracing smart collaboration helps companies recruit, engage, and retain great people (Chapter 2: The Talent Case).

Part 2, *Assessing Your Collaborative Starting Point*, presents a set of methodologies for judging the strength of your collaborative foundations. The organizational diagnostic, Chapter 3 (Enterprise-Wide Diagnostic), presents a powerful approach to assess your company's collaborative opportunities and prioritize actions to deliver a return on your efforts. We have also developed a toolkit, available through Harvard Business Review Press, with practical templates, instructions, and approaches for applying the concepts in your organization.[2] Chapter 4 (Individual and Team Diagnostic) presents a new way of looking at the behaviors underlying smarter collaboration, so that every person can understand how to use their natural way of operating as a strength to contribute to collaborative teams.

Part 3, *How-To's and Use Cases for Smarter Collaboration*, provides a holistic approach to the *who* and *how* of collaboration.

Starting with building a collaborative talent pool, Chapter 5 (Collaborating to Succeed at Hiring and M&A) shows how collaboration helps solve a major problem that has stumped organizations for decades: making sure that the people you bring aboard—whether through recruitment or acquisition—actually stick around, become profitable, and thrive in the long run.

No matter how you grow your employee base, how do you motivate people to engage in collaboration rather than individualistic endeavors? Chapter 6 (Paying People to Collaborate?) presents a comprehensive three-part system that combines aspirational goals and performance metrics, discussions aimed at performance improvement and development, and a revamped annual compensation review.

Even the most motivated performers need strategically aligned structures to help them take full advantage of their collaborative efforts. In Chapter 7 (Collaborating through a Sector Lens), we explore how a company can adopt sector-oriented structures that encourage people across the organization to integrate their unique views and generate more holistic solutions that are tailored to a customer's industry. Since all of those transformative efforts require significant ongoing vigilance and leadership, Chapter 8 (Leading and Sustaining a Collaborative Transformation) tackles the challenge of supporting collaborative efforts over time. It lays out a practical approach to embed collaboration so that it takes root and thrives long term.

This sets the stage for the final chapter in this part (Chapter 9: Collaborating with Outside Partners). Truly smarter collaboration involves recognizing the limits of your own organization and then finding external partners with complementary expertise. We show how to cultivate a collaborative ecosystem well beyond your own borders.

The other side of "how" is "how not to." *Troubleshooting Collaboration Challenges* is the fourth of our four parts. Chapter 10 (Watch Out: The Illusion of Inclusion) is purposefully provocative. We argue that mismanaged collaboration, especially when it is used to provide a veneer of diversity, can actually marginalize certain workers. Without strategic oversight and measurement, collaboration can create the appearance of diversity without real inclusion.

Mismanaged collaboration creates pitfalls beyond inclusion. In times of crisis, the strain on individuals and teams can destroy trust and weaken collaboration. Chapter 11 (Watch Out: Pressure Undermines Collaboration) shows how to sustain a collaborative culture during crises, which can help separate your organization from the pack and set you up for a strong postcrisis rebound.

Chapter 12 (Watch Out: The Overcommitted Organization) explores the roots and perils of asking people to take on too much in the name of collaboration. For example, some companies throw teams nonstrategically at every problem, on the assumption that *if some collaboration is good, more must be better.* But spreading resources too thin and overusing teams for routine work leads to bottlenecks and burnout. We describe steps that can be taken on three levels—senior leader, teams, and individuals—both to head off overcommitment and to manage it when it arises.

Our concluding chapter, Chapter 13 (The Next Frontiers of Smarter Collaboration), foreshadows the exciting future of smarter collaboration, presenting overarching principles that we derive from the preceding chapters.

This leads us to one last introductory thought: *smarter collaboration should be at the top of every senior leader's agenda,* because it is essential for addressing the highest-value challenges and opportunities in today's complex, data-rich, war-for-talent setting.

At the end of the day, collaborative success hinges on leadership focus and strategic execution. We hope that *Smarter Collaboration* helps you get there.

# PART ONE

# THE CASE FOR SMARTER COLLABORATION

$$\left[\ 1\ \right]$$

# The Business Case for Smarter Collaboration

Picture a huge, multinational consumer electronics company headquartered in Europe. We'll call it PremierTech.

By all accounts, PremierTech in the early twenty-first century was a highly siloed operation, characterized by a command-and-control management style. When Jen Baker arrived as the new chief technology officer for the audio/video division, she often found herself stymied by divisional and functional barriers. The company had products in more than a dozen separate divisions—audio/video, health, home products, personal care, and so on—each of which was run as a separate P&L. Each had its own empire to support it: production, software development, sales, distribution, and so forth. This siloed structure meant that PremierTech was very fragmented, without much benefit from shared design thinking or interoperability, and with limited scale and innovation.

Initially Baker pulled together an informal team of about two dozen disparate individuals, including software engineers, product designers, manufacturing experts, and people from the procurement, finance, and legal teams. "We had conversations about innovations we were starting to see at trade shows and in the market, and the team members would build off each other," says Baker. "These were people who had worked at PremierTech for twenty years, and for the most part still didn't know each other. But they knew our products, and they understood the market. We realized that we were making many, many, many suboptimal decisions because those decisions were all being made in isolation."

Baker and her team of renegades hit on the idea of a home automation hub, drawing on their disparate perspectives to figure out what capabilities various residential customers would be interested in. Someone would pose a question (*What can our system do to help elderly people in their homes?*), and representatives from multiple functions would work together to answer the question. The home automation hub that eventually emerged from this process wound up being packaged into many of PremierTech's home, health, and personal care products, drawing together formerly disparate groups to an unprecedented degree.

"It was such a novel way of working for us," Baker told us. "We tapped into all the brains that were needed, and it produced really strong financial results. Plus, people were thrilled to be working on this. For the first time in ages, our innovations were market-leading, and it made everyone from engineers to marketeers proud to be part of PremierTech."

This was a success in and of itself. But even more important, it persuaded the company's leaders to rethink how they organized and operated, because they realized how much more innovative and successful they could be when they broke down silos and transformed work.

PremierTech got lucky.

They were lucky that Baker was a determined change-maker. They were lucky that she was able to build a network of colleagues across multiple functions and geographies, and that those colleagues shared her interest in coming up with creative solutions to the company's challenges. As a result, PremierTech had the opportunity to move from counting on luck to relying on a new way of working—effective, cross-functional collaboration, which we refer to as *smart collaboration*.

Smart collaboration involves highly specialized experts working together across traditional business silos to define and solve more complex problems—and pursue more lucrative opportunities—than any single group could do on its own. This chapter makes the case that smart collaboration is a significant driver of five major outcomes at the organizational level: *revenues and profits*, and the equivalent mission-driven outcomes for nonprofit organizations; faster *innovation* and better adoption; *customer loyalty* and retention; higher *efficiency*; and transparency and *risk reduction*.

Many companies think they're already doing a lot of collaboration. This raises the question, *If collaboration is already common, why do we need to win over more people and organizations?* Well, first, not everyone has been persuaded. Most organizations still have holdouts who believe that operating independently gives them the greatest degree of power and therefore increases their chances of getting ahead. And second, even in organizations that have embraced collaboration generally, there is often a significant gap between what the corporate strategy proclaims ("Collaboration is one of our four strategic pillars!") and the extent to which employees actually collaborate ("It's not really part of my day job; it's more like the thing we get around to when our real work is done").

So we still need to make a compelling business case for why leaders should embrace and promote collaboration. Let's review each of the foregoing arguments in favor of smart collaboration in turn, starting with money: How does collaboration help the bottom line?

## Smart Collaboration Boosts Revenues and Profits (and Performance Outcomes for Nonprofits)

Simply stated, collaboration across functions, business units, and geographies leads to better financial outcomes for companies. Let's consider revenues first, followed by profits. Then we'll look at similarly consequential performance outcomes for organizations that are not driven by profits.

### Revenues

Let's take a commercial real estate company as our first example. When they provide a single service to a client—say, leasing to a retail chain—that service might generate $x$ dollars: a straightforward fee for service. But what if they can make that service part of a larger property management lifecycle solution, focused on how to optimize a client's real estate portfolio over time? What if they can offer a solution that necessarily includes planning, finance, leasing, acquisition, disposal, consulting, property management, and more? If that happens, the leasing activity becomes more valuable, because it is integrated with other disciplines to create a differentiated, value-adding strategy.

Stated differently, leasing alone can be viewed as a commoditized offering; but in combination with other disciplines, it becomes strategic. And we don't mean to pick on commercial real estate leasing here; the same considerations and calculations hold true across a broad range of disciplines. Those disciplines are more valuable when they are integrated, and less valuable when they are freestanding. Capturing that exponential value requires experts from each of those separate disciplines (planning, finance, property management, etc.) to come together in a way that we call smart collaboration.

Figure 1-1 depicts this. It shows rising revenue per customer even as five, six, and seven business lines become involved. Note that as more units collaborate on a client project or product offering, the average annual revenue from that offering (the bars) increases almost exponentially, over and above what each unit would have earned from providing services in a discrete, siloed way (the flatter, hypothetical trend line at the bottom of the graph). In fact, in this company, we saw that revenues were 7.1 times higher for accounts served by three business lines than by a single one. Those customers served by five business lines generated fees 20.4 times higher than those with just one kind of service.

Our work reveals this pattern time and time again across a wide array of organizations, ranging from technology companies and financial institutions to traditional professional services firms like law and accounting. The underlying principles apply to both companies that are international and those that are entirely domestic and that range from very small to giant.[1]

Why? Where does the upside come from? It's not about a simple cross-sell, as in, *Do you want fries with that?*[2] Having a broader range of people—executives, product managers, client-service experts, technologists, and finance managers—involved with a client in a

**FIGURE 1-1**

## More collaborators, more revenues

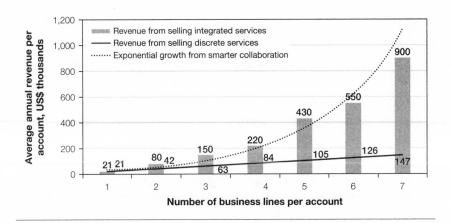

coordinated way gives you more information about that client's needs, priorities, and preferences. If your account teams communicate effectively among themselves (and that's a big "if" that can't be left to chance), you can leverage these insights to spot opportunities to support the client (and generate revenue) that your less engaged competitors might overlook.

Of course, some of the new work may be discrete projects or products—in the case of our commercial real estate company, for example, a contract to handle building maintenance for all of a client's properties in one city. But the big value-add opportunity arises when those individual units bring together their intel—that is, what they picked up in the course of the simple project—and *think together* about the customer's more complex challenges. That's how they start to identify the big questions and answer them in innovative, sophisticated ways.

When you address the bigger, more complex challenges of the sort faced by chief-level officers, you gain access to more senior executives who have broader responsibilities, larger budgets, and more sophisticated needs. And, of course, the more excellent work that you do for very senior executives, the greater your reputation and perceived legitimacy inside the client organization.

That said, you don't need to be working at the board level for smart collaboration to have a major impact on revenue. One global retail

## GROWTH THROUGH STRATEGIC PARTNERING

Relationship growth is a long-term endeavor. Not every new piece of business immediately drives big increases in revenues, given that the next opportunity may be with a small product or from a smaller region. What the data shows, however, is that as you expand your product or service offerings within a given client, the revenue grows *exponentially*. Why? Again, because you become a more strategic partner.

Let's look at a simple example of DrinkCo, which sells its extensive product line into a global hotel operator. The first sale was to the customer's "all suites" brand. As DrinkCo's reputation grew, it started selling into the hotel chain's premium brand, budget brand, and golf resort brand. Of course, the "acquisition" of each of these new brands brought in incremental and welcome revenue. But more important, DrinkCo's account leaders started quarterly business reviews with each brand's executive team in which they discussed strategy and operations, focusing on how the DrinkCo product lineup, distribution, and promotional offerings could better support the hotels' seasonality and other fluctuations.

With this deeper understanding, DrinkCo deliberately *evolved* its product. It addressed the unique needs of each brand and meanwhile created solutions across the businesses, which allowed the hospitality group to tap into better data, generate insights, and deliver both cost savings and better guest experiences. That strategic value allowed DrinkCo to not only sell an expanded line of products but also experiment with more innovative offerings that commanded premium prices.

---

bank we worked with provides a clear demonstration of this phenomenon. Our research uncovered patterns of collaboration that distinguished the highest-performing branches, where different kinds of bankers played discrete roles in collectively generating higher-quality, integrated offerings for customers. In these branches, the frontline bankers used a combination of data, personal interfaces, and targeted outreach to identify customers' needs and generate interest in the bank's products. Product specialists then leveraged their expertise to create customized offerings that generated higher value for the customer.

FIGURE 1-2

## Outcomes of collaboration within bank branches

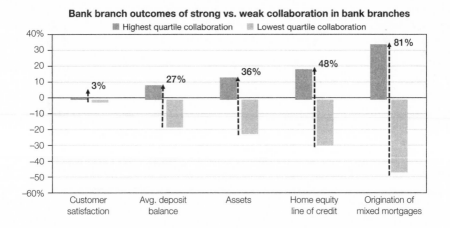

Bank branch outcomes of strong vs. weak collaboration in bank branches

■ Highest quartile collaboration　　■ Lowest quartile collaboration

*Note*: "0" on Y axis is average level of collaboration.

After controlling for a host of related variables, including the relative affluence of the neighborhoods and the number of nearby competitors, our analyses showed not only that more collaborative branches ultimately generated significantly higher revenue with those specific products but also that the deeper and broader relationships translated into greater customer loyalty. Figure 1-2 illustrates the difference between more and less collaborative branches.

Not surprisingly, these kinds of outcomes required significantly higher effort and genuine collaboration at the branch level, which presupposes both focus and motivation. Guidelines from headquarters direct the branch manager's attention toward creating an environment in which employees work together to achieve collective goals: an example of the end-to-end goals we discuss in Chapter 6. The product specialists, who serve multiple branches, play a critical role in spreading institutional wisdom and motivating the front line to make these additional efforts. "The jelly donuts make a difference," one executive observed. "A mortgage specialist who brings treats to a branch builds stronger relationships with the frontline bankers. It's the power of the team that ultimately makes the difference."

FIGURE 1-3

## Firm X portfolio: Collaborating for clients

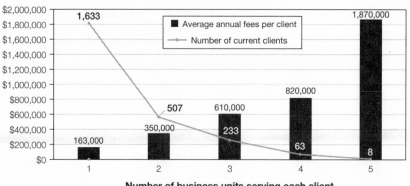

Number of business units serving each client

Our analyses show that most companies leave *enormous* amounts of money on the table when their business units don't collaborate. Figure 1-3 is pretty typical across the organizations we've studied. As we saw earlier, revenues increase dramatically with each additional business unit that joins the mix. The descending lines show that this company serves most clients with just one offering and has fewer and fewer clients as the service offerings broaden (the "long tail" problem). In Chapter 3, we dive into ways to run thought experiments with your data to quantify just how much potential upside is there for you to capture. Everywhere that we've conducted this exercise, the resulting number has been eye-popping.

For multinational companies, is *cross-border* collaboration more lucrative? Generally, yes, because cross-border work is often especially complex and demanding—whether it's a software company supporting the complex regulatory requirements in myriad countries, a logistics company providing global support to a multinational manufacturer, or an investment bank supporting a multicountry merger and acquisition deal. Realistically, each new region may not provide an exponential revenue bump; as a bank expands internationally with its customers, it may grow from serving only the customer's London headquarters to serving their far-flung operations around the globe. Winning the Malaysian business will be a smaller victory than securing the UK business, obviously. But by growing with the customer, the bank becomes a more deeply embedded strategic partner.

These kinds of gains tend to be enduring, as well—especially because collaboration generates higher customer retention and customer satisfaction, as we discuss later.

## Profits

Let's move on to profits. The kinds of holistic solutions developed through collaboration create the ability to not only deliver more solutions to existing buyers at your customer but also be more profitable. As you move up the food chain at your customer, work for the C-suite is likely to be the most critical and therefore the most valuable and highest margin. Further, expanding your relationship with existing customers is less expensive (total cost of sales including marketing costs, time, etc.) than landing work with new customers. In other words, this is a win along two key dimensions: higher-margin work with a lower cost of sale.

One senior manager at a consulting firm described it in these terms:

> When a board needs advice, I guarantee they're not asking the procurement department's permission on whom to hire. Recently some headlines hit about forced labor in a certain country, and my client's board commissioned a supply chain review that required collaboration across experts from human rights, operations, regulatory, data science, and lots more. We could never have sold this in at a lower level, and the margin was excellent.

Generally, "moving the client to the right" (to reinvoke the results shown in Figure 1-3) broadens the *scope* of work toward more sophisticated, multiline solutions. Again, this move takes you out of the commodity game and into the realm of differentiated products and services.

Let's look at a simple example from a tech and data provider we'll call ReachPro. The company's core product was data that tracked the effectiveness of marketing campaigns, which subscribers downloaded and analyzed. Most customers used a third-party's data-visualization software to help them detect patterns in the data. But integrating these two software packages was a cumbersome process, so when

## COLLABORATION ON THE INDIVIDUAL LEVEL

Our main focus in this chapter is on the corporate/organizational level. But we should also emphasize that engaging in smarter collaboration delivers real benefits to individuals, too.

Check out the results for two senior people inside one organization. They share so many demographic and professional similarities that we jokingly refer to them as "twins": they hold the same level and role inside the same department of their firm, they're both men of the same age who joined the company at roughly the same time. Yet their collaborative patterns are very different, as you see in the figure on the facing page.

Every dot represents a peer of the twins (the twins are circled), and the lines connecting them show that those people have worked together on at least one project for a significant amount of time in the year we studied them. Notice that Twin 1 worked with six colleagues this year, three of whom were within his department. Twin 2 collaborated with more than thirty other people, nearly three-quarters of whom were outside his department.

Here's the kicker: we measured a set of business outcomes for each twin, such as the revenue growth and profitability of clients they led, customer satisfaction, and team health. *Twin 2's outcomes were more than four times better than Twin 1's.*

---

ReachPro began offering a data-visualization tool optimized to analyze the data it provided, uptake was dramatic. The new ReachPro tool was easy to use, and it came prepackaged with reports and graphs directly linked to the marketing data, allowing the company to charge a slight premium over the generic products in the market.

Because ReachPro was selling exclusively to existing data customers, moreover, the cost of sales was low. Most executives understand intuitively that expanding existing relationships is one of the most cost-effective ways to grow. If companies had a way of capturing the true cost of sales—and many don't actually track this number accurately—most would find that it requires less time, effort,

What our empirical analyses (and those of many other scholars) repeatedly show is that a broad-based network generally helps a person reap many of the same benefits that collaboration generates for organizations: stronger innovation, more opportunities, better financial outcomes, and so on. Of course, these results hinge on a person's ability to *use* their network effectively, which is the focus of many of our upcoming chapters.

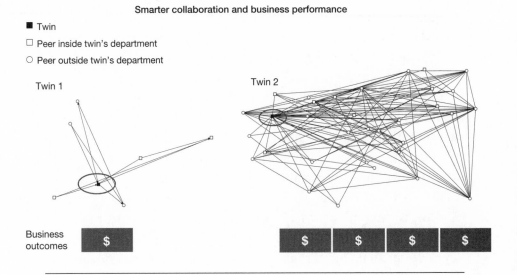

**Smarter collaboration and business performance**

■ Twin
□ Peer inside twin's department
○ Peer outside twin's department

Twin 1

Twin 2

Business outcomes

marketing expense, and risk to convert an existing customer into a one that uses the full breadth of services than it does to woo a brand-new customer of equal size away from a competitor.

The bottom line: *collaboration helps companies grow their profits.*

## Mission-Critical Outcomes beyond Profit

What if your focus isn't revenue and profit, but other kinds of performance outcomes? Maybe you work for a government agency tasked with enhancing the nation's cyber security. Or perhaps your work in the medical field focuses you on patient outcomes. In these examples, and in many other corners of the not-for-profit world, smarter collaboration can drive better results.

Let's take a quick look at health care. Patients are what matter most, and in most health-care scenarios, positive patient outcomes absolutely *demand* collaboration. When surgeons partner with patients, caregivers, nurses, case workers, and advocates to coordinate patient-care activities and communicate the right information to the right people at the right time, all the players are better positioned to provide safe, appropriate, and effective care.[3]

In fact, this kind of collaboration across hospital functions and occupations can reduce hospital readmission rates—in one documented case, by nearly 20 percent.[4] This was a clear win-win: not only did patients enjoy better outcomes—who wants to go *back* to the hospital?—but providers saved an average of $15,000 per patient, enabling them to serve more patients and serve them better.[5]

Successful collaboration in the health-care field not only occurs in traditional settings; it sometimes extends all the way to your wrist. In an innovative collaboration between technology and health-care providers, wearable remote monitoring devices allowed nurses, nutritionists, and health-care specialists to offer their patients individualized support and education, all drawing on multiple clinical specialties. A pilot study conducted with over five hundred patients, for example, used secure messaging to increase adherence to treatment and improve outcomes for chronic myeloid leukemia patients.[6] As a result of this innovative digital collaboration, pilot participants were 22 percent more likely to stick to their treatment regime.[7]

Again, this is only a quick sampling in two corners of an enormous economic sector. But it serves to illustrate our larger point, which is that even in realms where the bottom line doesn't necessarily involve dollars, collaboration leads to better outcomes—and may also save money.

## Smart Collaboration Accelerates Innovation and Adoption

Many of us were raised on tales of the lone scientist burning the midnight oil, working against long odds and universal skepticism, until he finally had a eureka moment and delivered a brilliant breakthrough to the world. A more recent version of the same story celebrates the single-minded entrepreneur beavering away in his garage, maybe in cahoots with a nerdy friend, and coming up with . . . the personal computer!

These tales inspire us, of course—that's what they're meant to do—but they are less and less reflective of today's reality. In nearly every domain, two trends work against the freestanding genius. The first is that, by necessity, our individual expertise continues to narrow into ever-deeper specializations. Meanwhile, the complexity of the problems that we're trying to solve continues to increase. The result is predictable. Research into patent applications over the last twenty years clearly shows that innovation happens increasingly among *teams* working together on a project.

See Figure 1-4. The average number of inventors per patent has grown steadily, almost linearly, from 1976 through 2020. Meanwhile, the number of patents with as many as seven contributing inventors continues to grow steadily.[8] Increasingly, breakthrough ideas require collaboration among individuals with diverse ideas and expertise. If the Day of the Lone Inventor ever truly existed, that time has passed.

These trends apply to innovation within companies as well. It's not enough to come up with a big idea; that idea also has to get to market. After all, innovation is applied creativity.[9] Organizations need to turn that idea into a product or service offering—often, a task that itself requires cross-silo work—and then bring that product or service to market, which requires further collaboration across multiple functional areas. In this complex sequence, intracompany collaboration increases the speed of discovery, the application of that discovery to products, and the introduction of novel offerings to the market.

In addition, innovation increasingly involves collaboration with third parties along every step of the process of making a discovery and applying it—creation, marketing, production, and distribution. In Chapter 9, we focus on the whys and hows of collaborating with third parties—up to and including partnerships with competitors. Through these kinds of partnerships, diverse organizations bring together their unique capabilities, intellectual property, services, and

FIGURE 1-4

# Average number of inventors per patent

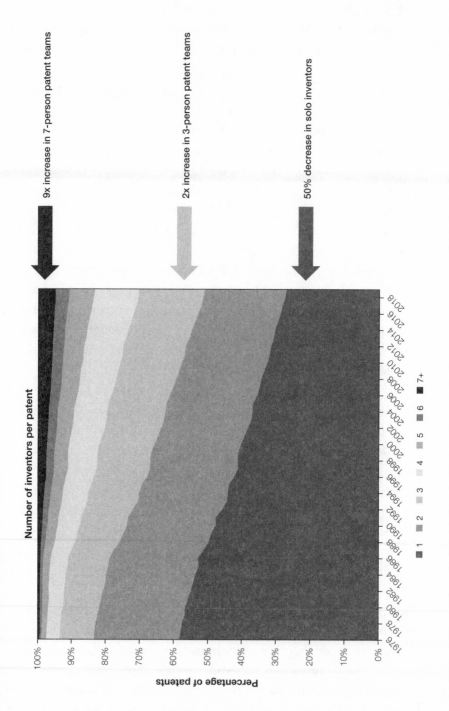

Source: D. Crouch, "Teams of Inventors: Trends in Patenting," Patently-O, January 30, 2019, https://patentlyo.com/patent/2019/01/inventors-trends-patenting.html.

products to develop a differentiated and specialized solution to target customer needs. Done well, that combination creates more value than the sum of its parts, and it can capture market share faster than traditional product-development approaches.[10]

And remember, collaboration is crucial for the kinds of innovation that may have far more impact than traditional business outcomes. For example, Terramera, an agricultural technology company based in Vancouver, Canada, has emphasized innovative collaboration at the heart of its operation. One of the company's key initiatives is to scale the practice of regenerative agriculture, which, says Terramera, results in wins for consumers, farmers, and the planet. The numbers are dramatic. Regenerative farming is estimated to be 78 percent more profitable.[11] It's better for the environment: every 1 percent increase in organic matter results in as much as twenty thousand gallons of available soil water per acre.[12] Finally, regenerative agriculture results in healthier crops, which yield, on average, 34 percent more vitamin K, 11 percent more calcium, and 15 percent more vitamin E.[13]

Despite the many benefits associated with regenerative farming, it is hard to persuade the world's farmers to go this route. It requires super-collaboration across many stakeholders to solve this challenge—including scientists, governments, farmers, agronomists, investors, universities, and many more.

To drive home the value, Terramera has brought together experts in computational chemistry, biology, machine learning, and advanced robotics to predict how molecules interact and behave in various states and climates. These insights allow Terramera to recommend how best to improve soil and plant health almost anywhere in the world. They are also essential to helping farmers quantify the value of the transition to regenerative agriculture.

To test and commercialize this technology, Terramera is working with leading experts, including farmers, soil scientists, universities, and agronomists, to get real-time input and feedback, with the aim of training data models that predict the optimal path in the regenerative transition. At the same time, in an effort to rapidly scale this work, Terramera is collaborating with investors and governments to expedite the creation of protocols for carbon credit generation, tools to support and scale regenerative agriculture, and methods to reach more farmers.

Who benefits from all this collaboration-driven innovation? Farmers are enjoying higher farm profits, greater soil health and water retention—resulting in resilience to weather changes—and access to new income streams, including from carbon credits. Investors benefit from their stake in a growing business. Consumers benefit from cleaner, more nutrient-dense food, the cultivation of which leaves farmland in better shape with each passing growing season. Society and the planet benefit from a reduction in pesticide use and a drawdown of carbon from the atmosphere into soil, where it builds and enriches soil health—which in turn presents the opportunity to begin turning back the clock on climate change.[14]

## Smart Collaboration Enhances Customer Loyalty and Retention

Customer satisfaction is a natural outgrowth of the deeper engagement, faster innovation, and better solutions that smart collaboration helps to deliver. For example, Jane Ashton, former president of the US division of a global telecoms company, recalls how her division's work to embed collaboration led to a significant uptick in the company's net promoter score (NPS)—the most widely used metric to evaluate the loyalty that exists between a provider and a customer:

> We were running global sales channels for technology, life sciences, and the remaining hodgepodge of customers we lumped into "business services." Each division operated in a silo, with no sharing or learning happening across the groups. Our NPS scores hovered in the 30s.
>
> When I became president, we launched a culture-change initiative to improve how we worked with each other and with our customers. We started having conversations that built on each other, seeking others' opinions, challenging, and even interrupting in the spirit of exploration, finding ways to improve our team, and serve our customers better. I paired people up across divisions for peer coaching. We built a healthy

spirit of challenge and collaboration to bring best practice to customers. And our NPS scores started climbing. After two years, they nearly reached 60, which for us was a historic high.

This telecoms company's outcome was no fluke. We've interviewed hundreds of buyers across a broad array of roles and industries: from a *Fortune* 50 company's chief technology officer who purchases hundred-million-dollar cybersecurity solutions to the general counsel of an African drinks manufacturer to the operations manager who sources facility maintenance services for a major retailer. In those conversations, we consistently heard that buyers believe they are better served when their suppliers are better at collaboration.

Not surprisingly, satisfied customers stick around longer—and that outcome is not just a feel-good reflection of a chummy relationship. As an account executive at a global civil engineering firm told us, "Generally, clients find it relatively easy to swap out individual mono-line suppliers with a similar replacement from a competitor. But finding substitutes for multiple services, especially if they are tightly integrated, is way harder." Over time, a self-reinforcing cycle emerges: the broader the team serving the client, and the more integrated the solutions, the higher the barriers become for a client to consider switching to a new provider.

One accounting firm reviewed its relationships with its three hundred biggest clients and uncovered a surprisingly large correlation between collaboration and client loyalty. Of those clients served by a single partner, roughly three-quarters said they'd consider moving their business to a competitor if their relationship partner left. In contrast, among those served by two or more partners, 90 percent said they'd remain loyal to their existing accountants. Figure 1-5 illustrates this point.

Across most industries, the more areas (product lines, regions, partners) that serve a given client, the more likely that client is to become "institutionalized"—embedded, as it were, across the organization, rather than narrowly connected through a single touch point. This substantially reduces the risk that the client will, or even *can*, make a change.

Does this lesson sound obvious? We would agree—except that in so many of the cases we've looked at, a company's key clients are

FIGURE 1-5

**"If your account executive departed, would you seek another provider?"**

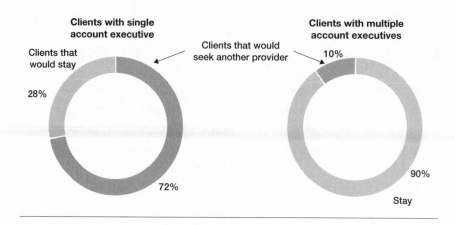

buying only a single service or product, which means that the loyalty of those clients is suspect, at best.

Have you reviewed the relevant data in your organization? What's eye-opening for most executives is that the majority of their customer relationships are controlled by a single team—and in many cases, by a single person. Figure 1-6 shows the recent distribution for the US client base of three major, well-regarded international companies.

These lessons apply well beyond professional services. State Street Bank's engagement with its investment-management clients provides a clear example of collaboration boosting customer retention. To investment managers, State Street provides a broad suite of operational services: custody, accounting, fund administration, data management, analytics, reporting, and trading. By increasingly integrating those services and offering them as "integrated solutions," the value to the client—and the stickiness for State Street—goes up. Mono-line competitors, even if they have a better price on an individual product, struggle to displace State Street. "Sure, I might save $100,000 by switching to a different accounting provider, but in terms of our overall spend and relationship with State Street, that's a drop in the bucket," said the chief operating officer of a global investment manager. "And I would have to integrate that accounting tool with everything else State Street does for me—whereas today, they handle it."

**FIGURE 1-6**

## "Across your customers, what proportion is served by one versus multiple senior people?"

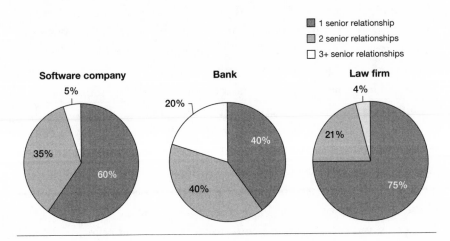

- ■ 1 senior relationship
- ▨ 2 senior relationships
- ☐ 3+ senior relationships

**Software company**
5%
35%
60%

**Bank**
20%
40%
40%

**Law firm**
4%
21%
75%

Again, a broad relationship gives you deeper insight into the customer and increases the likelihood you will be seen as a strategic partner relative to other possible providers. This buys you time when a challenge arises. As an executive at a consumer products company said, "I'd always give my strategic partners the chance, multiple chances, to fix something before I make a change. That's not the case with a smaller, less strategic vendor."

To summarize, bringing the full suite of services in a deeply collaborative way is key when it comes to institutionalizing clients. The broader those relationships are across different service lines, departments, or geographies, combined with integration that makes that suite of capabilities difficult to replicate, the more likely the client is to remain with the provider.

## Smart Collaboration Promotes Greater Efficiency

*I don't have time to collaborate.*

This is one of the most common explanations we hear for why people decide to stick with standalone, non-collaborative approaches to work. And we are quick to agree that there's a grain of truth underlying that blanket statement. The truth is, collaboration incurs startup costs—including, for example, the time it takes to build your network of trusted collaborators and the time it takes to learn your customer's business well enough to tackle complex problems outside any single contributor's expertise. Again, it's true: you have to devote the time that's needed to get past those startup costs.

The unwelcome news is that most of the tangible benefits of smarter collaboration—such as increased revenues and profits and higher customer satisfaction scores—accrue slowly. So at the outset of the collaboration, the costs are very likely to outweigh the benefits. At this point in the process, if someone complains that collaboration is inefficient, they may well be right. The good news is that these startup-phase costs drop over time as people gain experience. Eventually, the lines cross and collaboration begins to pay off. At that point, you don't have time to *not* collaborate.

Take the case of software development. Typically, software developers write their code and then someone else tests it and provides feedback, and the coder makes edits in response to that feedback. San Francisco–based Pivotal Software takes a different and more collaborative approach.[15] It invests heavily up front to train its developers to code in pairs. Rather than following the linear approach just described, the paired coders work simultaneously in parallel on the same code. Seeing each other's work more or less in real time, they learn from each other and catch issues as they go. The ultimate output arrives more quickly and has far fewer bugs.

Another powerful example comes from Roche, a 122-year-old biotechnology company with ninety-four thousand employees in more than one hundred countries. Tammy Lowry, global head of talent innovation, shares an example of radically streamlining the drug development process through more effective collaboration:

> The average time to get a drug from discovery through FDA approval had been twenty-one months. Every minute of that time, you don't have a drug in the market that could be helping patients. We set ourselves a goal of radically shortening that time.

In Roche, the development-through-approval process was owned by three different siloed groups. At each handover from one part to another, there was a very controlled approval stage-gate process, with people scheduling formal meetings, creating presentations, meeting again, etc. It wasn't a fast process.

We piloted a different approach: cross-functional, cross-organizational teams that from the beginning work through every step of the process in collaboration. We got the right people involved from the beginning, working together and accelerating everything. We eliminated artificial organizational boundaries, stripped out the bureaucracy, and removed all the siloed approval processes. The new process reduced the time to FDA approval by 50 percent.[16]

Efficiency matters in the nonprofit world as well. Anyone who has written a grant application knows that the efficient and effective use of resources is a key criterion for grant providers.[17] As Jeff Raikes, the former chief executive of the Bill and Melinda Gates Foundation, puts it, "Simply, we have to help people do more with less."[18] And that efficient use of resources can quite literally help save lives. Professor Melissa Valentine of Stanford University found that nurse and doctor teams collaborating smarter in a hospital emergency department improved patient throughput time by 40 percent.[19] This obviously matters to the patients who need treatment as soon as possible, and it is also good for the hospital. Past the startup costs, collaboration creates that kind of efficiency.

## Smart Collaboration Facilitates Transparency and Risk Management

Rogue actors, regrettable employee turnover, cyber threats: companies today face an unprecedented array of risks, ranging from the merely damaging to the truly existential. In many of those situations, effective collaboration is essential for mitigating risks—and even for preventing future exposures.

Let's start with a major headline-grabber: the rogue employee. We're thinking, for example, of the celebrated case of the London Whale, which led to losses for J.P. Morgan of more than $6 billion. How did it happen? Due to a lack of oversight and collaboration between managers in risk, audit, compliance, and the investing team, traders were able to engage in speculative and risky derivatives trades that were not in line with the bank's investment strategy.

Although such intentionally bad behaviors are relatively rare, they're on the rise—and when they *do* occur, they can be fatal.[20] The good news is that this kind of aberration simply can't arise in a highly collaborative environment, in which colleagues engage in open dialogue and invite input into their work. Transparency lowers the risk of illicit rogue behavior by wrongdoers.

Stepping back from rogue actors, collaboration across an organization is crucial for helping to reduce risk before, during, and after a major event. All three of these stages require internal collaboration from top to bottom—from boards and executive management through the line workers—and across silos. Meanwhile, external collaboration is also essential, because including outside advisers who have cross-industry expertise can help you identify your blind spots.

Many organizations, and particularly those engaged in financial services, have started conducting "premortems." These analyses start with the end state: What could happen in the future that would create a major shock to our organization? Typically, members of the C-suite kick off the process by working with subject-matter experts to imagine a set of catastrophic events, then use reverse engineering to consider the conditions that would get them there. In this kind of scenario-building, cross-functional expertise is vital. Also valuable may be engagement by board members, whose experience in a range of companies, industries, or geographies may help unearth complex interactions that can create systemwide risk.

Ultimately, this broad-based, senior learning gets pushed down to the business-unit level. When it does, leaders throughout the organization can make the necessary adjustments to prepare for the future.

Looking at present-day risks is all about identifying small problems before they become bigger problems. A cross-functional team, in many cases led by a chief operating officer, works to create a culture in which the organization learns to become open about issues. It's rarely easy. "You're fighting human nature," observes risk expert James Lam. "When there is good news, everyone's willing to talk about it. But when something bad happens, people try to just quietly fix it. You lose transparency, which means you lose the chance to lower risk."[21]

Collaboration in this stage means surfacing risks and working across silos to analyze them and find ways to mitigate them. Why? Because risks rarely exist within a single silo. For example, losing one customer seems like a small loss. But if you don't understand that the departed customer left for a new competitor whose technology is fundamentally more advanced and cheaper to use, then you will fail to see that your company is stalled on the tracks and the train is fast approaching.

Finally, there's the collaborative "postmortem" stage, which is probably the most common way of bringing different brains into the risk-analysis process. One common practice is creating a loss-event database. By cataloging all losses, cross-functional teams can analyze them for patterns, assess the outliers and potential black-swan events, and conduct root-cause analysis to understand the drivers of losses. The objective, as Lam explains, is to "really understand how we make mistakes, how we suffer losses, and use that insight to shape risk mitigation strategies going forward. This requires deep cross-functional collaboration."

For example, one global bank started cataloging all losses above $10,000. The team involved soon found that analysis so valuable that they dropped their cataloging threshold down to $5,000—a remarkably small sum for a bank that generated more than $100 billion in revenues in 2020.

One more time: risks can, and *must*, be managed. Increasing your internal transparency is an important contributor to that effort—and collaboration fosters transparency.

## Serving All the Bottom Lines

The bottom line? Smart collaboration is good for the bottom line, no matter how you define that bottom line.

For many people, the most important outcome of smart collaboration is that it can help organizations achieve a higher purpose. In August 2019, 181 CEOs from the Business Roundtable redefined the purpose of a corporation as being to promote not only shareholder returns but also equity and social justice. Focusing on a broad range of stakeholders—employees, suppliers, and communities—the Business Roundtable emphasized the positive role that corporations can play in society. "Major employers are investing in their workers and communities," said Jamie Dimon, CEO of J.P. Morgan, "because they know it is the only way to be successful over the long term."[22]

Delivering on that vision will require organizations to work within their walls to develop their people and create opportunities through increased diversity and inclusion—and at the same time, to work outside their walls with customers, suppliers, and communities. Whatever else happens, the bottom line will surely benefit from smart collaboration.

# The Talent Case for Smarter Collaboration

I n the last chapter, we laid out the evidence that smarter collaboration propels the success of companies and nonprofit organizations facing complex challenges. Smarter collaboration makes it possible for organizations to innovate faster and more effectively, build customer loyalty, and minimize risks—all of which contributes to enhanced revenues and profits, or similarly attractive outcomes for nonprofits.

Now we present the case that smarter collaboration directly enhances the people who deliver that success, and helps their employer to get the most out of their talent. More than mere teamwork, smart collaboration creates a virtuous circle through its elements of *why*, *who*, and *how*. It focuses collective effort on transformational goals, giving people a sense of bigger meaning and purpose. It brings in people with varied expertise and experiences, who can use their diversity as a source of strength. It's highly inclusive, so that people feel valued by their managers and coworkers.

Smarter collaboration is also deliberately developmental, so that people can learn and grow on the job. This way of working creates highly engaged employees, who are more prone to lean into the big, tough problems with their teams. The cycle becomes self-reinforcing.

So how do you get there? This chapter delves into five ways that smarter collaboration boosts the workforce: both the individual employees and their organization's ability to draw out the benefits of a strong talent base. We start by showing how smarter collaboration enhances engagement, which is a much-vaunted element of talent management but currently under serious strain. Smart collaboration can also help an organization reach its diversity, equity, and inclusion (DEI) goals, and it has direct effects on people's physical and mental well-being. Then we look at how to use smarter collaboration to improve the integration of people you bring into the company, whether through hiring or a merger. And since today's most dynamic companies no longer even *try* to get lifers, we wrap up with a new twist on hiring: showing how smarter collaboration with today's employees can improve your chances of making them "boomerangs," who return later as employees, brand ambassadors, or future customers.

## Collaboration Drives Engagement—and Engagement Drives Results

What is engagement? It's your employees' enthusiasm and sense of connection to their work, and their willingness to commit their physical, cognitive, and emotional energy to it.[1] Engagement stems from a chance to contribute and be valued for those contributions, and from opportunities to learn and grow.[2]

If you think this is fluffy, think again. A large body of research shows that high engagement not only boosts productivity, revenues and profits, and talent retention but also promotes psychological and physiological benefits.[3] (See Figure 2-1 for empirical findings on the impact of engagement on outcomes.)

Unfortunately, engagement in the workforce is generally low across the globe.[4] Thirty percent of employees worldwide, and 67 percent in the United States, report that they are *not* engaged.[5] And the momentum may be in the wrong direction: Recent studies suggest that

FIGURE 2-1

## Engagement by the numbers

*Gallup research shows a remarkable difference in business outcomes depending on employee engagement.*

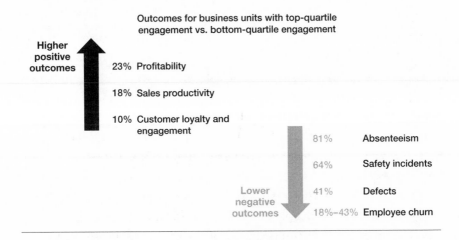

Outcomes for business units with top-quartile engagement vs. bottom-quartile engagement

**Higher positive outcomes**

23% Profitability

18% Sales productivity

10% Customer loyalty and engagement

81% Absenteeism

64% Safety incidents

Lower negative outcomes

41% Defects

18%–43% Employee churn

remote working, so significantly expanded and accelerated during the Covid-19 pandemic, can have an adverse effect on engagement.[6]

The seismic shift to remote or hybrid working came as a jolt for many people who never planned to work from home and for managers who preferred to have their teams working closely together in the office. Working remotely can cause people to feel isolated from their colleagues, out of sync with their teams, and out of sight from their managers. Particularly for new joiners or new teams, creating bonds and starting to feel enmeshed in the culture can be far more difficult.

We propose that a fundamental shift toward smarter collaboration will help to turn those numbers around and produce sustainably higher engagement, whether working in person, remotely, or somewhere in between. Smarter collaboration is by its nature inclusive, which makes people understand that their managers and coworkers appreciate their contributions. And as noted earlier, smarter collaboration is also deliberately developmental, meaning that people can learn and grow on the job.

An engaging job is one where you *play to your strengths*. The Gallup organization has conducted annual studies on engagement involving millions of people on more than one hundred thousand teams across fifty-plus industries. They've found that one agree-or-disagree statement is a critical indicator of an employee's level of engagement: "At work, I have the opportunity to do what I do best every day."[7]

Smarter collaboration not only allows this, it *demands* it. It demands that people understand their own strengths and—equally important—admit where they're *not* all that brilliant. It demands that people find others who possess complementary strengths, then work effectively with them to tackle important challenges. That's how everyone gets to play to their strengths, and no one is forced to lean on their weaknesses.

It's not enough for a person to *want* to contribute by using their strengths. They need people around them, including their supervisors and colleagues, to understand, appreciate, and draw on those strengths. Gardner's dissertation research clearly showed this. She worked with more than six hundred people in one hundred project teams over the course of nearly a year.[8] Her analyses clearly showed that some teams have a serious problem in actually using their members' knowledge, even when it's genuine experts who are speaking up and trying to contribute. Those teams, not surprisingly, performed relatively badly—not only in terms of their members' engagement but also in satisfaction ratings from their clients.

What went wrong on those teams? First, leaders failed to create the kind of environment where collaboration thrives—for example, devoting time for team members to learn about one another's technical and market knowledge, and especially about how that expertise related to the current client's specific needs. Second, team members undermined one another's ability to play to their own strengths. For example, they often mistakenly overrelied on the inputs of higher-status team members rather than listening to people who knew the clients deeply or had other important ideas. Videos of some team meetings showed that up to 65 percent of these missed opportunities were caused by team members (not the leader) talking over, ignoring, or even physically turning their backs on experts who tried to contribute.

These findings highlight a key element of smart collaboration: leaders play a major role in shaping the context (as we explain in depth in Chapter 8), but individual team members have to be constantly vigilant in drawing out and drawing on each other's strengths.

Let's look at a case in point. One midsize private equity–backed consumer goods company, BeautyCo, wanted to expand into new customer segments and geographies to achieve its ambitious growth goals. Toward that end, it identified five major initiatives. Meanwhile, the company's CEO announced that he wanted a new approach to execution planning. Rather than having the executive committee take the lead on building launch plans, they would create and rely on working groups that spanned all levels of the company, including recent joiners.

An outside group trained the teams to conduct a rigorous project launch. Each member really got to know everyone else's expertise and experience—not just their role but also how their personal background contributed to a deeper customer connection and how what they had learned in prior roles could apply to the new project.[9] Members also learned to periodically revisit ways to use each other's strengths as projects evolved or as team members changed.

It worked. One of the projects got to market months ahead of schedule by using an outside technology provider that a younger team member had previously worked with. Another expanded into a new region based on the in-depth knowledge of some team members who grew up there.

Given these successes, the collaborative approach soon spread to other parts of the organization. The concept of allowing people to use their strengths and do what they do best every day was adopted in the language of the company and implemented in little ways every day. Confirmation came in feedback from the employee engagement surveys. As one product manager said, "I like that we ask questions like, 'Where can you have the most impact on the project?'" Unsurprisingly, engagement scores started to rise. (See the related sidebar on engagement.)

## THE REALITIES OF "ENGAGEMENT"

Many of the companies that embrace the idea of "engagement" do so only in superficial ways.

Yes, they conduct engagement surveys, but in many cases, the effort stops there. In other cases, the survey results are alarming enough (clear signs of widespread disengagement!) to prompt short-term actions aimed at making employees feel more satisfied. Dress codes get relaxed, and new opportunities for informal socializing get invented. But this is like taking aspirin to bring down a fever rather than tackling the underlying illness. Engagement is a *measure* and therefore can't be cast as an "initiative."

And engagement can't be the sole province of human resources. Yes, HR can and should help measure change and track its impacts, but the change itself has to come from deeper within the organization.

---

BeautyCo's leaders helped push project teams toward truly smarter collaboration, not only by making sure people had the opportunity to play to their strengths but also by taking a deliberately developmental approach. This is key: smarter collaboration helps boost engagement because it gives people the opportunity to learn and grow. Our surveys of thousands of team members consistently show that they value collaboration in part because it provides them content knowledge, such as market intelligence and a broader understanding of their customer's business.

Working closely with colleagues also enhances their skills in areas such as problem-solving, leadership, and effective communication. The more that people grow and learn through collaboration, the more they can shape the direction of their work and careers, and the more they can help others around them and gain status for their enhanced knowledge. When people see those outcomes, they put more brainpower and emotional energy into their roles. The more engaged they are, the more they contribute to an organizational culture that encourages curiosity and genuine interest in other points of view. And that, in turn, promotes diversity and inclusion, which we turn to shortly.

Parallel developments in the human-resource field reinforce this kind of progress. For example, leaders no longer need to wait for the annual company-wide survey to understand where engagement is strong and where it isn't. More and more companies have been moving toward team-level "pulse" surveys—that is, short, frequent check-ins that are usually conducted online. Technology now allows leaders to understand organizational sentiment near real time through the analysis of communications within the company. In particular, chat tools like Microsoft Teams and Slack can be analyzed to understand how team members are feeling, and pick up early warning signs of issues, while still maintaining individual anonymity.

## Enhanced Diversity and Inclusion through Collaboration

Uncertain and complex problems are best tackled by a diverse team of complementary talents, organized and led in a way that puts that diversity to effective use. But simply putting diverse people on teams probably won't help you solve tough problems, and it certainly won't help a company reach its DEI goals. Teams need to engage in truly smarter collaboration, which means encouraging everyone to contribute as their authentic selves—that is, to draw on their strengths—and creating an environment in which their contributions can be heard, valued, and integrated into the team's work.

For example, by taking time at the launch of a project to discuss the task goals and how each person's life experiences and aspirations can best contribute—like the BeautyCo teams learned to do—the team gets the most from its resources. This level of inclusivity helps people achieve their individual professional outcomes like promotions and raises, because they are deeply involved, not token representatives, in the company's core work. This involvement allows people to learn, get coached, find sponsors, take on stretch assignments, and ultimately progress in their careers. These outcomes create a positive cycle: diverse people who get ahead stick around longer and serve as role models and mentors, bringing more diverse people into the company and up the ranks.

Unfortunately, though, this kind of inclusion has gotten harder with the growth of remote work. The virtual workplace inevitably slows and complicates the development of interpersonal relationships, which even in a normal work environment can be difficult to develop among people with differing backgrounds. Trust, including both interpersonal trust and competence trust, is an essential element of effective collaboration, but it becomes far more difficult to develop and maintain when the social interactions of the traditional work environment are gone.[10]

The combination of remote work and the associated erosion of social interactions hits marginalized groups hard, and pushes those groups further toward the periphery. Research on cognitive bias shows that certain kinds of people who are "out of sight" are also likely to be "out of mind": women, minorities, and others who are on the outer edges of the team are less likely to have access to information or resources and therefore have less influence on the team leader.[11]

These challenges increase further during periods of high stress, because anxious people tend to turn to others who are most like them in terms of age, gender, ethnicity, socioeconomic status, and personal beliefs. Researchers call this phenomenon homophily, and it is manifested in ways that can be subtle and not so subtle.[12] When a problem bubbles up, who hears about it first, and how? Is there an informal inner circle, and if so, how did it emerge and how representative is it? If there's a fire to be put out, who gets involved only after the fact, and why?

Smarter collaboration doesn't eliminate homophily, which seems to be hardwired into the human brain. But by explicitly underscoring the team's true complementarity of talents, smarter collaboration can make it less likely that a person or group will become marginalized, and this has very positive implications for DEI initiatives. Some companies are starting to use technology to analyze collaboration almost in real time, flagging emerging problems of exclusion before they escalate. For example, analyzing patterns of email or contributions to a digital platform like Microsoft Teams can alert a project manager if nearly all the team conversations become concentrated within a small subset of a team's members.

Truly inclusive collaboration isn't easy. Done badly, collaboration can backfire on DEI efforts. We cover these potential issues in Chapter 10. Done wisely—with a strategic and holistic view of actions across the organization—collaboration can advance the DEI cause.

## Smarter Collaboration and Well-Being

When we go into a company and start talking about smarter collaboration, we sometimes get challenged by a skeptic in the group who tells us that the workplace isn't an appropriate setting for touchy-feely stuff. Instead, the skeptic asserts, work should be about delivering hard, quantifiable organizational and commercial benefits.

We have two responses. First, that's exactly what smarter collaboration is all about: delivering quantifiable benefits to the company and to the people who work there. Second, science tells us that there are real advantages to the mind—and the body—when we work with close colleagues, especially on tasks that we're all invested in.[13] The result can be a healthier workforce, which benefits the organization in ways ranging from lower absenteeism and health-care costs to longer tenure and higher productivity.[14]

How does this work? The sense of connectedness that grows out of smarter collaboration directly improves personal well-being, in part by lowering the risk of loneliness. Many of the thousands of people who participated in our survey research reported that the most important benefit they derive from working on team-based projects is the opportunity to meet new colleagues and to deepen existing relationships.

Conversely, being left out of collaboration can be both painful and harmful. Brain scans show that when people feel left out—as minimal as being excluded during an online game with "peers" who happen to be robots—their brains react in the same way as when they are stimulated by physical pain.[15] Neuroscientists have also shown that social isolation detrimentally affects the way our brains function, and a growing body of research shows the serious health risks of social isolation and loneliness.[16] In one study, for example, participants were voluntarily exposed to a cold virus. Those who were socially isolated were 45 percent more likely to become ill.[17] Longer term, abundant research shows that loneliness has serious consequences for our bodies, including increasing cortisol and inflammation (which lowers immune response), heart disease, and even cancer.[18]

Overall, collaboration helps promote mental and physical well-being and is an essential avenue to a healthy workplace.

## Collaboration Makes Your Experienced Hires Successful

Have you ever hired someone with a brilliant track record and a sterling résumé, only to find that they sputter along, fail to deliver the goods—whether the hoped-for goods are faster innovation, increased sales, or otherwise—and leave your company long before they even start making money for you? If so, you're not alone.

Research around the globe and across industries shows that nearly half of all new hires fail within eighteen months.[19] Companies are generally quite poor at integrating senior hires in a way that makes them more productive. For example, the Wharton School's Matthew Bidwell—in a study of lateral hiring aptly named "Paying More to Get Less"—looked at six years of personnel data from the US investment-banking branch of a financial services corporation. He found that lateral hires were far more likely than internal workers to leave their job, either because they quit or because they were fired.[20]

Dismal as this sounds, you probably can't avoid external hires. Developing and promoting internal talent is essential, but probably insufficient to meet your talent needs in an incredibly fast-moving and competitive market. McKinsey used to have a strict policy of developing its own talent, but that has changed significantly. When it needed to move quickly into the hot area of data and analytics, for example, it chose not to wait a decade to develop the talent internally and instead started aggressively hiring from outside.

By now, you won't be surprised to hear that our prescription is smarter collaboration—and that this prescription is backed up by research. Our studies, and those of other scholars, show that if experienced hires aren't engaged in serious collaboration in the first six months or so, they have a radically increased risk of leaving the company soon afterward.[21] Even harder, the collaboration that needs to happen in that short time must be *reciprocal*. First, new joiners need to get pulled into the organization's core work. Those in the department they enter, as well as other stakeholders, need to understand the new joiner's role and capabilities so that they can proactively draw them into important projects. Second, new hires need to reach out and initiate mission-critical relationships. Then the circle needs to close: tenured employees need to be responsive when the new joiner asks for help on their work. This sounds obvious, but we've seen many examples where new joiners were perceived as competitors and deliberately boxed out.

If either of those two directions of collaboration (that is, both incumbents and newbies initiating the joint work) is missing, then experienced hires are at a much higher risk of leaving; if neither happens, they're almost certain to be gone by their two-year anniversary.

For example, a talented social media executive was hired by a consumer goods company looking to build out its data and analytics capabilities. To give her freedom and agility, her projects were set up independent of the core business and separate from her peers in functions like product development, brand management, and so on. "People liked the idea of data and analytics," she said, "but nobody actually wanted to engage. I was stranded on an island." Frustrated and struggling to gain traction, within fifteen months she left to join a competitor. Despite the importance of her initiatives, after her departure those projects were shut down, and the company fell behind its peers.

And it's important to look at the all-in cost of failures in this realm. Research in labor economics suggests that the cost of each failed external hire is more than double the individual's annual compensation.[22] Many experts suggest that the *total* cost—including, for example, the opportunity costs of people's time spent interviewing and onboarding the short-lived new joiner—is even higher.[23] Beyond the financial costs, moreover, losing external hires creates internal disruption, slows the pace of execution, and risks undermining client confidence.

But let's switch back to the positive side of the ledger. Beyond mere retention, collaboration helps experienced hires generate value sooner.

It typically takes three to five years for new joiners to reach the level of performance achieved at their old organization, let alone achieve greatness.[24] In research across companies including financial services, software, consumer products, retail, manufacturing, and life sciences, Babson College professor Rob Cross found that new joiners need to gain legitimacy and visibility with their peers before their ideas are even considered.[25] Collaboration—direct work with other people on increasingly important, central work of the company—is the way to build this credibility and two-way trust, which is the surest way for the organization to capitalize on newcomers' fresh ideas and expertise.

Here is another area where technology plays a role. The near-ubiquitous use of communication software allows managers to easily analyze how widely engaged their new hires are—within specific projects and across groups. One health-care company, for example, tracks a whole range of digital interaction patterns across its employees: how often they post requests for help and what proportion of their requests get answered, how often they share knowledge or respond to others' posts or chats, and so on. By zeroing in on groups of new joiners (rather than specific individuals), they can identify parts of their business where entrants are not sufficiently integrated and alert managers to take action.

In Chapter 5, we also expand on the ways that smarter collaboration enhances the success of even bigger groups of newcomers: people you bring into an organization through a merger or acquisition. Getting employees from the two legacy companies collaborating on the core work sooner is a powerful way not only to achieve the outcomes that drove the merger rationale in the first place but also to create a more compelling, unified culture that helps to retain people in the longer term.

## Building a Stronger Alumni Network through Collaboration

Your firm can't and won't retain everybody you hire. Maybe that shouldn't even be your goal. Most cutting-edge companies today embrace the notion of a fluid career path. Rather than viewing departed employees as traitors, these organizations cultivate ongoing relation-ships with "alumni" who leave to broaden their experiences and develop new skills. While these alumni are elsewhere, they may pro-vide a rich pool of talent to collaborate with. And if these so-called boomerangs return from time on sabbatical, with a startup or even at a competitor, they are likely to bring back fresh ideas for innova-tion, deep knowledge of how other companies (including customers) operate, new sources of external partnerships, and a renewed energy. But for this to work, organizations need to ensure their people are *engaged*, both while they are with you and while they are away. Col-laboration is the way to achieve both.

Done right, you can also save huge amounts on hiring. As Andrea Legnani, Citi's global head of alumni relations, recently told us, "Companies can save between $50,000 and $75,000 on each return-ing alumnus, compared to other external hires. At last count, return-ers at Citi numbered about twenty thousand—that is, 10 percent of our workforce." In other words, *rehiring alumni saved Citi at least a billion dollars.*

And at Citi, according to Legnani, boomerang employees onboard faster: "I like to say that they already know where the bathroom is, which is my shorthand for the fact that they know the system, they know the people, and they already have a network." For these and other reasons, on average Citi's boomerangs tend to stay longer, are happier, and perform better than their peers who were hired from the open market.[26]

Are you wondering if this alumni strategy only works for knowledge-based companies? The answer is no. Consider Sodexo, the global food services and facilities management company. Its US alumni network has nearly nine thousand management-level employees. The program's strength lies not only in the company's ability to maintain ties with former colleagues—who often refer other qualified candidates for jobs—but in convincing them to return. About 20 percent of the exter-nal hires Sodexo makes each year are former employees. "It is one of the largest candidate pools that we pull from with our external hir-ing," says Lisa Inserra, Sodexo's director of talent acquisition.

But people who've left your organization become loyal, beneficial alumni only if you get them fully contributing and networked while you employ them. And that's where smarter collaboration comes in. Decades of psychological and sociological research show that the higher the number of formal or informal connections that exist among individuals and their colleagues, the more committed those individuals will be to both their job and their employer. Smarter collaboration fosters working relationships that make employees self-identify with the organization—so that they'll say, for example, "We do it this way," rather than, "The company does it this way." Simply stated, the person who feels deeply and meaningfully tied into the organization is more likely to behave as a "friend of the firm" after he or she has left. In that spirit, Deloitte calls its alumni "colleagues for life."

The companies with the best track records in this area start to build a network affinity before they even recruit candidates. Then they work to enhance commitment among their employees and foster postemployment loyalty in a whole variety of ways. Companies like Citi, Bain, Microsoft, Google, and Coca-Cola have developed a range of diverse channels to keep collaborating with their alumni—as a gig-work labor force, customers, strategic partners, and members of alumni advisory boards.

Even if your alumni don't return, those strong ties imply that in subsequent years, they can help the organization in myriad ways: as brand boosters, sales advocates, market informants, and sources of recruitment.

No, these benefits are not the result of collaboration alone. But they are definitely among the downstream benefits of it, for both the company and the individuals involved.

## Making the Link

Simply bringing great talent in the door isn't enough—or close to it.

Creating a deep-seated sense of engagement is critically important for the *retention* of that talent. But as the numbers show, engagement is an elusive goal for most companies. People want to do their best work—they're *eager* to do their best work—but in all too many cases they aren't allowed or encouraged to do so. They want to work on an effective team, and at the same time, they want to be recognized for their individual contributions. They want to learn, and grow, and become even more valuable contributors. They want to be healthy and satisfied in the workplace—and of course, their company wants the same thing.

Smarter collaboration can help on all these fronts. It can also make your company's DEI initiatives more likely to succeed, and increase your chances of tapping into a satisfied alumni network. But all these benefits accrue only if your company purposefully links collaboration to its strategy: the subject of our next chapter.

# PART TWO

# ASSESSING YOUR COLLABORATIVE STARTING POINT

# [ 3 ]

# Enterprise-Wide Diagnostic

U p and down the hallways of a fast-growing enterprise software company, TechStar, the race for growth was becoming increasingly challenging.[1]

Early on, the company's innovative software was wildly popular in the market, and bagging new logos was easy. But as the business matured, its leaders realized that sustaining high growth by acquiring new clients was unrealistic. The pool of attractive new clients was shrinking, onboarding large numbers of complex new accounts was difficult, and many existing clients were grumbling, *loudly*. Tech-Star's CEO, Rick Jones, realized that many current "wins" focused on narrow parts of the client's enterprise—say, a single division or country. TechStar clearly wasn't maximizing its share of the wallet and was leaving good money on the table.

TechStar's strategy, as Jones reminded his senior colleagues at one of their weekly meetings, was to help clients generate deeper insights by integrating all their data and providing one window into their business. "Our technology is really good," Jones said. "But if we don't figure out how to expand across the clients' silos, we're never going to claim that money on the table."

Things kept getting worse. Strategic clients started leaving because the original promise of integrating client information to generate insights wasn't being delivered. TechStar was increasingly perceived as a resource for solving narrow problems, rather than a strategic partner.

"I *know* we can do better," Jones told his operating group. "We've got the smarts. Collectively, we can think like our clients and serve them better. But we just don't seem to work together in ways that bring our big guns to bear on our clients' toughest problems. And we're running out of time."

. . .

Although he didn't use the word, Jones was talking about *collaboration*, or the lack of it, at TechStar. We'll return to TechStar later in the chapter; for now, we'll simply observe that Jones was on the right track. Our most recent research has revealed an eye-opening statistic: more than 70 percent of forward-thinking companies have now embraced the concept of collaboration as a core pillar of their strategy.

Of course, we applaud that as a signal of good intentions. At the same time, a strategy only works if it is put into practice. For many companies with those good intentions, the question now on the table is *how* to implement a strategy of smart collaboration. What practical steps should you take to get from here to there?

The first step, as we explain in this chapter, is to design and conduct a rigorous, data-driven, smart collaboration diagnostic.

## Why a Diagnostic?

Maybe this will sound self-evident, but let's risk it: the reason to conduct a diagnostic is to make sure you understand where your problems are. All too often, organizations that feel themselves to be "under the gun" jump right to the presumed solution without really identifying the problem. Their leaders make decisions based on a set of *assumptions* about what is holding their company back. When we conduct research inside organizations, however, we often find that those assumptions are only partially supported by the data. This gap that can render those leaders ineffective as change agents in the collaboration zone.

Why are leaders' views about collaboration so often disconnected from their organizational reality? One answer is that those views can be skewed as a result of the leaders' relatively lofty positions: research in social psychology confirms that people's views change when they attain greater power.[2] But it's more than a mere perceptual challenge. For several reasons, *the leaders' experience of collaboration is often genuinely different from that of others in the organization*. First, leaders often are long-tenured within their company, meaning that they have had ample time to build broad-reaching, productive networks of colleagues. Second, many were promoted to senior leadership in part because people trusted them along the way—and as we'll explain later, trust is a critical foundation for collaboration. Finally, few people say no to an executive's request to collaborate.

The upshot is that *people at the top actually face fewer collaboration obstacles*. Their positive experience, reinforced on a daily basis, creates a chasm between their perception of collaboration in the organization and everyone else's reality. But as one CEO said, "Until I had a clear-eyed, data-driven view of our starting point, I couldn't fathom why people wouldn't just pick up the phone and pull in their colleagues."

An objective understanding of the company's launching point for a new or modified strategy helps the company leaders pinpoint how and where to spend their energy—and more important, how to direct others to do the same. Leaders must constantly reinforce the idea that "smart" collaboration is a means to a much larger end: providing holistic solutions to complex issues. If people feel that they are being asked simply to "collaborate more," then they are likely either to waste time and effort or simply to ignore the mandate. A call for unfettered collaboration can be counterproductive, and even irresponsible.[3]

Again: to pinpoint specific interventions, you need to conduct a thorough diagnostic. In our experience working in multiple organizations across North and South America, Europe, and Africa, we have found that this initial diagnostic phase sets up leaders for success in six ways:

- aligning the efforts to the business strategy

- helping those leaders diagnose the perceived and actual barriers to collaboration

- discovering and analyzing "bright spots" where collaboration already happens, and thereby providing examples that can be used to help shape a collaborative culture

- generating compelling evidence about the potential upside of making changes (ideally expressed in monetary terms), which often is essential for motivating high-autonomy leaders to even consider new ways of working

- building in the customer's perspective—certainly needed for *all* product and service offerings, but especially important for collaborative initiatives

- setting priorities based on both the anticipated upside (return on investment in financial terms, plus other benefits such as customer satisfaction and engagement) and the challenge of implementation (e.g., friction points that can hinder the capture of return on investment)

Let's look at each of these steps in turn. And for anyone who wants more detail and tactical guidance about how to conduct this diagnostic in their own organization, we have developed the Smarter Collaboration Diagnostic Toolkit, available as a companion to this book through Harvard Business Review Press.[4]

## Aligning Collaborative Efforts with Your Strategy

Because collaboration is a means to an end, you have to clearly articulate how collaboration helps the company achieve its strategic goals. To pinpoint specific areas of the company where cross-silo collaboration would provide the most benefit, you can ask questions like, *Where do we lack business momentum? Where do we see anti-collaborative behaviors? Where are competitors moving ahead? Where do we see high attrition, low employee engagement, or a lack of progress toward diversity, equity, and inclusion (DEI)? Where are we coming up short in terms of innovation?*

Capturing the kinds of business outcomes we laid out in Chapter 1 may come from integrating a specific function, such as risk management, into the rest of the business. Or you may need broader collaboration in a specific process—such as getting sales, operations, legal, and customer service involved in product development—to capture an opportunity.

## Diagnosing the Real and Perceived Barriers to Collaboration

Identifying the barriers to collaboration requires a two-pronged approach, using both surveys and structured discussions. Both generate broad-based inputs from across the company, which are needed not only to ensure that you are collecting and interpreting views from a variety of employees but also to build a sense of participation across the entire senior leadership group. Research clearly shows that "having voice" is crucial for helping people feel invested in a change effort.[5] Together, the prongs give leaders a true understanding of the obstacles—including structural, cultural, and interpersonal issues—that inhibit effective collaboration.

We should offer an upfront caution: because this work relies on qualitative research, some of your colleagues may believe that it is as simple as asking a few questions (as in, "I'm excellent at interviewing candidates; surely this is even easier"). Because we are all exposed to surveys on a near-daily basis, it's tempting to think that the survey process is easy and obvious. But in fact, conducting qualitative research is a well-developed science, and laypeople commonly make mistakes that can seriously bias a survey's results. For example, asking a person to provide identifying information (e.g., gender) at the wrong place in a survey may dramatically skew their responses—and may even impede their ability to answer questions correctly.[6] On the other hand, asking simple, *open-ended* questions about perceived barriers to collaboration makes it far more likely that you'll generate compelling and high-quality data. To do this piece right, you need an expert in qualitative research to help you design the survey, then follow up with rigorous methods to code the results.[7]

The second prong of the barriers-identification process involves focus groups and in-depth interviews. Test your understanding of those barriers by arranging a set of one-on-one interviews with selected leaders. Make sure to include thought leaders whenever possible, since the strategic selection of interviewees can help build commitment to the project and provide organizational momentum.

Although every organization is unique, our work within a wide variety of organizations has surfaced a number of typical barriers. These include the following:

- **Lack of knowledge of the company's capabilities and expertise.** It's often hard in organizations to know what capabilities (technology, products, functionality) and expertise (who can do what, and how well) exist.[8]

- **Lack of competence trust.** To collaborate, you need faith in others' capabilities—not only technical skills but also broader competencies like client-handling ability and negotiation skills.

- **Lack of interpersonal trust.** Are people worried their colleagues are going to undermine them? That lack of interpersonal trust—how much faith you place in someone's character and intentions—may be rooted in previous observations (and therefore possibly well founded) or simply in a lack of familiarity (and therefore not well founded).

- **Lack of time or inefficiency of collaboration.** The collaborative process can be logistically challenging—for example, due to different time zones and language or cultural barriers, and to the time required to explain the task to someone else. Sometimes companies find specific culprits, such as outdated technology, that make collaboration far too cumbersome. Elsewhere, the real question is not whether people have time to collaborate, but whether they choose to spend it that way. This barrier arises when people think they get more benefit from working in a silo than from collaborating, which leads to our next point.

- **Poor incentives and key performance indicators.** Sometimes the problem is a misguided incentive system, like the one in a company we advised: "We're all handed individual sales quotas. There is no team component, and we can't split the credit. Why would a colleague help me close a deal when they get nothing out of it?" Let's be clear: Every compensation system has both known trade-offs and unintended consequences. But some systems are more broken than others—especially the ones that rely on formulaic calculations of individual outcomes.[9]

- **Lack of collaboration capabilities and confidence.** Collaboration is a metacapability: a set of mindsets, behaviors, and abilities that collectively equip someone to engage in effective cross-silo working (see the sidebar). To enhance collaboration, you need to assess your people and develop their underlying skills that add up to a collaborative mindset and approach.

Wherever possible, your surveys should inform and stimulate your in-person inquiries. For example, we often find it helpful to use some of the respondents' verbatim quotes from the open-ended survey questions to illuminate the barriers discussions in the focus groups and interviews. These examples often spark useful conversations about deeper issues that the respondents didn't write about in the survey. Direct quotes are also useful for leaders to use when explaining the results of the survey, because they demonstrate that people have been heard.

## Discovering and Analyzing Bright Spots

You might be surprised by the places where great collaboration is already happening in your company. Leaders who feel a strong sense of urgency may be tempted to skip this step and "get right to the problems we need to fix." But capturing these success stories is important for two reasons. First, stories are the backbone of human culture. In organizations, culture is created and spread by sharing real-life examples. Do you celebrate the sales hero who singlehandedly bags a new account? Well, fine—but do you also acknowledge the team that did the research, helped prepare the pitch, and then flawlessly implemented the solution? Turning bright-spot episodes uncovered in the

## FOUNDATIONAL SKILLS FOR SMARTER COLLABORATION

To enhance collaboration, you need to develop the skills that add up to a collaborative mindset and approach.[a] Through our research, we have defined three major categories of those foundational capabilities:

- **The ability to identify issues that truly warrant collaboration.** The ability to see a complex problem *holistically*, and not just through a single functional lens, is the difference between starting down a path of smart collaboration and taking a subpar, siloed approach. Underlying capabilities include, for example, *root cause analysis* (identifying the underlying systemic issues of a given challenge, which are often far more complex than the presenting symptoms) and *framing issues* (taking multiple sources of ambiguous information and distilling those inputs into a clear statement of the challenge).

- **Interpersonal skills.** Collaboration often requires people to work with people in different parts of the company, or even other organizations, which means they need interpersonal skills that will enable them to navigate complex organizations. One is the ability to *exert influence*, rather than power, because the collaborator needs to gain commitment from colleagues over whom they have no authority. *Conflict management* is essential because collaboration inevitably involves clashes of viewpoints and often engenders power struggles; people

---

diagnostic into stories that get told and retold allows leaders to shape the culture in collaborative directions—and implicitly defines a set of anti-collaborative behaviors that should be avoided.

Second, stories summarizing specific actions that have worked in your company can be critically important in convincing skeptics not only that collaboration is already delivering returns but also that it can be replicated.

### Generating Compelling "Upside" Findings

Despite starting a diagnostic expecting to find untapped potential, most leaders are shocked to find how much money they are leaving on the table.

need the skills to seek out a diversity of views and create an environ-ment of trust in which those views can be shared.

- **Self-management abilities.** Because smarter collaboration requires people to get out of their comfort zone and embrace change and complexity, the kinds of skills that support a personal transformation are fundamental for fostering collaboration. Broadly, these skills include directing one's own behaviors, thoughts, and emotions in a conscious and productive way.[b] This involves demonstrating *comfort with ambiguity and change* (retaining an open mind and seeking new opportunities for development and growth), *self-reflection and authenticity* (understanding your own behavioral tendencies so you know what to flex on and what to reflect on), and *curiosity* (actively exploring new ideas and engaging with a diverse group of people to identify new opportunities and create connections across ideas).

a. We are grateful to the several dozen chief learning officers who participated in our research on this topic.

b. More than half the companies surveyed by the World Economic Forum in 2020 agreed that these skills will be even more in demand by 2025. World Economic Forum, *The Future of Jobs Report 2020* (Geneva: World Economic Forum, 2020).

How do you quantify the upside? Let's go back to the kind of exam-ple we discussed in Chapter 1. In one business, we saw that revenues were *5.7 times higher for clients served by three business lines than by a single one.* Those clients served by five business lines generated fees *17.6 times higher* than those with just one kind of service, as shown in Figure 3-1.

First, calculate the average revenue generated per customer based on the number of offerings they purchase (as in Figure 3-1). Next, cal-culate the upside from a realistic shift in your portfolio. Your aim isn't to serve *every* client with your full range of services each year, nor necessarily to eliminate low-revenue clients (see sidebar on "chopping the tail"). Instead, how much is it worth if you shift just 10 percent of

FIGURE 3-1

## Revenue impact of smart collaboration

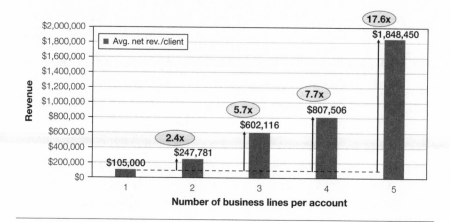

clients in each category to the next-higher category? The numbers below the bars in Figure 3-2 indicate the business lines bought by each customer; the numbers in the circles show the hypothetical customer profile and revenue if 10 percent of clients in each category move one step to the right. For this company, the incremental revenue of this shift adds up to nearly $43 million.[10]

Note, too, that in this example, the vast majority are making a move from one to two products, where the incremental value is relatively low. As you consider where to focus, think about deepening your larger relationships where the relative bump in revenues is highest. Making that kind of move with your customers who already buy multiple services is also more likely to succeed: they already trust and value your company to provide more sophisticated services, and you almost certainly have more buyers inside the client and more insights that will make you a top-choice provider for their highest-level needs.

This top-line shift is typical across the organizations we studied that are collaborating well—that is, doing complex work for clients that results in appropriate levels of increased revenue. Many businesses are missing out on an additional 15 percent of overall revenue by not figuring out how to make this shift.

FIGURE 3-2

## Hypothetical new portfolio and upside

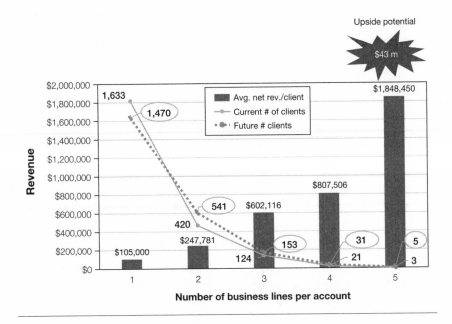

The punch line: saying, "We could realize an extra $43 million in revenue by collaborating better," serves as a compelling argument for collaboration.

## Building in the Clients' Perspective

If you want to alert your company to the importance of collaboration, just talk to your clients. You will hear that they want deeper engagement with their strategic partners, and in most cases, they aren't getting it today. The "voice of the client" is one of the most powerful ways to drive home the need for collaboration, assess the gaps that exist today, and better understand what might give your business a competitive advantage through more skillful collaboration.

First, a caution: Remember that you aren't trying to sell anything in these conversations with your customers. You're trying to answer the question, *Where can we add more value to the client by bringing to bear the full breadth of our company's capabilities?*

## DON'T JUST "CHOP THE TAIL"

Your analysis will inevitably show a long tail of low-revenue single-offering clients. Don't succumb to the knee-jerk reaction to "chop it off." This focuses people inside your company on what they're *losing*: inevitably, some people are very attached to certain clients in that group, because they've worked long and hard to develop the relationships. And as Daniel Kahneman's Nobel Prize–winning work clearly shows, people will overfocus on what they're losing, even if there's some upside to gain.[a] That sense of loss will kill collaboration.

The upshot? Leaders need to be transparent about decision criteria for shifting the portfolio to help people see the strategic rationale. Ideally, client-facing employees will be involved in these decisions, helping them become invested and committed.

Start by dividing low-value clients into segments depending on how collaboration could allow you to harness their potential. The following are some examples:

- Some offerings simply aren't needed, at least not all the time (e.g., litigation from a law firm, crisis management from a PR firm, custom software development services from a tech company). Nevertheless, make sure your salespeople who consistently call on the clients are helping to keep channels open for colleagues who can provide these intermittent services.

- Other clients who use niche services are great names for you. One public relations executive told us, "We'd never give up Richard Branson as a client just because he doesn't use our digital offerings." Collaboration can help leverage that brand for marketing across your areas.

- For businesses that are too small or simple to require multifaceted service, can you collaborate internally, or with external partners, to develop more cost-effective business models to serve them?

Your aim isn't to serve every client with your full range of services. Instead, you need to figure out how and where collaborative investments will pay off.

a. D. Kahneman, *Thinking, Fast and Slow* (New York: Macmillan, 2011).

FIGURE 3-3

## Clients' vs. partners' assessment of collaboration

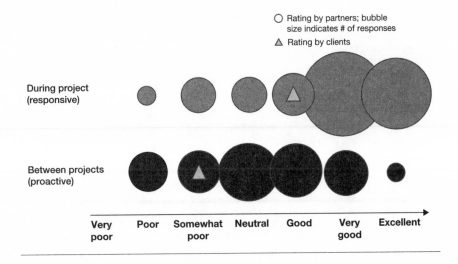

Don't assume your people already know what the clients are looking for or have a good sense of their own performance. In study after study, we've seen providers radically overestimate how good they are at delivering their company's full value to their customers. Figure 3-3 shows one example that came as a rude shock to a Big Four accounting firm: when asked to rate their collaboration "on deal" (during a live project), most partners scored themselves as very good or excellent; for "off-deal" collaboration (times when they kept in touch with clients to check in or add a nugget of insight), partners rated themselves as neutral to good. Clients' estimates, however, were consistently at least a full point lower. One said, "They never bother to reach out unless there's a clear piece of work on offer."

Another pitfall to avoid: don't repurpose customer interviews that have already been conducted as part of other initiatives. Typical "voice of the client" interviews almost never focus on collaboration. Your goal is to identify and analyze specific situations in which the client was or wasn't served in a cross-silo way by your business, and whether more holistic opportunities exist.

See Table 3-1 for a sampling of themes to listen for during these kinds of customer interviews.

TABLE 3-1

## Clients' vs. partners' assessment of collaboration

| Theme | Illustrative quote |
|---|---|
| Deeply, proactively invested in understanding the client's business | "Understanding us—our business units, our industry, the ecosystem—is critical. We expect a provider either to have consulted with his peers and arrive with the accumulated institutional knowledge or to bring colleagues along to have a real rich conversation." |
| Deliver the value of the organization | "Don't just try to cross-sell another product. I have lots of vendors. Show me why buying two things from you is better than if I buy them separately." |
| Integrated global client service capability | "You have expertise around the world. When you bring it together we really see the benefit. But, it wastes my time when we get calls from multiple people in your company who want to talk about basically the same thing." |
| Trust-based, candid relationship with the client | "I can just be really honest with them and say 'Listen, my CEO is in a rage. I'm going to go get my head handed to me on a platter if I give this advice—you have to raise it and take the pain for me.' And they do." |
| Consistent proactivity | "It is not about calling me to have coffee—it's the discussion during coffee. Figure out where I am going, and be the 'door opener' for innovative tools and capabilities, other brilliant minds in the field I can learn from." |

If you are reluctant to "ask a favor" of your clients, consider this: many appreciate this signal that you want to serve them better. We sometimes help our clients with these conversations, and in our experience, most of these interviews run well past their scheduled time. Why? Because people are excited to engage in a deep conversation about collaboration.

Combined with your internally derived survey and interview insights, these customer conversations should help guide your focus on areas for growth through collaboration.

## Setting Priorities

Once the organization has linked the priorities to the business strategy, the specific initiatives need to be prioritized. In our client work, we use a simple two-by-two matrix (Figure 3-4) to facilitate conversations around prioritization.

FIGURE 3-4

## Setting collaborative priorities

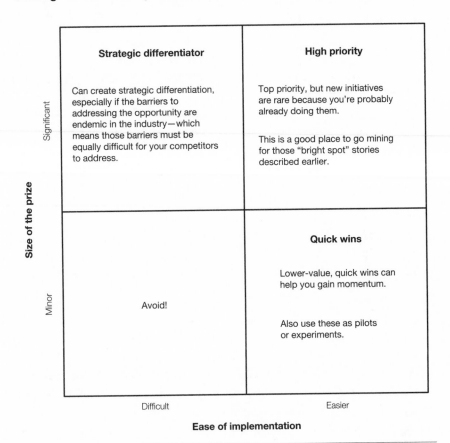

"Size of the prize" is often expressed in financial terms: increased revenue, cost reduction, error or loss reduction, client retention, and so on. Other opportunities (such as enhanced reputation, client satisfaction, innovation, and progress toward DEI goals) may require different approaches to quantification. Mapping these onto a single two-by-two matrix may require subjective judgments, but the goal is to always link them back to their impact on the business strategy.

Along the *x* axis, we're asking and attempting to answer the question, *Which of our potential opportunities can we collaborate on*

## EXPLOITING THE HIGH EASE/MINOR PRIZE (I.E., QUICK WINS) ZONE

Even though "quick wins" may not sound compelling, we can point to two solid reasons to explore this zone. The first is to run carefully structured pilot programs, which will allow you to quickly learn about both content and process. You'll need to collect before-and-after data so you can replicate (or alter) the initiatives in the broader rollout. Ideally, you'll run several pilots concurrently to figure out what works best as quickly as possible.

The second reason to explore this zone is that quick wins can help show early momentum and galvanize an organization to take on the tougher but higher-value opportunities.

As a rule, it's OK to "over-support" these pilots and experiments, vis-à-vis what you'd do on behalf of broader rollouts. At this point in the process, your company may need to see just that kind of commitment from senior leadership.

---

*most easily?* "Easier" opportunities include areas where the company already has the required expertise and resources, complexity is low, similar initiatives have been successfully completed in the past, or the initiatives have a short implementation period. Conversely, initiatives involving engagement from a large number of internal groups or external parties, new skills or expertise, a longer timeframe to execute, or greater uncertainties will fall into the "difficult" box.

### Identifying Additional or Alternative Benefits

The preceding six sections summarize the many advantages to the typical business of conducting a "collaboration diagnosis." But what if your strategic goal for collaboration is not revenues and profits? The good news is that you can still use a modified version of our diagnostic tool to identify compelling benefits for *your* organization.

For example, you may choose to quantify the benefits of reduced risk (regulatory fines, operational errors, etc.), or the financial and quality-control upsides of improving employee engagement and reten-tion. Hospitals and other health-care providers might choose to focus their analysis on metrics like patient outcomes. Government agen-cies, nonprofits, and foundations might focus on the time needed to implement new programs and deliver new services. If you go this route, be sure to capture some of the less obvious and direct benefits—for example, an enhanced reputation in the DEI space. In all cases, the goal is to use your hard-won diagnostic data to assess your full potential arising from smart collaboration.

## Disseminating Your Findings

Let's assume that you have run an appropriate diagnostic for your organization, and you have powerful findings in hand. Now what?

There are many compelling answers. The diagnostic can be a power-ful tool for turning up new opportunities. It can also serve as a potent tool for generating momentum for change. Because Chapter 8 provides much more detail about leading and sustaining collabora-tion, here we focus on how to wrap up the diagnostic to get the most impact.

Depending how you reveal your findings, you can radically increase the excitement level. One media and entertainment company we worked with—let's call them PrimeTime—timed the conclusion of the diagnos-tic to coincide with its annual leadership retreat for the company's top 1,200 executives. As we were wrapping up the diagnostic, we held a series of small-group and one-on-one discussions to gain the commit-ment of leaders throughout the company. We asked a number of them to participate in the presentation at the leadership retreat.

The CEO kicked off the retreat by reiterating how PrimeTime's strategy hinged on smarter collaboration. We then shared a recap of the findings, including the potential benefits and missed opportunities: higher profits, faster product innovation, increased job satisfaction, expanded career opportunities, and so on.

Verbatim quotes—especially some of the snarky and colorful ones from anonymous survey responses—and short videos from employees and clients around the world livened up the presentation. The CEO then confirmed specific actions the company planned to take, and described the resources that would be allocated to make effective collaboration a reality. Various leaders explained the action plan at a detailed enough level to give confidence to the more concrete thinkers in the audience.[11] Each subsequent session of the retreat wove in key themes about collaboration, making it clear that this wasn't merely a sideshow but rather the core way going forward to deliver PrimeTime's most important goals. People came away not only fired up about the collaborative direction but also clear about specific changes they needed to champion and committed to leading it within their own groups.

Even if you can't mount a major retreat, figure out which elements you *can* replicate on a smaller scale: cascading commitment throughout the leadership team, championing change from the top, using evidence to communicate the rationale for change, and convincing people to make specific commitments for collaboration-enhancing actions.

## Back to Our Case in Point: TechStar Conducts Its Diagnostic

Earlier, we introduced TechStar: a software company whose leaders, including CEO Rick Jones, were pretty sure that they were leaving good money on the table by failing to work collaboratively on their key clients' most pressing problems.

To understand what was holding them back, TechStar conducted a diagnostic. It surveyed the organization to get a feel for the pulse of collaboration and conducted internal interviews across functions, levels, and geographies, including external advisers and the board. Through these concurrent processes, three key barriers emerged. First, the sales team was primarily driven by individual revenue targets. "I have my own quotas to hit. I can't afford to spend time helping other people hit theirs," said one sales executive. Second, coverage of the large, complex clients was siloed across multiple salespeople calling on different divisions and markets. "We don't look great when several of us are at the client's office and we didn't even know it. What's worse, if the client's issue cuts across divisions, who's on point?" asked another salesperson. Finally, functions like product management and development were internally focused and rarely had direct client access. The diagnostic showed the result: they spent far more time addressing Tech-Star's need for efficiency than on client-relevant improvements.

The news wasn't all bad. One of TechStar's largest clients was a midsize global bank, and the diagnostic illuminated how that account had grown so much. "We are serving almost all their divisions in multiple markets," CEO Jones commented. "The difference with this client came from Cindy Wentz, one of our sales leads, who had developed relationships with the COO [chief operating officer] and CTO [chief technical officer]. She was operating above the level of the client's own silos, and also coordinating across all our sales efforts. That made a huge difference."

"The client wants one TechStar," Wentz confirmed in a subsequent conversation. "By pulling our salespeople together, we could talk about strategic solutions that bridged multiple silos."

Interviews with clients validated many of the challenges, and also uncovered several new issues. One strategic client with a low satisfaction score said, "Most times I don't know who to call. We have multiple salespeople calling on us. They're all good, but no one is pulling it together. And nobody's reaching out proactively." In contrast, an executive at the global bank commented, "TechStar came to us with a future-state model that integrated a dozen of our countries into a single global service model. To pull it off, we worked closely with their teams in Canada, the UK, and India, as well their product team, to fill some of the functional gaps. Cindy did a great job herding the cats, and they now support our European business."

With those insights, TechStar identified three priorities for maintaining growth through enhanced collaboration:

- Designate one salesperson as the point for each strategic client. That person's responsibility would be to grow overall global sales at the client in conformance with TechStar's strategic client plan, acting as the central hub of coordination across salespeople, geographies, and functions.

- Set business development goals for existing clients as well as new logos, and give all salespeople associated with a given client a shared goal of growing overall revenue at that client, rather than just their own product line.

- Formalize client feedback and client satisfaction ratings with an emphasis on collaboration between TechStar and the client, and give all groups touching the client (sales, service, etc.) a goal of increasing client-satisfaction scores.

Jones launched the new strategy at a town hall meeting. "I brought in the COO of one of our global bank clients," Jones recalls, "and he talked to the whole company about how our two organizations had worked together to create a new capability, and that had made a real difference to the bank."

That presentation was inspiring both because of the successful process it documented and because of the real-world impact of the innovation. The COO explained that his bank wanted to increase lending to disadvantaged communities. "We created a joint team with your data experts, product managers, and tech wizards alongside our teams," he told participants at the town hall meeting. "Together, we figured out how to use new sources of data about our customers to better identify potential needs and analyze risks. We made a huge leap forward—doubling our lending to these communities in just fifteen months."

## Time Well Spent

To sum up, Jones and his TechStar colleagues used their diagnostic process to change the way their company competed in a tough marketplace. They listened hard to their clients, found and celebrated bright spots, and set three concrete goals for collaboration in the future. The entire process took just under three months. Yes, that's an eternity in the software environment—but given TechStar's ominous slide toward playing a niche role in its marketplace, this was time well spent.

Let's assume that you've conducted a diagnostic at the organizational level, and you now know where you're going strategically and how you're going to get there. Your next challenge is making sure that your teams know where their personal strengths lie, and that they can use those strengths to effect the needed transformation. Our next chapter provides a novel and scientifically supported way to make that happen.

$$\left[\begin{array}{c} 4 \end{array}\right]$$

# Individual and Team Diagnostic

*N*o one collaborates alone.

Self-evident? Maybe so. But let's dig a little deeper into the implications of this seemingly simple statement.

If today's most important business problems are indeed highly complex, then strong teams have to be brought together to work collaboratively on tackling them.

But how do these strong teams *really operate*? To answer this question, we need insights on two levels: the team and the individual. First, the team leader has to understand the talent on that team. We generally steer away from sports metaphors, but in this case it's pretty hard to avoid one. Who wins the World Cup, the America's Cup, the World Series, or the Tour de France? The answer: the team that most effectively combines a group of star contributors with different and complementary skills, and knows how to *use* each person's strengths as part of that team.

Self-awareness is the starting point for individual insights. Team members, and their managers, need to understand how they tend to act at work. For example, is it more natural for them to take control of a project, or to delegate readily and easily? Are they better at launching a new initiative, or at refining one that's already in progress? Some of those insights arise merely through reflection, but people tend to miss some critical "ah-ha" moments unless guided in their reflection.

And then comes the second tough challenge. Someone has to *manage* those stars, making sure that the team dynamics are pointing the team toward victory. Generally speaking, this means getting people to play to their strengths and to focus consciously on using those strengths to improve collaboration and capitalize on its advantages.

In the following pages, we explore how both individual attributes and team dynamics contribute to understanding and using collaborative strengths. We'll begin with individual attributes, emphasizing a tool that can help people understand their own particular strengths.

## On the Individual Level: The Seven Behavioral Dimensions of Smart Collaboration

Human motivation is complicated, and it's sometimes tempting to interpret collaborative behavior as an undifferentiated blob of be-nice impulses. But our decade of research (see sidebar) shows otherwise. We can identify which behaviors really matter, and how to use them to foster collaboration.

We have identified seven key behavioral dimensions, as summarized in Figure 4-1. The first four relate to the way a person tackles the *issues* on which the smart collaboration is focused. What kinds of problems is a given team member attracted to, and how is he or she inclined to tackle them? The next three relate to the *group-centered* behavioral components of smart collaboration—in other words, how the team member tends to interact with his or her peers in general.

Before we dig deeper into these seven dimensions, we should make it clear that when it comes to collaboration, *none of these tendencies is inherently "good" or "bad."* They can all be strengths if used deliberately—that is, thoughtfully deployed to promote collaboration. But if your tendencies show up in the wrong way—for example, taken to the extreme when you're under pressure—then they can block collaboration. As a rule, a winning team calls on a mix of these behaviors; conversely, the team that lacks such a mix may be headed for trouble.

FIGURE 4-1

# The seven dimensions of smart collaboration

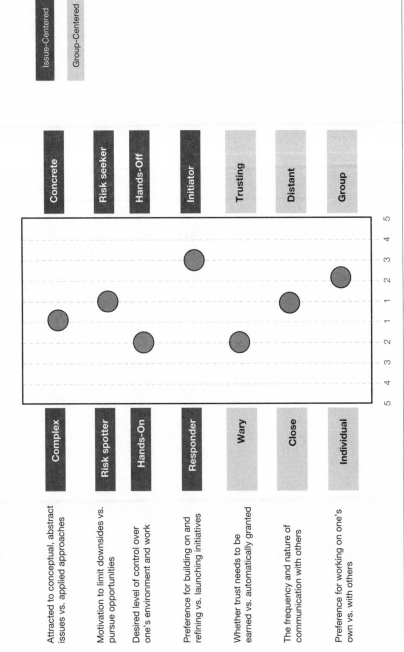

Attracted to conceptual, abstract issues vs. applied approaches

Motivation to limit downsides vs. pursue opportunities

Desired level of control over one's environment and work

Preference for building on and refining vs. launching initiatives

Whether trust needs to be earned vs. automatically granted

The frequency and nature of communication with others

Preference for working on one's own vs. with others

Issue-Centered

Group-Centered

Concrete / Complex

Risk seeker / Risk spotter

Hands-Off / Hands-On

Initiator / Responder

Trusting / Wary

Distant / Close

Group / Individual

## THE ORIGINS OF THE SEVEN DIMENSIONS

To understand the individual foundations of collaborative behavior, we pursued data on several fronts. First, we conducted a survey that involved respondents from more than fifty countries. This survey generated more than four thousand responses, which we assembled into a unique database—one that relies heavily on respondents' answers to open-ended questions about their experiences of collaboration, including both actions that have helped them reap the benefits of collaboration and actions that have created barriers to collaboration.

At the same time, we spent two years digging deep into the reality of one specific workplace: a global organization with units across sixty-five countries. Through a series of diagnostics, interviews, observations, focus groups, and analysis of archival data, we identified a group of individual behaviors that help foster cross-silo collaboration, and a second group of behaviors that can impede collaboration. Whether done intentionally or not, acting in these anti-collaborative ways can encourage silos, reduce trust, and discourage people from working together.[a]

Bringing all the research efforts together, we developed a model of seven behavioral dimensions that are the foundation of the Smart Collaboration Accelerator psychometric tools, described later in the chapter.[b]

a. For more details on the surveys, interviews, and verification events we conducted to develop the seven-dimensional model, see "Part I, Quantitative and Qualitative Field Research: Core Behavioral Dimensions of Smart Collaboration," in the technical report of the Smart Collaboration Accelerator, available on request through Gardner & Co. (https://www.gardnerandco.co /contact/).

b. Details of the tool available through Gardner & Co. For early background research, see H. K. Gardner, "Teamwork and Collaboration in Professional Service Firms: Evolution, Challenges, and Opportunities," in *The Oxford Handbook of Professional Service Firms*, ed. L. Empson et al. (Oxford: Oxford University Press, 2015), 374–402; and H. K. Gardner, "Effective Teamwork and Collaboration," in *Managing Talent for Success: Talent Development in Law Firms*, ed. R. Normand-Hochman (London: Globe Business, 2013), 145–159. Over time, we have revised and refined the model to crystallize the current seven dimensions and their relationships to specific aspects of smart collaboration.

For example, a consumer-products company we worked with had a strong bias toward recruiting Initiators and Complex thinkers. Why? The company's leaders believed that the business needed people who were innovative and who could drive their teams to launch new products and solutions. As it turned out, their teams were indeed great at conceptualizing and jump-starting lots of projects, but without Responders and Concrete thinkers to move projects along, those products were slow to get to market. Those innovative teams were jumping ahead to the Next New Thing before the last good idea could be implemented. By using the framework, the manager was able to restructure the team with a stronger balance of skills.

Now let's look at the seven dimensions in turn, beginning with what we call the "issue-centered" individual behaviors. We'll do so from the perspective of an individual team member. How do you approach working with a group?

## Issue-Centered Behaviors

The four issue-centered behaviors relate to the way a person tackles the issues on which the smart collaboration is focused.

### Complex/Concrete

This dimension explains how you approach problems. Do you enjoy exploring abstract ideas and digging into ambiguous issues that have multiple causes? Do you draw on conceptual models and your past experiences to make connections across a range of topics, sometimes to the extent that the people around admit that they feel a bit baffled, or even put off? If so, you are on the Complex end of this spectrum.

Or, during a theoretical discussion, does your mind move ahead to questions like, *How would we put this into action? What resources would we need?* Or maybe even, *So what?* If so, you're more on the Concrete side.

People with these two very different approaches can really get on each other's nerves in a discussion. (Maybe you've been involved in such a fracas!) The Complex thinkers look down on their Concrete colleagues—*They're so mundane! So predictable!*—while the Concrete thinkers grumble that all these abstractions floating in the air are a big waste of time, or a shameless exercise in grandstanding, or both. The truth, however, is that both approaches are essential for innovation. Why? Because innovation is more than just mere creativity. Creativity doesn't qualify as innovation until it gets applied successfully.

## Risk Spotter/Risk Seeker

Risk Seekers are the ones who examine a problem and instantly look for ways to turn it into an advantage or opportunity. Risk Spotters, by contrast, look at the same situation and see mainly downsides or even threats. The fear of failing is one dividing line between these groups: Risk Seekers will risk failure in pursuit of a perceived great opportunity; Risk Spotters will circle the wagons to head off the possibility of failure.

If you are a Risk Spotter, you are likely to be the one responsible for reality-checking new ideas. Yours can be a very positive influence—for example, by helping the team avoid being overly optimistic and stay out of the trap of group-think. But it's incumbent on you to be a *constructive* skeptic. Yes, point out the risks, but also be ready with solutions. To meet one CEO who learned to turn his Risk-Spotting tendencies into a strength by partnering with a complementary chief operating officer (COO), see the sidebar.

If you're a Risk Seeker, you're in a good position to help the team manage the inevitable setbacks, put those failures in a broader context, and keep the team focused on the goals. Encourage the discussion of challenge and risks—even if that's not your default mode—and don't react emotionally if people challenge your ideas. Remember: smart collaboration requires differing perspectives.

## Hands-On/Hands-Off

Which is better for promoting collaboration: being Hands-On or Hands-Off?

It's not a trick question, but neither does it lend itself to an easy answer. Hands-Off people give others lots of room to operate

## COMPLEX THINKER, RISK SPOTTER

Markus, a C-level executive with a global beverage company, had a rocky start in his position. Although he had strong ideas about solving production challenges in the early days of the pandemic, he had never reached the point of making a single recommendation to the company's board. One stumbling block: Markus constantly obsessed about *all the pieces that could go wrong,* as he saw it.

His fortunes started to change when he got to know the company's new COO, a natural Risk Seeker and a more Concrete thinker. With the COO as his sounding board, Markus realized how his efforts to mitigate all possible risks became a roadblock to his conceptually powerful solutions. The way the COO framed the same situation opened Markus's eyes to the wide range of potential *upsides,* as well the risks. By embracing those different perspectives, Markus's ideas were able to be captured in well-rounded, compelling proposals that were welcomed and valued by the board.

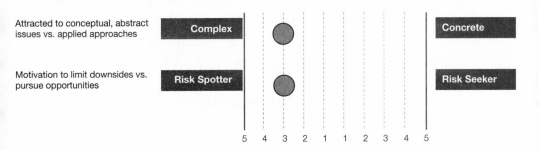

independently, but at the same time, they may fail to give sufficient guidance and feedback. In a remote-work context, moreover, the truly Hands-off team member runs the risk of simply . . . disappearing. Hands-on people, meanwhile, are likely to give clear direction and coaching, and are unlikely to drop out of sight. But when stressed, they tend to roll up their sleeves and get the job done themselves. Taken to an extreme, the result is micromanagement, or even the exclusion of other team members.

Many people locate themselves in the middle of the spectrum along this dimension. If you're one of them, it's worth reflecting on *when* you're more likely to be Hands-on or Hands-off. For example, make sure you're not instinctively jumping in to "help" the team member who happens to have a strong accent. Also be aware of the unintended (and maybe unwelcome) consequences of Hands-on behavior. If your colleagues come to anticipate that kind of behavior from you, they may be inclined to sit back and wait for you to set out the action plan on your own: the opposite of smart collaboration.

### Responder/Initiator

Who goes first, and who goes second?

If you're strong along the Initiator dimension, you're always looking ahead to spot future problems or opportunities, then working proactively to shape them.

If you're a Responder, by contrast, you're comfortable with not being the first mover. "Going second" gives you the chance to build on others' initiatives, perhaps helping to take them from being unworkable to viable. And if you're an effective Responder, you can be counted on to carry the work through. Your willingness to pitch in and support new initiatives is a boon to teams. Along the way to the larger solution, you react to *actual* problems, rather than wasting time caught up in what-ifs.

A word of caution to the Responder: Make sure your contributions are recognized and valued. In many organizations, it's the Initiators who get the glory (think about the "heroic" deal makers whose teams never get any credit for doing the hard work of executing). And while it's fine for them to get their due, make sure to use ongoing group communications to build a suitably broad base of ownership for success—and share those comms as broadly as possible.

Now let's look at the four group-centered behaviors.

## The Group-Centered Behaviors

The three group-centered behaviors relate to how the team member tends to interact with his or her peers.

## TWO RESPONDERS AND AN INITIATOR

The three presidents of an international mobility technology company are peers, with each leading a division. Despite the company's siloed business approach, the three leaders have developed strong bonds through a combination of leadership meetings, calls, and offsites. During one of their conversations, President 3 proudly reported on her team's favorable reputation: "When folks have an idea and want to get it done, they come to us. We are brilliant closers." President 1 chuckled and said, "Ditto!" Both leaders had figured out how to leverage their strengths as Responders.

President 2 laughed too, but she was intrigued. She wanted to understand their "secret sauce" for finishing new projects. As a high-powered Initiator, she often found herself exploring forward-looking ideas, but far less often saw her team carry those idea across the finish line.

On the advice of her peers, P2 expanded her collaborative network to include more colleagues who could help shepherd her product development to completion—a group that included both P1 and P2.

Preference for building on and refining vs. launching initiatives

## Wary/Trusting

When you meet new colleagues, do you assume that they have a high degree of integrity and are fully capable of doing their jobs? Or do you take a "wait-and-see" approach, extending your trust only after your colleagues have proved themselves? If you are in the Trusting category—that is, if you're the kind of person who assumes that your colleagues are often right and generally have good intentions—you may jump fairly quickly into collaboration. If you are more Wary—tending to rely on data and evidence to assess whether others are really up to the job and are in roles that play to their strengths—you may get to collaboration more slowly.

## HIGH TRUST AND HANDS-OFF: WHAT COULD POSSIBLY GO WRONG?

We recently worked with the leader of a team handling the rollout of a new 5G-related technology for a major telecoms company. Here, we'll call her Ann.

At a point when they were well along in that project, Ann had a major lightbulb moment: Based on her Smart Collaboration Accelerator results (a tool detailed later in this chapter) and discussions with a coach, she learned that she was both highly Trusting and highly Hands-off. Because she trusted in people's competence, she instinctively believed her team members could handle the major stretch assignments they were taking on. But because she was also inclined to be Hands-off, she rarely gave those colleagues any effective direction or coaching. She was surprised and frustrated that they frequently were coming back with solutions that were different from what she had envisioned. Masking that frustration, she'd say, "Well, this isn't quite right. But obviously you guys are great at what you do, so why don't you give it another try?"

In other words, she was failing to provide concrete feedback on what she was looking for, or how to approach the problem differently. Instead of empowering the team members who were reporting to her—which was her natural inclination—she was actually putting them in a position of having to read her mind. Yes, the team appreciated her trust and their resulting autonomy, but on balance, it wasn't working. She had taken her behaviors too far.

Ann realized that she needed to try a different approach—one more focused on ensuring that she and her teammates were aligned on the vision for projects, that they would all be open to thought-partnering as the work progressed, and that she was giving more frequent coaching and direct feedback.

For the innately Trusting, use your high trust level to welcome new viewpoints onto your teams and thereby increase the diversity of thought. This might involve welcoming someone in as a regular contributor—or even as a one-off—to share a new perspective and enrich the group's thinking. Remember that those around you may be more Wary and you may need to moderate your enthusiasm to earn their trust.

For the Wary among you: listen to those Wary tendencies! Your skeptical eye—whether it is focused on people, organizational politics, or commercial situations—can help spot small issues before they become more substantial ones. Early detection and correction can enhance trust by letting people know that it's safe to admit errors and that their colleagues will support them. Meanwhile, be careful not to appear overly negative, argumentative, or unsupportive of others.

## Close/Distant Communicator

This dimension focuses on communication style. Let's imagine one colleague of yours who always gets right down to business, with no preliminaries. One result of this approach is that you may not know anything about this colleague's personal life, despite the fact that you've worked together for years. People like this are what we call Distant. They engage when they need to push work forward but not for socializing. They tend to be hard to read. You frequently feel like you don't know where you stand with them.

Now let's conjure up a Close colleague. He or she is the person who injects energy into a meeting, frequently drops by your office, shares a photo of the kids, discusses plans for the weekend, and seems quite comfortable with being "easy to read."

Both Distant and Close communicators can be powerful collaboration boosters. If you are more Distant, you can use that as a strength to let others have more visibility and more of the limelight. (Generally, though, you *do* need to open up enough to ensure that colleagues can figure out what's on your mind.) If you are a Close communicator, you most likely have a relatively large network of active relationships. This means that you can be a powerful connector—helping others build their own networks and welcoming those kinds of people (such as new arrivals or members of formerly underrepresented minority groups) who might otherwise find it hard to get tied into the organization.

## Individual/Group

Where do you fall on the spectrum of preferring to work as part of a group as opposed to working independently?

## HIGHLY CLOSE

Jeffrey, the new president of a large, public university, was hired to design and implement a top-to-bottom turnaround effort. Part of the problem, he was told, was its uncollaborative culture. Tensions ran high, and key performance indicators kept sinking.

Given the seriousness of the issues, Jeffrey—hired in part because he had a reputation for being collegial, "super friendly," and personable—adopted a task-oriented, rigorous, Distant leadership style that he felt was better suited to the task at hand, reinforcing the notion that *he meant business*.

It didn't work. While his plan was acknowledged by most to be spot-on, he struggled to get people engaged and progress was minimal. Jeffrey's increasing challenges led to a series of deep, reflective talks with a few trusted advisers. Based on these talks, Jeffrey realized he had abandoned his strengths and tried to lead in a way that was not authentic. Once he embraced his natural, warm self, the organization responded swiftly, and the turnaround began.

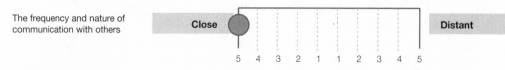

The frequency and nature of communication with others — Close / Distant — 5 4 3 2 1 1 2 3 4 5

A highly Individual person prefers to work on their own and be self-reliant. Drawing on our own experience, we have a seriously Individualistic colleague who sees collaboration as inefficient, even describing it as a "tax"—something that occasionally may be necessary but is generally unwelcome and expensive. Other colleagues, conversely, gravitate toward team meetings. They love the energy of being with others and solving problems by sharing and debating ideas. They are what we call Group oriented.

The challenge for the highly Individual person is to make a conscious, and *fair*, assessment of when group work is worth it and when independent work is likely to be more effective. In our experience, even the most hardboiled Individual eventually admits that certain complex projects benefit from the wisdom of others—just as die-hard

## INDIVIDUAL

Sujin, the CEO of a global software giant, was surprised to learn that her reputation across her team and the larger executive branch was that she "just doesn't care" and "doesn't participate." As a deeply passionate leader who wakes up in the morning determined to make every day count, Sujin couldn't understand where these assessments were coming from. She thoroughly prepared for each of her meetings and always arrived at them with at least one well-thought-through plan that the team could use as a springboard. She felt she was a valuable contributor to the team's work—so where were these negative perceptions coming from?

Sujin's blind spot was not understanding how colleagues interpreted her frequent "disappearances." For example, while others extended kick-off meeting debates throughout lunch "just to keep thinking aloud together," Sujin retreated to her office to organize her thoughts and push her own thinking. Why? She felt that until she had put in enough solo thinking time, group discussions were time poorly spent, for her.

The change began when Sujin started openly disclosing why she "disappeared"—it was not to be anti-collaborative but rather to think deeply. This transparency helped the team understand her natural way of getting started, especially when it came to topics that really mattered to her and her department.

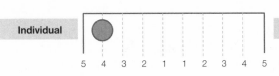

collaborators admit that some relatively uncomplicated tasks are best performed as solo efforts.

In contrast to the individual, the highly Group-oriented person can be a visible role model for collaborative behavior. Actions like sharing speaking time, actively listening, encouraging colleagues to contribute (especially the Distant communicators), soliciting input from experts around the organization, and focusing on execution help develop a positive group climate.

As we said earlier, none of these three behaviors is necessarily hostile to, or at odds with, collaboration. By extension, no single type of person is best at collaboration. Perhaps this seems counterintuitive. Wouldn't the best collaborator be the charismatic networker who lights up a room? Not necessarily: research shows that people who are more private have an advantage at intellectual problem-solving. Susan Cain, author of *Quiet: The Power of Introverts in a World That Can't Stop Talking*, found that introverts sit still more, reflect more, and are more reserved, making them knowledgeable about many subjects and appropriately slow to process decisions.[1] Because collaboration requires genuine listening (not just waiting for your turn to make a point!), a person with a strong individual tendency can be a great collaborator.

Conversely, isn't a highly Wary person going to be uncollaborative? Again, not necessarily. Imagine a team that's stacked with highly Trusting people. They assume that everyone is trustworthy and competent. But what if that's not uniformly true? A Wary person asks questions like, *Does our negotiating partner truly have a win-win mindset? If not, does that argue for us taking a new approach to these negotiations? Does our team have the skills required to negotiate in some new way?*

The consumer-products company mentioned earlier ultimately addressed its execution issues by restaffing its teams with a mix of Responders, Initiators, and Complex and Concrete thinkers. It then took steps to ensure that the members of the teams understood their colleagues' strengths, and to encourage those people to be their authentic selves, even in the face of conformity pressure.

A final thought to close this section: everyone has natural tendencies, as just outlined, but not everyone is extreme, or even fixed, in those tendencies. Suppose that you show up in the middle of one of the spectrums we've just described. That doesn't necessarily mean that you are "average" in your outlook and instincts. Instead, it may mean that you're more likely to flex in response to a given pressure-filled situation: sometimes you're this, and sometimes you're not this.

This sort of flexing can be a good thing—and even critically important in a team context. The key is to flex *intentionally. What's the pressure we're under? What do I know about the strengths of the people around me, as they come under pressure? How can I complement their strengths by playing up one of my own?*

To answer these kinds of questions—and to locate yourself along the seven dimensions we have described—you may find the tool we describe in the next section to be helpful.

## Accurately Identifying Your Own Behavioral Tendencies

How do you figure out what your strengths *really* are, and how do you tap into them? We emphasize "really" because it's not a question of how you'd like to be seen. (We all have an idealized self-image that we'd like to live up to, but often don't.) Instead, it's a question of how you are likely to behave, especially under the pressures of a work environment. What are your natural tendencies—and how can you use them intentionally, so they can serve you as strengths?

The best way to learn about your behavioral tendencies is to use a psychometric test.[2] Through this kind of assessment, people discover their underlying, natural behavioral styles. These research-based insights can be essential, because so many of us have blind spots about how we actually operate at work. Removing the blind spots sets us up to be more effective collaborators.

We've developed a psychometric tool that focuses specifically on the seven dimensions described here, and which we call the Smart Collaboration Accelerator.[3] Based on research with thousands of participants in organizations around the globe, the Accelerator psychometric helps people use their strengths for smarter collaboration. The test itself is simple enough: an online self-assessment, requiring only about ten minutes to complete, at the end of which you receive a report showing your profile. For teams, multiple individual profiles can be compiled into a team profile providing insights into the behavioral dynamics of the group.

Then what? The online report not only reveals your profile but also provides personalized recommendations about ways to turn your natural tendencies into concrete behaviors that can foster collaboration—and ways to avoid having your strengths hinder collaboration. In our work with people ranging from senior executives of global corporations to junior lawyers and software engineers, we have found the data generated by these tools to be powerful—especially for those kinds of people who think of themselves as rigorous and data driven.

Let's assume that you have your test results, including some recommended strategies, in hand. What's next? Your overall goal here is to turn your *potential* strengths into *actual* strengths, which will allow you to be a better collaborator and also help bring out the best in the people around you. To some extent, you can undertake this challenge on your own. You might set interim goals for yourself, and also set target dates for peer feedback on your progress—for example, a 360 feedback exercise a year from now.

But as we noted at the opening of this chapter, *nobody collaborates alone*. Much of the necessary work is likely to take place in the team context: the subject of our next section.

## Understanding and Using Collaborative Strengths on the Team Level

Differences are powerful.

All too often, discussions of diversity trivialize or diminish that power. When we advocate for smart collaboration on teams, it's not because we believe that people should be tolerant of those who are different from themselves—although certainly we do believe that. Instead, it's because the right diverse team, managed adeptly, can get things done that neither the solo contributor nor the homogeneous team can accomplish.

In this section, let's take the team leader's perspective. As indicated earlier, a useful first step is to *do your own homework*. What does your personal profile tell you about your leadership style and its impact on collaboration? The earlier sidebar describes a telecoms company team leader, Ann, who learned some important lessons about herself and adjusted her team-leadership style accordingly.

Let's assume that you've received not only your own profile but also an aggregate psychometric profile of your team, with individual but anonymous profiles sketched out and quantified. (In other words, you know that you have a certain number of Responders and a certain number of Initiators, but you don't know who they are, based on the assessment results.) What now?

First, focus on the *distribution* of strengths, rather than averages. (Averages wash out the diversity that you're trying to draw on.) Next, hypothesize about how any imbalances in that distribution might be hindering the team's work. Then look for evidence that this may actually be happening. We worked with one global renewable energy company in which the thirty-five most senior executives were massively skewed toward Risk Seekers. This revelation, in turn, helped surface an uncomfortable truth: the team was regularly steam-rolling its five members who were trying to inject doses of realism into their group discussions. What was most interesting about this sequence of events was that most participants knew the problem was real and important—but most were engineers, who needed to see the supporting data.

Some of the most powerful changes happen in a group when the team members can see how their own profiles fit in with those of their colleagues. When team members understand their overall composition, they are far more likely to seek out the strengths of others—for example, calling on a Complex thinker to help break down and explain a vexingly ambiguous issue. That's the end goal. So what practical steps can you as a team leader take to get there? Here are some suggestions:

- In the context of a facilitated workshop, kick off a candid discussion of strengths. What is the profile of the team? Do we have gaps in our profile? Is there a dominant profile along one dimension and an individual outlier whose voice we need to hear? How can we use the strengths of each individual to drive forward on our goals? Note that this is important not only for new teams but also for stable teams, on which assumptions about skills and experience can be seriously out of date.[4] How much do we know about our colleagues' past experience, whether in prior roles, companies, outside work, education, or even a relevant hobby? How might that experience come to bear?

- Also in the group setting, encourage people to reflect on their preferred ways of working—both in routine interludes and at times of crisis.[5] Note that we've called for a "facilitated" workshop. If you're not confident that you have the skills to run such a workshop on your own, get help. There are skilled coaches out there who can take the pressure off you and thereby increase your chances of success.

- Either independently or in consultation with other team leaders and your superiors in the organization, assess your team's gaps. Are additional experiences and perspectives needed? If the answer is clearly yes, how and when will those resources be acquired?

- Meanwhile, allocate tasks to strengths—and consider deliberately defining "stretch" responsibilities for people who appear to have the potential to rise to new collaborative challenges. If you are a Hands-off leader, make sure someone is there to help the stretched individuals—for example, the coach or a Hands-on colleague.

- Throughout this change process, maintain an environment of transparent feedback and constructive challenge. This should happen through both one-on-one huddles ("Are you leveraging your strengths?") and team meetings ("Are we leveraging our strengths?").

## Getting and Keeping the Great People

Once again: addressing truly complex problems requires integrating the collective wisdom of individuals with diverse expertise and experiences and allowing them to play to their own strengths—or in slightly different terms, to engage with their work as their "authentic selves." Research confirms that when people believe that they can put their own strengths to work, both they and their company wind up performing better. This is true across a wide range of dimensions, including customer satisfaction and employee retention.

The converse is also true. When people are expected to fit into the prevailing work culture, rather than acting authentically, performance declines. They're unhappy, and unhappy people tend to leave organizations at higher rates. The pattern is particularly clear among people of color and other underrepresented groups, whom in many cases companies are trying very hard to recruit and retain.[6] But it also comes to bear on "diversity" more broadly defined—and here's another place where understanding and using collaborative strengths can help. We recently sat in on a company's LGBTQ training, during which a team member who had recently gone through two smart collaboration workshops said, "I honestly can't understand the lifestyle, but I do understand that getting different perspectives is valuable and we will be better when everyone in the team can contribute their perspectives." The Smart Collaboration Accelerator training helps people understand the importance of leveraging behavioral differences and allows them to reapply that way of thinking to other kinds of differences as well.

Our next chapter explores the challenges of integrating talent—both those new joiners whom you hire on their own and those who join as part of an acquisition—and how a focus on smart collaboration can help.

# PART THREE

# HOW-TO'S AND USE CASES FOR SMARTER COLLABORATION

# [ 5 ]

# Collaborating to Succeed at Hiring and M&A

I t was a truly big deal: on December 3, 2017, CVS Health and Aetna, Inc. announced their intention to merge. If approved by the Department of Justice and other federal and state regulators, the $70 billion transaction would be the biggest health-care-sector merger in US history, and it would propel CVS into the number five spot in the *Fortune* 500.

Final approvals from Washington came in the fall of 2019. Then, early in 2020, the Covid-19 pandemic erupted on a worldwide scale. Karen Lynch, an Aetna veteran who was named CVS's new CEO just before the pandemic took hold, recalls those turbulent months in early 2020:

> So we had just embarked on the formal postmerger journey. And as with any integration, you try to bring the teams together in a very deliberate and disciplined way, and you take care to do it over a period of time. And certainly, in terms of culture, bringing two companies together takes a while.

But then, only a few months into that process, the pandemic hit. That really accelerated everything, including the cultural change. We had to move *fast*.[1]

Imagine the challenges inherent in bringing together more than three hundred thousand people, most of whom know little to nothing about one another, in one of the most complex sectors of the economy. Then throw in the worst global pandemic in more than a century, which would almost certainly require major, unprecedented initiatives on the part of your newly merged company.

In this chapter, we focus on how companies integrate newly arrived, experienced talent—whether those people join en masse as part of a merger or come aboard as single hires or in small groups. In all of these instances, the speed and depth of talent integration is a major determinant of success, *and it has to happen quickly!* As we outlined in Chapter 2, newly hired people have about six months to engage in reciprocal collaboration with their new colleagues. Doing so determines whether they will thrive in their new roles and produce a return on investment for their company—and ultimately, whether they will stick around or leave. Figure 5-1 shows the essence of reciprocal

FIGURE 5-1

## Collaboration and experienced hires: Two paths

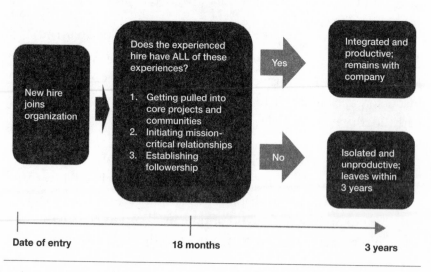

collaboration, which determines whether new hires get on the successful or unsuccessful path.

## The Three Stages of Hiring

With the growth of remote working and the continued rise of geographically dispersed organizations, we now see a significant portion of experienced hires entering a company without having met a single colleague face-to-face. And many may *never* meet their peers in person. Without traditional ways to get on board, how can these newcomers build trust with colleagues, learn about the culture, or even know about what work they could get plugged into? Lacking any serendipitous hallway encounters, how do they learn about new collaboration opportunities with different colleagues or on upcoming projects?

It's probably fair to say that engendering collaboration for experienced hires has never been trickier, or more important. New hires who collaborate with colleagues on important, meaningful work build their own credibility and reputation; at the same time, they learn about their peers' expertise and who's best to work with. This two-way trust helps the organization capitalize on newcomers' fresh ideas and expertise. Because their contributions make them increasingly valuable, they get drawn further into the collaborative networks, which heightens their engagement and likelihood of staying.

So how can organizations improve their chances of getting experienced hires sufficiently integrated into collaboration? We've conducted research across more than a hundred organizations worldwide, including technology giants and startups, utilities, educational institutions, financial institutions, professional services, and beyond. When we break the hiring process into three stages, we can analyze how the most successful organizations use collaboration to make it happen:

- **Stage 1:** laying the foundation for post-hire collaboration

- **Stage 2:** recruiting truly collaborative talent

- **Stage 3:** integrating new hires through smart collaboration

Let's look more closely at the kinds of actions that companies should take at each stage to help experienced recruits get integrated into collaborative networks so that they can thrive and succeed.

## Stage 1: Laying the Foundation for Post-Hire Collaboration

Doing your homework *before* you start the recruitment process will help create the necessary foundation to hire collaborative people and get them integrated deeply and rapidly into your core work. If people push back because they lack the time or energy, point out the obvious: your organization is going to expend enormous resources—direct financial expense, time and effort, and cleanup efforts—whether this new hire flourishes or flames out. Spending the time up front to get this right is another investment you need to make to promote smarter collaboration.

- **Clarify the role and build support.** Existing employees need to understand how the new joiner's role is different from what they are already doing, or else they might react defensively rather than collaboratively. Even if you are just filling an empty slot, don't assume that you can skip this step. New joiners will bring in unique skills, different ways of operating, and fresh perspectives from the outside. Leveraging these insights in collaborative work is not only how you get the most out of a new hire, it's also how you get them to feel valued and included (and therefore give you a return on your hiring investment).

- **Uncover pockets of "churn and burn."** Analyze your company's hiring data from the last five years, focusing on who pushed for or sponsored the request and how well each of those new hires fared after joining. Your analysis might reveal pockets of high turnover shortly after hiring—churn and burn—which show that something is going wrong. Do experienced hires need support to start collaborating sooner and better?

- **Develop a tailored strategic plan before you start the process.** Whom do they need to collaborate with across the organization? For example, which customers will they meet, and in what sequence? Who's going to arrange those introductions and ensure they are pulled into projects? Assign clear responsibilities to those people who will need to support the new hire, and make it clear that this is part of a larger system of accountability.

## Stage 2: Recruiting Truly Collaborative Talent

You certainly already have well-established practices for recruiting new hires, but what you are likely missing is the focus on a candidate's *collaborative capacity.*

- **Fine-tune the screening algorithms.** Whether you are using AI-powered résumé screening or automated video interviews, make sure your algorithms are optimized to look for clues on strong collaboration.

- **Use structured, behavioral-based interviewing.** The best in-person interview practices today involve asking candidates to describe particular situations they have faced, how they handled them, their personal emotional response to the situations, and perhaps what they learned from them. For example, "Can you provide me with an example of when you faced a major challenge?" Follow-up questions might include, "How did you approach it? Whom did you work with and why? Would a broader perspective earlier in the process have helped?"

   Effective interviewing requires training and practice, which many will resist. If so, they should consider this: many of the same probing, listening, analyzing, and empathy skills that are essential for interviewing are the *same ones that skilled executives use* to uncover and understand complex business issues. Done right, this approach elicits valuable insights into the candidates' aptitude and attitude toward collaboration.

- **Immerse the search firm.** If you're using a search firm, make sure it is well briefed on your demands for collaboration and is prepared to prescreen candidates for this quality. Candidates should be closely questioned about their teamwork experiences, both as leaders and as followers, and they need to understand that they won't be considered strong applicants unless they have a strong collaborative track record with demonstrable outcomes.

- **Use self-selection.** Once the candidate is in the chair, describe the company's expectations for collaboration, with as many specific, successful examples as possible. Be clear about how collaboration will be measured and rewarded, both financially and otherwise. Explain the extent to which the organization values and rewards activities like mentoring, marketing activities, recruiting, volunteer work, and so on. Again, clarity helps weed out non-collaborative candidates through self-selection: a very efficient way to weed.

- **Look for the candidate who understands the value of networks.** Groundbreaking work by Harvard Business School professor Boris Groysberg showed not only how crucial the *network* is to the success of someone who is changing employers but also how often professionals (especially men, his research showed) take their network for granted.[2] Because they failed to appreciate how much support they'd been getting from their colleagues in their old company, they believed they were more independent and "portable" than they actually were. Unfortunately, the failure to grasp the value of peer collaboration meant that many new hires failed to invest enough in building ties with new colleagues once they landed in a new company.

Overall, make non-collaboration a deal-breaker. Don't compromise "just this one time" to bring in a hotshot who you believe is likely to poison the culture with toxic, me-first behavior. If you want your people to collaborate, don't hire people who don't value that process and are hard to work with. To put it succinctly: *don't hire jerks!*

## Stage 3: Integrating New Hires through Smart Collaboration

Collaboration helps new joiners get integrated and become productive members of the community—and ultimately thrive and stick around.

This is no sure thing: one study showed that after professionals in the banking sector switched employers, their average performance fell dramatically and hadn't reached pre-move levels even five years later.[3] Why? One answer is implied in the foregoing discussion: they lost the internal networks that had helped make them so productive in the first place.

The remedy: experienced hires need to get integrated into the organization's core work, *quickly*, and this happens most successfully through a structured approach to collaboration. Numerous researchers have reached similar conclusions. Proactive, comprehensive integration increases job satisfaction, expedites individual productivity, and more easily promotes an inclusive culture.[4] But this is a two-way street: the receiving department and other stakeholders must actively draw the new joiner into their projects, and that newcomer needs to actively seek ways to involve new colleagues in his or her work.

The reality, though, is that many companies are pretty mediocre at this. One large-scale study found that only 12 percent of employees in Fortune 1000 companies strongly agree that their organization does a great job of onboarding new employees.[5] That's discouraging, but it also means that fixing the integration process represents the proverbial "low-hanging fruit." Here are seven specific steps you can take to increase the odds that an experienced hire will engage in smart collaboration soon after joining:

- **Help them build competence trust.** Even the most careful vetting of candidates' skills doesn't guarantee that they will be seen as competent once they join the firm. Why? Those skills need to be brought to bear within a new context, which means the newcomer needs to learn how to effectively operate in the new company—without existing networks, and again, *quickly*. Meanwhile, their new colleagues have to find scarce time to get to know new joiners and plug them into existing ways of working. For new employees entering a hybrid or remote environment, it's especially crucial to set clear performance expectations, for the first one hundred days and beyond. Leaders must explain to both the new joiner and their teammates how the individual's capabilities can propel the group toward higher performance. This clarity helps them demonstrate their abilities, leading others to trust them sooner.

- **Help them build interpersonal trust.** Let's face it: we're human, and we're quick to perceive threats to our established orders—and to the members of the existing hierarchy, the arrival of a new player on the scene creates just such a threat. New senior hires usually arrive with fanfare swirling around them. After all, a major investment has been made, and leaders want to generate excitement about the new hire both inside and outside the company. But what about the people who are already in place? They may see this turn of events as a door that is closing for them. Given that firms generally pay much more for a hotshot brought in from outside, those hotshots are often "overpaid" relative to peers at the same level. And all of this, especially a perceived injustice, fosters jealousy and undermines interpersonal trust. Whether the new arrival has earned it, he or she very often is digging out of an interpersonal "trust hole."

  Again, there are no shortcuts, and the incoming hire has to do much of this heavy lifting for himself or herself.[6] But building interpersonal trust is especially difficult for anyone who is working remotely themselves or has teammates who do. Leaders must help the people build more personal knowledge about one another (personalities, preferences) and the team (norms, expectations). For the leader, start with self-disclosure. Let the team see you as a person with aspirations, concerns, and a personal life. And encourage the team to voluntarily do the same.

- **Use "guides" to weave them into strategic relationships.** In Stage 1, you should have secured commitments from specific people in the hiring group who are responsible for introducing the newcomer to predetermined accounts or facilitating other strategic contacts—all with an eye toward collaboration in the longer term. Require those guides to report on their progress to the appropriate manager, whose feet you will subsequently hold to the fire as needed. Again, the key is creating a context of *specificity* and *accountability*, rather than clinging to the vague hope that people will "do the right thing" by the new-comer. Think about all the other pressing concerns on their plates. Will helping to set up the right collaborative relation-ships for the newcomer be high on their agendas? Not unless you put it there.

- **Define a two-way collaboration plan.** Feeling pressure to prove themselves, many newcomers try to go the "solo hero" route. Don't let that pattern get established; instead, let those newcomers know that they'll be seen as more valuable if they collaborate successfully. Work immediately with new hires to develop strategic work plans that identify specific opportunities for them to engage with and involve their new colleagues. Again, you and other leaders should facilitate those introductions and make it clear to incumbents that they are expected to participate.

- **Define and underscore accountability.** For managers who have hired people into their unit, base part of their performance assessment on how successfully they integrate each new joiner. Managers are ultimately accountable for using the tools at their disposal—collaboration plans, internal communications, guides, and data—to ensure their new hires' success.

- **Use technology as an early warning system.** Data analytics will help uncover whether new hires are engaged in collaboration and whether it is sufficiently reciprocal. For example, the Australian collaboration-analytics company SWOOP has studied data from Microsoft Teams for almost one hundred thousand teams across thirty-three organizations. SWOOP shows how data from platforms like Teams can be used to assess how broadly a person is integrated into the organization—whether people are answering newcomers' questions or build-ing on their comments in group forums, replying promptly to their emails, and including them in channels for core projects.

The best companies build dashboards where employees can see their personal behaviors and ways to improve their collaboration through platforms like Teams and Yammer. Because reciprocal communication is a strong indicator of collaboration, social connection, trust development, and engagement, seeing measures of those behaviors will also help managers troubleshoot where they need to provide extra support to newcomers.

- **Actively manage remote working.** For groups that don't have opportunities to physically coalesce—and engage in all the spontaneous ways of sharing laughter or worries or of learning about a new joiner's personality and aspirations—leaders need to work to create a sense of team cohesion. When new people join a group or department, it provides a natural time to reset some of the team norms and ways of operating. Connect hearts and minds by uniting around a common goal. A sense of belonging depends on not only the frequency of interactions but also the quality of relationships that these interactions form. More important than co-location, people need to feel included in the group—recognized, engaged, and up to date.[7] This kind of truly smart collaboration not only helps newcomers thrive, it boosts the morale and performance of the whole team.

To summarize, new joiners face an especially difficult task as they set out to collaborate in a new setting. But as we explained in Chapters 1 and 2, successful collaboration is great for the organization and also great for the individual. For all these reasons, companies need a well-designed plan for helping new colleagues land on their feet, build strong new networks, and collaborate successfully.

## The Three Stages in the Mergers and Acquisitions Context

Now let's run through the three stages of talent integration in the context of mergers and acquisitions (M&A): a special challenge and opportunity for collaboration. You need to set the stage for talent

# BOOMERANGS: OPTIMIZING A SPECIAL RESOURCE

If your company has been living by the rules we laid out in Chapter 2—that is, using collaboration to build strong ties of loyalty among employees and between employees and the company—you have created a pool of alumni who might be willing to return under the right circumstances.

Recruiting these potential "boomerangs" should be a high priority. Not only is recruiting them significantly less expensive than recruiting total new-comers, it should radically enhance how well and how fast they integrate because they know your culture and have pre-existing networks. That said, you can't take it for granted that they'll automatically be able to collaborate well. They've changed while they're away, and so has the company culture and many of the folks they'll work with. Here's how to get them plugged deep and fast into collaborative projects:

- **Focus interviews on uncovering new talents.** Don't short-cut the rigorous interview process and assume you already know what returning people are good at. Instead, ask a range of people to interview them and focus on their recently acquired knowledge and skills.

- **Help update their image.** Some boomerangs told us that they had a hard time shedding their prior persona once they returned. If they left a relatively junior position, for example, they were still viewed as a junior when they came back. Coach the boomerang to talk about their experience elsewhere in ways that will help enhance competence trust. To build their collaborative credentials, they need to showcase their newly acquired capabilities and, at the same time, underscore their willingness to help their new team succeed.

- **Invest in an "update roadshow."** Returning alumni need to know what's changed at the company, in a way that doesn't undercut their stature. An update roadshow, thoughtfully designed, can help achieve that end—and at the same time, reintroduce the boomerang to a wide range of teams and people.

integration, bring aboard the truly collaborative talent, and then help make collaboration happen. Given the dramatic and sensitive nature of M&A—including, for example, regulatory constraints on how many people can know about a deal before it's publicly announced— the first two stages might be less sequentially delineated than they are in the hiring process, but both imperatives remain. Then, once the deal is sealed, you have to move quickly and deliberately to generate the kinds of collaboration that will draw out the full value from the combined enterprise and create a culture where people want to stay and contribute. We'll draw on the CVS-Aetna merger, introduced at the beginning of the chapter, to put these prescriptions in a real-world setting.

## Stage 1: Laying the Foundations for Collaboration in the M&A Context

Most companies spend enormous effort planning for a merger or acquisition. But the due diligence phase of M&A transactions still focuses primarily on financial, operational, and legal aspects of the deal. Where most companies fall down is focusing on how their talent will collaborate across legacy companies once combined. We have three prescriptions to help you determine your own organization's readiness to absorb large numbers of new people and take steps to enhance that readiness:

- **Assess your company's "organizational health."** According to McKinsey research, "Leaders considering a large acquisition should first assess their organization's own health to better gauge whether or not to take the merger plunge."[8] Specifically, are they adept at helping new joiners collaborate quickly and integrate well? And can they do it at the scale M&A would require? Two years after an acquisition, companies with the strongest organizational health showed 22 percent higher total returns to shareholders compared with unhealthy companies.

  Of McKinsey's nine organizational dimensions that indicate a healthy culture, the one that best predicts successful M&A outcomes is talent management. Why? Because the moment the M&A process starts, you are going to need to select the best, most collaborative people, without bias, from both organizations (Stage 2, in our parlance). If you have a principled process for identifying and selecting the best talent for a role in your own company, then this capability will serve you well as you combine.

- **Conduct collaborative due diligence on the target company.** How do your potential colleagues think and talk about working across siloes? What's the evidence that they do so? Do they demonstrate the kind of learning culture that stimulates curiosity and a desire to collaborate with new people? Since smarter collaboration hinges on inclusivity, you need to dig into sources that can help you understand whether diverse employees feel that their differences are embraced and their perspectives are valued.

- **Build internal support.** Leaders need to engage in *extensive communication* ahead of time. You are communicating to build buy-in and commitment—not only for the strategic plan that this acquisition represents but for the associated integration plan that will get people collaborating across legacy companies.

Again, *do as much foundation-setting as possible up front.* In the case of CVS and Aetna, it's useful to remember that this was a story that played out over time. "It helped enormously that the management teams both on the CVS and Aetna sides knew each other very, very well," explains chief strategy officer Thomas Moriarty. "Because Aetna had been one of CVS's top customers—as a buyer of pharmacy services—for about seven years, we had an ongoing working relationship, and so we knew each other's culture, we knew where the talent was, and we understood the state of play in terms of collaboration."

They also took advantage of the extended regulatory delay to continue their Stage 1 work of deepening relationships between the organizations. In this preliminary period, regulators allowed only a small group of representatives from both companies to engage in certain kinds of discussions. As that integration team plowed through meeting after meeting with federal regulators and officials in some twenty-eight states, their relationships naturally broadened and deepened. They had to work across functional and company lines to analyze reams of data and answer tough questions. Beyond formal weekly meetings, team leaders at the two companies created open channels of communication—within legal bounds—that helped to forge a sense of joint enterprise.

Federal courts gave their blessing to the deal in September 2019: almost two years after the initial announcement. This was a relatively long interval, which helped the two companies build on pre-existing ties. If you don't have an established relationship or extended courtship period during which to conduct all the Stage 1 activities, you will need to put a lot more emphasis on due diligence, to understand who you are tying up with, and then you will have to invest to quickly build trusting relationships.

## Stage 2: Selecting Truly Collaborative Talent in the M&A Context

A merger or acquisition nearly always includes significant shuffling of people and roles, so use this opportunity to elevate and advance those employees who excel at collaboration. After all, they are the ones who are most likely to promote the kind of cross-silo exploration and value capture that drove you to the combination in the first place.

If both companies have previously implemented the kind of comprehensive performance management system that we describe in Chapter 6 (unlikely!), then managers will have access to a rich set of data to help understand each employee's collaborative history. Otherwise, some combination of line managers and human resources talent (perhaps including external consultants) will need to derive insights into your people's problem-solving approaches and emotional intelligence. How do they react to challenges and opportunities? What experience do they have with successful collaboration? Are they open and curious about how the larger organization provides a platform for enhanced customer outcomes (or whatever your company aims to do)? This is also the time for leaders to identify potential gaps in the new organization's collaborative capacity and start making plans to enhance the underlying capabilities.

Leaders at CVS Health/Aetna took the bold step of naming people to key positions in the combined company well before the merger took place. Although it risked losing the commitment of people who were *not* named, this courageous move reduced the politics of executives jockeying for positions, and the risk of the knock-on effect of "rival camps" springing up. Of course, this preemptive move didn't *guarantee* collaboration, but it certainly set the stage for a more collaborative environment.

Formally setting out the future power structure also empowered a wider range of leaders at the two companies to start planning their own collaboration-enhancing steps, such as selecting their own teams and starting to build familiarity and trust between teams. These Stage 2 actions are especially important in a merger context, when leaders tend to be laser-focused on meeting the financial targets. The "harder stuff" is more or less guaranteed attention; the human side of the deal needs the same level of thought and care.

A final lesson to be drawn from the CVS-Aetna merger concerns the power of explicit statements in shaping expectations about how important collaboration will be in the merged company. The leaders declared, up front, that the business going forward would be different from its premerger incarnations. "Simply stated," recalls chief strategist Moriarty, "we would move away from a directive management model to a collaborative one." Leaders spotlighted that change explicitly and used it to describe their vision of the future company. Self-selection now came to bear: those who wanted to work more collaboratively stayed, and those who didn't voted with their feet.

## Stage 3: Making Collaboration Happen in the M&A Context

We should restate a key point from the beginning of the chapter: a major determinant of whether your merger is likely to be successful is whether you can get enough people collaborating deeply and broadly enough within the first year. Let's face it: numerous studies report post-M&A failure rates at between 70 percent and 90 percent. Even in the most conservative of the published numbers that we could find, one study shows that after five years, 1,829 M&A deals had succeeded and 863 had failed, a failure rate of approximately one-third.[9] If you don't like any of those odds, especially given the size of the bet you're making, you need to push hard on postmerger collaboration.

And this is where having thought about Stages 1, 2, and 3 as part of an inseparable whole will serve you well. By the time the deal is closed and integration has begun, you should already have a set of initiatives on the drawing board that are designed to advance your strategic goals through enhanced collaboration. Based on available resources, what will you address first? Where can you generate the near-term "wins" that will reassure your combined workforce—and not incidentally, your investors—that this merger was a brilliant move?

Stage 3 for CVS was mostly defined by the Covid-19 crisis. Barely six months after regulators approved the merger, the newly merged company had to send more than one hundred thousand employees home to work remotely. It was a major test of the combined company's operating systems. By all accounts, those systems performed extremely well.

At the same time, the pandemic compelled the newly combined company to put early (and perhaps unexpected) weight on its collaboration model. Karen Lynch, named CVS Health's new CEO just before the pandemic hit, recalls the challenges of integration in those early days:

> We were still in the midst of integration, still learning about each other, still trying to figure out how the people in the combined company could work together—when the pandemic hit, and we had to bring the entire company together in a hurry.

> So we radically accelerated the pace of integration. It probably could have taken five years for people to learn about the other parts of the business. But we just didn't have that time. So we came up with four guiding principles—keeping our colleagues safe, making sure that our customers were front and center, ensuring business continuity, and consistently looking around the corners—and used that as a framework. And then we brought together all our functional leaders and those

whose decisions would affect our customers on a daily basis and talked about what needed to be done. That level of collaboration was make-or-break for us.

Much of this was about what might be called "just-in-time collaboration." For example, CVS Health decided that it could and should take the lead in Covid-19 testing across the United States, which meant leveraging operations, datasets, physical assets, and the already hard-working IT infrastructure to invent entirely new systems from scratch, at a massive scale.

How and where would tests be administered? How would the nearly two hundred thousand frontline workers running those testing sites in the retail contexts be protected? (Vaccine development had barely started at that point.) How would new vendor relationships be set up in an economy that had largely ground to a halt? Again, from Lynch:

> We were very candid about the fact that we didn't have all the answers, and that *no one* had all the answers, and that we needed to figure this out together. We stressed that we had to use this as an opportunity for the individuals in the company to learn from each other.

> People at the center began learning more about how our field operations worked. The people on the insurance side began learning about supply-chain concepts for the first time, as we thought aloud about how we could get [personal protective equipment] to our colleagues and customers without disrupting our ongoing drug-supply chain.

> We essentially had a full-scale effort, with the entire company focused on our four overarching goals, and jointly figuring out how to get there. So it was a big effort—a big collaboration.

And as Lynch implies, the collaboration moved *quickly.* The first Covid-19 testing site opened in the parking lot of a CVS Health store in Shrewsbury, Massachusetts, on March 21, 2020, with testing initially focused on first responders and health-care workers.[10] "We had planned for everything but the pouring rain and the blowing wind," she recalls. In less than a year and a half, that pilot program had been expanded to include 4,800 test sites in forty-five states, collectively conducting some twenty-nine million tests—which incidentally added up to a billion-dollar business.[11]

It's a remarkable story, and it's only one facet of CVS Health's efforts to collaborate in the context of a crisis. We will return to that larger subject in Chapter 11.

## The Cultural Challenge

Focusing on the complex realities of a company like the postmerger CVS Health brings us back to the question of *culture*. At the beginning of this chapter, Lynch stressed the importance of corporate culture and—even outside of the context of a global pandemic!—devoting enough time and energy to its development.

Most of us can bring to mind an example of a work group rejecting a newcomer who seemed not to respect the culture that the group embraced and depended on. We've advocated in this chapter for creating collaborative opportunities that will help defuse these kinds of cultural landmines, many of which arise and have to be dealt with early in the game. Collaborative activities help individuals join, and change, a culture.

Certainly mergers and acquisitions demand that special attention be paid to cultural issues. What aspect of the acquired company's culture are you hoping to retain? How does that overlap with your larger plans to succeed through collaborative initiatives? If people have to learn about collaboration, who will be the student and who will be the teacher? How will existing business areas collaborate to create new opportunities for themselves—perhaps drawing on supportive cultural strands from both the acquired and acquiring organizations—even as resources are heading off in promising new directions?

All of which raises the question, *How do we incentivize people to collaborate?* In the next chapter, we look at a new collaboration-centric approach to performance management and development.

# [ 6 ]

# Paying People to Collaborate?

As the advantages of smart collaboration begin to become clear within a company, people tend to raise an obvious question: *How do we pay people to collaborate?*

Good impulse—but wrong question. You aren't paying people to collaborate; you're paying people to *achieve strategic objectives through smarter collaboration.* This may sound like a semantic quibble, but it's actually an important distinction. Dozens of studies over the past several decades have shown conclusively that people who expect to receive a financial reward for completing a task don't perform as well as those who expect no reward for achieving the same goal. In general, the more that the task at hand requires cognitive sophistication and open-ended thinking, the worse that people who are working for a reward perform. (See the sidebar on paying for collaboration.)

No, we're not arguing that financial rewards don't matter. They certainly do! You have to pay your people in ways that both reflect marketplace realities and are perceived internally as fair. But if you want your people to collaborate consistently and effectively, you need to implement a comprehensive performance management system that embeds collaboration as a means to an end, rather than an end itself.

## COMMON FLAW #1: THE PROBLEMS WITH PAYING DIRECTLY FOR COLLABORATION

Why can't you just pay people to collaborate? Because it will backfire.

When people are promised a monetary reward, they tend to lose interest in what they need to do to *earn* the reward. Tangible rewards undermine intrinsic motivation, and as a result, people put in less effort, seek out short-cuts that may help them hit their numbers, and—perhaps worst of all, from the point of view of collaboration—take a less risky path that steers away from exploration and creativity.

Being paid a direct reward for behaving in a certain way sends a poten-tially negative message about both past behavior and the task at hand, and it certainly signals an effort to control behavior going forward.[2] "If they have to bribe me to do it," the recipient of the reward assumes, "it must be some-thing I wouldn't want to do." Numerous studies confirm that the larger the incentive we are offered, the more negatively we will view the activity for which the bonus is being paid.[3]

But the biggest peril in compensating directly for collaboration lies in short-circuiting the processes of invention. Whenever people are encour-aged to think about what level of compensation they'll receive for engaging in a task, they become less inclined to take risks or explore possibilities, play hunches, or consider weak signals and incidental stimuli. "The number one casualty of rewards," as the late Cornell University professor John Condry put it, "is creativity."[4]

---

A siloed approach to performance management is one of the top barriers to collaboration in a wide range of companies, according to our research with more than eight thousand senior employees in sec-tors ranging from biotech to automotive, banking, consumer products, energy, and law. Throughout this chapter, sidebars elaborate some of the most common flaws we've uncovered. But don't despair! We also lay out a pragmatic way to shift your system so that you reward and recognize talented people who achieve collaborative outcomes— and can fairly, objectively, and powerfully identify the lone wolves who undermine collaboration. Our system consists of three mutually reinforcing components:

- A four-element set of interlocking goals and performance metrics, designed as an integrated scorecard across roles and silos

- Discussions aimed at performance improvement and development

- The annual compensation review

These three building blocks are certainly familiar to most managers. What may be new is how these time-tested managerial tools need to be revamped so that they help to foster smarter collaboration.[1]

## The State of the Art: Effective Performance Management

Maybe the easiest way to summarize where performance management systems stand today, and also to summarize some of the shortcomings of traditional systems, is to look briefly at a real-world example.

Our case in point is Gap, the San Francisco–based clothing and accessories retailer. Several years ago, Gap's leadership realized that their traditional performance management and reward system, centered on a year-end review with performance rankings on a forced curve, undermined collaboration and wasn't driving the engagement and performance that leadership wanted. Rob Ollander-Krane, senior director of organizational performance, realized that "a ranking and rating process can be effective at improving productivity. But that model was created to increase productivity in a factory-like environment. We were trying to drive creativity, innovation, and cutting-edge design thinking."[5] In other words, they needed outcomes that demanded collaboration.

Based on that insight and other indicators, the company blew up its traditional annual planning cycle and related performance management system. Gap completely eliminated the year-end review process, rating system, and forced rankings—which, again, are antithetical to collaboration because they are based on competition—and instead put in place a company-wide performance standard that all headquarters staffers were expected to aspire to. It changed its goals from a laundry list of tasks that needed to get done to a short (no more than eight-item) set of outcome-oriented goals with stretch elements—in other words, a new focus on the *why*. The new goals aligned to the reality of a fast-moving business world and included a mix of shorter-term goals and longer annual or multiyear goals that were reviewed and recalibrated on a monthly basis. Performance discussions moved to a less formal monthly "touch base" and managers received training on developmentally effective ways to give feedback. The explicit goal was to create a learning culture going forward.

Finally, the company's bonus structure was weighted toward collective (rather than individual) performance, with 75 percent of the bonus being based on business outcomes and 25 percent on individual performance. The new approach shifted performance management to a tight list of dynamic goals, enabled regular development feedback, and increased the emphasis on team-based outcomes while still allowing for variable compensation based on individual outperformance (or underperformance).

These changes at Gap reflect a larger evolution across the global business landscape. The classic "annual planning" cycle is becoming passé, largely because in a complex and constantly evolving business environment, strategy has to move faster than that. Likewise, the traditional annual review process is widely scorned—employees and managers dislike the conversations, which often fail to translate into learning or growth opportunities; employees are demotivated by the numeric ratings; the reviews create a sense of zero-sum rewards and competition among staff; and the process ultimately has no measurable impact on performance. Deloitte, for example, found that 58 percent of its executives felt that participating in old-fashioned annual reviews was not a good use of their time.[6]

Clearly, as Gap's leaders recognized, the review process can and should be done better. We argue that *those improvements should have collaboration at the core*, so that they create an environment in which people are intrinsically motivated and rewarded by the collaborative outcome—and, of course, share in whatever financial benefits also accrue. Toward that end, let's turn to our three components, which serve as the foundation for a robust performance management system: a scorecard with four interlocking elements, ongoing performance improvement and development discussions, and a reconceived annual compensation review.

## Goals and Performance Metrics That Foster Collaboration

Leaders of a fast-growing marketing analytics software company we'll call TechCo couldn't understand how so many new customers ended up seriously dissatisfied when every single department was hitting its metrics for the sales and installation process. Digging in, the executives of the company discovered that each department was measuring its performance in carrying out its own task, but none was incentivized to ensure all the pieces fit together—that they customized the software to generate accurate marketing analytics based on each customer's specific requirements and that they went live on time. Customers complained that the software wasn't delivering on their more complex and specific requirements.

More detailed analyses revealed one root cause of client dissatisfaction: a disconnect between clients' nuanced business requirements and what TechCo actually delivered. The overall process of satisfying new clients was breaking down between silos. Its sales reps all hit their individual revenue targets but were so fixated on getting the deal signed that they didn't accurately or completely document the client's needs, often glossing over the more complex requirements and TechCo capability gaps to get the orders closed quickly. Its engineers then started working on detailed implementation plans, but the lack of clarity in the sales process had confused the customer about the promised scope of work and functionality. What's more, because the implementation engineers were measured on installation time, they were motivated to cut corners. After the customer was "live," TechCo's customer service team was left to clean up the mess.

This problem is all too common. When companies cascade their broad corporate goals down through the ranks, they often use scorecards that incentivize managers and employees to take an overly narrow, short-term view of performance. In scrambling to hit their own

## COMMON FLAW #2: KEY PERFORMANCE INDICATORS THAT AREN'T FOCUSED ON CUSTOMER SATISFACTION

Companies typically set big, overarching, collaboration-dependent goals, such as revenue growth or faster innovation, and then create a cascade of myriad, increasingly narrower targets for functions and divisions and units within them. But the narrower targets often are based on the conventional wisdom that people should be measured and held accountable only for outcomes they directly control, which causes them to focus on optimizing their own results and not consider the impact of their actions on other parts of the business. This system can motivate people to hoard resources, such as people or knowledge, pit groups against each other, create a blame culture, undermine employee engagement, and leave customers dissatisfied and angry.

---

particular numbers, people lose sight of the big goals and compete with colleagues for resources or credit. Unnecessary competition contributes to stress and burnout.

As Darrell Rigby, one of the gurus of the agile methodology, told us: "Traditional management has mistakenly focused on fomenting competition to spur individual effort rather than fostering collaboration to achieve team success. Cooperative groups almost always outperform aggressive individuals—not necessarily by defeating them in battle, but by adapting more effectively to rapid changes in environmental conditions."[7]

Instead, companies that want to encourage collaboration should use a scorecard with four interconnected elements that will collectively drive employees to work together on strategic targets but also still make individuals accountable for delivering specified results.

- Element 1: Ambitious, annual cross-silo goals

- Element 2: Team-based goals

- Element 3: Individual goals

- Element 4: Collaborative building blocks

Each of the four elements needs to be weighted relative to its importance in helping the company reach its strategic aims. We recommend overweighting the collective goals to counteract people's natural tendency to focus on their individual metrics. To direct people's attention and focus them on what the organization truly values, each of the four scorecard elements should have no more than one or two goals.

## Element 1: Ambitious, Annual Cross-Silo Goals

The aim of these broadest goals is to break down structural silos and get teams working together *across functions* to solve big challenges by creating metrics that focus on the end result that your company desires to achieve. Separate from the very long-range goals that form Element 4, these goals can be accomplished within an annual performance cycle. They might be halving the time to market for new products or doubling revenue from certain customers by selling multiple offerings. Including only a limited number of goals makes sure that they really stand out and employees don't get overwhelmed. To identify such goals, it's often easiest to start with the customer: What is the overall experience and outcome the customer wants? If a goal doesn't directly involve a customer, try identifying a strategic outcome—for example, diversifying your supply chain. As you build your scorecards, determine which groups influence the desired outcome and embed that goal in each of their scorecards.

Once the alarm bells had sounded at TechCo, its leaders decided to pilot a new scorecard approach to tackle the lack of collaboration across silos. They created a four-element scorecard for functional executives, regional managers, and employees in three departments— sales, implementations, and client service. For each role, the goals were linked to a common objective. In this case, they set a bold goal: *increase new customer satisfaction ratings by 25 percent in twelve months.* This was the only goal in Element 1 of the scorecard for every role, and Element 1 was the most heavily weighted element (40 percent) on everyone's scorecard. Each role had a customer satisfaction metric to measure progress against this strategic goal: for individual contributors, it related to new accounts they directly worked on, for regional managers it encompassed all new accounts in their region, and for the top execs it was for all new US accounts.

Because none of the three functions could improve overall customer satisfaction alone, the shared goal forced the sales, implementation, and client service teams to consider how their own actions affected the next steps in the overall process. The shared goal motivated them to look beyond their specific remit (such as closing the sale) to work with other teams to find ways to improve the client experience.

After the new scorecards were implemented, the leaders of the sales and implementation teams took three actions. First, they jointly redesigned the order intake forms to document client requirements more granularly. Second, they formalized the client sign-off process so that everyone was aligned on what was to be delivered. Third, the leaders of the implementation and customer service teams agreed to get their people involved earlier in the sales process to uncover and resolve any potential gaps or misunderstandings about capabilities and ensure the client would be satisfied with the final product.

Some might argue that embracing a narrow, more targeted goal that is clearly linked to individual performance is preferable. Why complicate things by creating more nuanced and explicitly collaborative goals? The answer is, *because not every dollar is equally valuable.* As explained in Chapter 1, a project that is strategically important for the client, solves a highly complex problem, and brings in multiple business lines is likely to be more valuable than a single-line sale. Furthermore, as described in Chapter 2, collaboration gives people a chance to learn and grow on the job, use their strengths, and find greater purpose and meaning in their work. Bottom line: even if individuals hit their personal targets, the organization most likely has missed out on both greater future potential with that client and the kinds of organization-building benefits that come from collaborating.

As one example of organization building, let's dive into the engagement piece for a minute. Overarching goals are powerful for a number of reasons. First, they're *ambitious*, which is inherently motivating. Research in goal-setting theory indicates that people who are given specific and challenging goals perform better than those who are encouraged, vaguely, to "do your best."[8] Second, by their nature, they *demand* collaboration. Participants in one study who were set collaborative goals stuck at their task 64 percent longer than their solitary peers. Ultimately, those participants also reported higher engagement levels and less fatigue, and they achieved a higher success rate.[9]

## Element 2: Team-Based Goals

Organizations do not only need to break down silos *across* functions; they also have to get people collaborating *within* functions: sharing best practices, learning from each other, and working to achieve its collective target. Measuring team-level results and holding people accountable for them signals the organization's expectation that everyone works to raise the performance of their whole working group, which could be a functional department, a key account team, a product development team, and so on.

Let's go back to the implementation teams at TechCo. Previously, individuals and project teams had no department-level goals that focused people on improving the quality and speed of *all* initial customer setups; instead, each project team was measured on only the customers it implemented. There was little motivation to share best practices or learn from others' mistakes, which meant that projects were frequently delayed while people "reinvented the wheel" each time.

In the new scorecard, each individual on the implementation team received the same metrics related to success across all projects within the region: the system needed to be fully functioning when it went live, and they needed to implement 95 percent of projects on time. Similarly, individuals in sales and client service had their own functional metrics (team-level sales and service-team responsiveness).

To keep team managers focused on sharing best practices and other collaborative actions with their peers in other regions, the metrics for team managers relate to the success of *company-wide* implementations. The functional executives' scorecard includes a metric for *worldwide* outcomes; it motivates them to collaborate with their global team—that is, their peers who lead the other regions.

The managers and executives also have people-related metrics tied to employee engagement and attrition: collaboration hinges on people's willingness to be creative and take some risks, and even the best KPIs (key performance indicators) can't engineer this kind of mind-set in a burnt-out, disengaged employee. This intrateam element was given a 30 percent weighting, the second highest, which further reinforced the importance of the collective goals that required collaboration.

Deborah, TechCo's head of implementation, told us, "Because the whole implementation team had this shared goal, engineers [across the department's teams] started helping each other more. They set up a community on our intranet so that they could share ideas about how to solve specific implementation problems, and they started standardizing best practices that made the process faster. During Covid, when we had lots of staff shortages, they set up an SOS system so that they could quickly swap resources between customers; in the old system team leads would have hoarded their people for their own projects."

These collective goals encouraged a sense of shared purposed among the teams in each department. "Rather than each engineer having a goal to implement their specific client install project on time, we are actually measured on our overall, collective performance across all the client installations," Deborah told us. "We are all focused on the mission of the team." Team goals encouraged information sharing and, conversely, discouraged individuals from hoarding information and resources in an attempt to outperform a peer.

There's also a little-understood diversity, equity, and inclusion (DEI) angle to collective metrics: team-based metrics can play to the strengths of disadvantaged groups. Research on the different approaches to collaboration across socioeconomic groups found that "groups from lower social-class backgrounds took more conversational turns while working together than groups from middle-class backgrounds, and had more active and balanced discussions."[10] As we've noted, balanced conversations are a crucial ingredient to high-performing teams because they allow diverse views to surface. "Including team-based evaluation metrics will . . . ensure that employees from lower-class backgrounds, who are more likely to display these [team-based] skills, have an opportunity to earn high marks and rise through the ranks in organizations, ultimately leveling the playing field."[11]

Above all, leaders need to role-model the right behaviors and nurture a culture in which people believe in "doing the right thing" for the organization, even if they aren't directly incentivized to do it. In that spirit, think carefully about what you celebrate. If your success stories focus on the individual performer—the alpha-type personalities who go all out to beat their targets—you imply to the organization that individual success is valued above collaboration. In Chapter 8, we will discuss effective ways of communicating change, and the importance of using storytelling to reinforce collaboration as a key theme.

## Element 3: Individual Goals

Well-designed, individual metrics not only promote personal accountability; they also should directly connect to the team-based and organization-wide goals and metrics. Then each person will understand how their specific actions contribute to higher-level success.

Let's look at TechCo's client service team. Every individual client service professional has goals related to their specific "day job" of handling inquiries for the specific customers they were assigned—for example, reducing the backlog of unresolved inquiries by 25 percent. All the individual goals added up to the overall team goal but ensured each individual was focused on delivering their part. The weighting, just 15 percent of their overall scorecard, ensured that they kept the focus on collaborating to achieve higher-level goals but was large enough to instill a strong sense of individual accountability.

Under the old system, individual help specialists had been measured on their efficiency: how long each client inquiry took and how many inquiries each specialist completed in a day. Those measures drove high productivity but not customer satisfaction. Service specialists weren't incentivized to improve the quality of TechCo's services or to help resolve the root cause of an issue, such as TechCo's failure to modify the software in a way that provided high-quality data based on each customer's complex and nuanced requirements. Had they done so, they would have been able to mitigate the problem's impact on other clients and reduce the overall number of customer inquiries submitted to the service team.

## COMMON FLAW #3: COMINGLING SHORT-TERM OBJECTIVES WITH VISIONARY GOALS

Many companies with major, long-term ambitions—opportunities such as achieving a carbon-neutral footprint or using artificial intelligence to create more dynamic and resilient supply chains—struggle to get employees to focus on taking action to move these projects forward. Their mistake is mixing these visionary goals into the scorecard along with more tangible, shorter-term, easily quantified objectives.

As much as people get excited about the major ideas, they focus on accomplishing the concrete, shorter-term actions because it's both more satisfying and more financially rewarding. Psychologists studying delayed gratification have long documented people's tendency to trade off future, big rewards when they are tempted to achieve a near-term gain. It's more gratifying to get frequent dopamine boosts from accomplishing what Harvard's Teresa Amabile calls "the power of small wins."[12] On the money side, managers tend to recognize and reward the more tangible achievements. When we recently analyzed multiple years of compensation outcomes for several professional service firms, for example, we found that they all espoused the importance of activities with longer-term payouts, such as developing significant new thought-leadership areas. But even though the firms collected data on the initiatives and included them in partners' scorecards, our statistical analyses showed that they had precisely zero effect on a partner's salary or bonus. The results had gotten lost because they didn't have a specific weighting assigned to those specific outcomes, so the managers ended up basing bonus decisions only on concrete wins that had near-term impact.

---

TechCo's new system motivated client service professionals—the people who have real-time, sometimes visceral perspectives on customers' experiences—to be proactive in identifying ways to solve those problems. These efforts represent the granular, individual-level actions that help TechCo achieve the overarching Element 1 goal of increasing new customer satisfaction. The scorecard for one client service individual who was assigned to a task force aimed at resolving new customers' data-quality problems included the metric, "As part of task force, propose solutions to reduce inquiries on two data-quality issues."

This metric would motivate the person to not only participate in the task force but also seek inputs from their client service peers about the underlying issues. The task force also included people from the other two departments. The leader of this task force was a regional manager who guided the project team day to day, and a functional executive sponsored it, a role that entailed coaching the regional manager and helping the task force obtain resources. Both were measured on reducing inquiries related to that specific issue.

Giving everyone in a team a personal target related to the team goals is important to discourage members from free riding or fearing that others won't do their share.

## Element 4: Collaborative Building Blocks

The first three elements of the scorecard focus on goals that can be largely achieved during a single annual performance cycle. To focus employees on longer-term, multidisciplinary initiatives that will take more than a year to carry out, a fourth section, with its own weighting, is needed. Examples of goals that fall into this category include developing white papers that showcase a company's cutting-edge ideas in order to build its reputation; completing significant pro bono projects that draw on an array of the company's skillsets, showcase its capabilities, and give members of the project team a chance to stretch their skills; and making significant, measurable progress on diversity and inclusions at all levels of the company.

McKinsey's research shows that women leaders, compared with men at their same level, are about twice as likely to spend substantial time on these kinds of activities that fall outside their formal job.[13] By measuring and recognizing Element 4 results, companies can better reflect these results in compensation and career advancement decisions, which in turn makes the performance management system more equitable for everyone who contributes to collaborative building blocks. Building trusting interpersonal relationships among the people who take part in these activities will also help fuel collaboration in future endeavors.

TechCo set a three-year goal to enter a completely new customer segment. The CEO tasked the three departments with creating a compelling proposition that they could effectively sell, implement, and service to these customers. The three functional executives worked together to select a team of regional managers and individual contributors across the three departments; they were chosen not only for their diverse expertise but also because their development review in the prior year noted that they would benefit from working on more complex projects that involved other departments. Their scorecards included metrics that could be achieved in the first year: completing a series of roundtable discussions with senior executives of firms that were prospective customers to glean an understanding of their unaddressed needs, the market segment's competitive dynamics, buying patterns, and so on.

To ensure that the task force didn't just go through the motions, the metrics included the seniority of the roundtable participants (to make sure they would have sufficient knowledge of the market segment) and their post-event feedback about the value of the roundtable. To make sure regional managers assigned to the project and the functional executives followed through on what the teams learned during roundtables, the former's metrics included securing three prospective customers to help codevelop the new product, and the latter's involved piloting the beta product with at least two customers.

A note of caution: *collaboration is good, but more collaboration isn't always better.* People need to decide which collaborative activities are going to have the biggest return on investment. People should justify each of these building blocks in terms of how it will move the organization toward achieving a strategic goal and how carrying out these activities will help build collaborative capacity such as skills, cross-unit knowledge, and trust. Each building block should have customized quantifiable metrics—in terms of not only what will be delivered but also the organizational impact it will have. See Table 6-1 for examples.

· · ·

To conclude this section, let's reiterate that you need to measure each goal you set (obvious, but often overlooked). You have systems in

TABLE 6-1

## Example of collaborative "building blocks"

| Initiative | Why it matters | Assessment |
|---|---|---|
| *Cross-functional "lunch & learn" sessions:* | | |
| Organize product managers from different divisions to explain how their offering works and brainstorm potential multiline customer opportunities. | It builds competence trust across silos and knowledge of the company's broader offerings, and it builds networks. It can also lead to near-term business development and longer-term innovation. | Recognize the people who organized the series, as well as guest speakers. Record specific initiatives arising from these events, such as joint customer follow-up calls. |
| *Customer roundtables:* | | |
| Convene customer executives for a series of short (probably online) discussions about market challenges or other hot topics. | Internal prep work (like identifying cross-cutting market themes) enhances knowledge across silos. Improved customer engagement can lead directly to new business. | Measure not just whether events were held, but also the seniority/relevance of attendee. Organizers get further kudos for helping to shepherd these deepened relationships into tangible outcomes. |
| *Pro bono work:* | | |
| Groups of cross-functional employees use their skills to engage in community enhancement. For example, a multidisciplinary team works with a large homeless shelter to improve its service delivery model. | If substantively linked to the contributors' core work, it gives them a way to sharpen their skills in a different setting. This kind of reapplication often leads to innovation, which propels future collaboration. | Assess both the completion of the project and what people learned from the experience and how well they applied those lessons to their core work. In the homeless shelter example, the team might see how to radically lower costs of service delivery. |

place to capture many of the quantitative outcomes your organization focuses on, such as revenue, throughput, and customer satisfaction. But it gets tricky: evaluating performance against a set of metrics hinges on having *data that people trust*. If there is a whiff of unreliability or inaccuracy in the data, then people will lose trust in the metric and confidence in the process. If you can't measure it reliably, you need to ditch the goal.

Another crucial point: the world is changing fast, and your goals need to keep up. What happens if you set a rigid annual target on January 1, and your employees realize by the end of February that some misfortune (such as losing their main customer because it got acquired, or the company missing a crucial regulatory filing that sets development back half a year) means they'll miss their yearly objective? Chances are good that morale and motivation will dip significantly for the remaining ten months. What a missed opportunity to turn it around! Regularly review and recalibrate goals, as Gap started doing on a monthly basis, to make sure your scorecard is relevant, motivating, and performance enhancing.

Finally, keep in mind that you're *not* trying to hit upon the "perfect goal," because it's not out there. Every goal can result in counterproductive actions or gaming of the system. But the upside of some goals (driving collaboration) will compensate for the downside of others (driving individual behaviors), which is why leaders need to construct a comprehensive and integrated set of goals that steer individual and team behaviors in the right overall direction.

## Ongoing Performance Improvement and Personal Development Discussions

Now let's look at the second of our three components of a robust, collaboration-enhancing performance management system: ongoing discussions aimed at performance improvement and development.

Note that we didn't say "performance reviews," which often have the feel of a summary judgment of one's worth as an employee. We said "discussions aimed at performance improvement and development," which are essential to supporting smarter collaboration. When people work together to tackle fast-changing, complex problems, they need to be constantly vigilant about spotting their own deficiencies and finding others whose strengths can offset those shortcomings. They also need to keep their skills sharp, so others have competence trust in them and want to draw them into team-based work. They need to be continually prompted to consider how their work is connected to the larger organization and how well they are working with others.

To that end, performance improvement discussions are to some extent backward-looking ("How did you do?"). More important, they are also forward-looking ("How can you improve?"). They're also supportive ("How can we help build your capabilities in order to achieve your goals?"). And finally, done right, these discussions not only support collaboration by building trust between the employee and manager, they are the essence of collaboration—two people integrating their perspectives to work through challenges (personal and professional) and generate solutions.

Note that we call for *ongoing* discussions about these topics. People need frequent input on their performance. It gives them a sense of their trajectory and allows them to course-correct if there are issues. Waiting until year-end allows poor performance to go on far too long without intervention, and fails to give people the chance to improve along the way. With these facts in mind, something like 70 percent of today's multinational corporations have moved toward regular conversations about development and feedback.[14]

At GE, for example, where annual goals have been replaced by short-term priorities, supervisors use frequent "touch points" to help employees ask and answer key questions: *What am I doing well? What should I continue? What should I change?*[15] Managers use this "start, stop, and continue" framework to provide coaching and access to developmental resources. Once these frameworks are understood to be nonpunitive, employees start *asking* supervisors for feedback rather than trying to avoid it.

The traditional performance review makes people want to hide their faults. What's needed instead is an honest discussion about where somebody has fallen short, which allows that person to surface the underlying capabilities gap and enlist the manager's help in figuring out what to do about it. Remember: not every gap needs to be filled. The point of collaboration is to team up with others who have complementary skills and approaches. For example, if you've been faulted for not taking enough initiative, maybe it's an opportunity to figure out how to play to your responder tendencies.

Certainly, these discussions need to take a clear-eyed look at where people are not delivering up to expectations. Helping people see where they have a knowledge or skills gap helps to trigger a sense of curiosity, provided that they feel supported rather than merely judged.[16] And curiosity is directly linked to collaboration. One study of call center workers by INSEAD professor Spencer Harrison showed that the most curious employees sought the most information from coworkers, and the information helped them in their jobs—for instance, boosting their creativity in addressing customers' concerns.[17]

Here's an unexpected argument in favor of frequent developmentally oriented conversations: *they're good for your health.* As neuroeconomist Paul Zak's research has demonstrated, engaging in frequent conversations causes the brain to produce oxytocin, the "social-engagement" molecule.[18] The brain rewards us for collaborating—both in the review process and in the normal flow of business.

When and how often should these development discussions happen? The most effective approach is to link the timing or cadence of the feedback discussions to the milestones in the work in question. For example, since a call center's workers have extremely short-term targets, such as daily call quality, their managers should sit down weekly with them to review those outcomes. To avoid losing sight of long-term goals—for instance, in the TechCo example, the company's ambition to enter a completely new customer segment—time the sit-downs to match strategic, interim milestones: for the individuals, these discussions could be linked to completion of half of the customer interviews; for the regional managers, to a milestone in the effort to codevelop the new product; and for the functional executives, to a milestone in the process for piloting the offering.

McKinsey instituted biweekly "Team Barometers" pulse surveys, which provide frequent and timely insights into which teams are performing well and which are struggling. The surveys are brief and easy to complete, which helps increase participation. Similarly, Google created an "upward feedback survey." Through rigorous analysis, Google identified eight behaviors that the company's best managers do well. Against these eight metrics, managers receive reports with numerical scores and comments from their teams supported by a development curriculum to help them improve.[19]

These tools enhance development and encourage collaboration because they are not just top-down. They ensure the entire organization feels a shared accountability for development—for their teammates, for the managers, and for the teams around them.

# A Reconceived Performance Recap and Annual Compensation Review

Now we turn to the third of our three building blocks in a robust, collaboration-oriented performance management system: the annual performance recap and compensation review. Getting a handle on the first two building blocks will make this step far less onerous for the manager, and far less stressful for the recipient, compared with the traditional annual performance review.

Let's assume that throughout the year, managers have provided ongoing feedback and coaching to their teams. At year-end, the annual review is a recap and summary of performance against goals that have been discussed over the course of the entire year. In other words, there are few surprises.

Even organizations that have moved to more ongoing feedback still find that they need a formal check-in point once a year to set compensation. Why? Because in nearly all companies, compensation is on an annual cycle along with the larger budget process. Let's look back at the example of Gap cited earlier: following the complete overhaul of its performance management and compensation systems, the company's end-of-year assessments summarized performance discussions that had happened periodically throughout year. Managers made decisions about compensation changes and bonuses based on their judgments about each employee's value to the company, and the HR function played a crucial role in helping to calibrate these decisions across business units.

## The Performance Recap (What and How)

Your review should include the performance against each of the types of goals we have discussed: big goals, team goals, individual goals, and building blocks. The organization needs to give managers guidance on how to weight these streams. We can't prescribe an "ideal" weighting, since this is very much context dependent. But your weighting should suggest how the company answers a key question: *What do your people need to focus on to accomplish your strategic goals, given the marketplace in which you operate?*

But this is more than just the numerical performance against each of the goals. Because you want to embed smart collaboration behaviors into your organization, your review process needs to be far more nuanced than a traditional formulaic aggregation of quantitative targets. You also need to consider whether *how* people delivered those results is aligned with the organization's values. One of those values should be working collaboratively. It is the manager's responsibility to understand whether the individual delivered on their goals in a collaborative way.

So where do you get the inputs about *how* people are achieving their objectives? Your job as a leader is to keep an ear to the ground, and to probe when you hear tidbits that might be concerning. "Pulse checks" and similar tools, described earlier, are also a potential source of insight into how people have behaved with their teams. For example, a pulse check may indicate that a manager is micromanaging a team, and as a result, the team's members don't feel empowered. The supervisor should discuss this feedback as it comes in, provide coaching, and then look for trends in subsequent pulse checks.

As crucial as they are, these insights can be subject to bias and idiosyncrasy. Some managers may be harsh or generous raters; others may put greater weight on elements that they personally find more valuable. This undermines trust in the process, which, in turn, undermines the incentive to collaborate. Given these risks, HR can play a vital role by norming these ratings across raters throughout the company.

How do you sum up all these pieces in a way that will be received as constructive and motivating? If possible, avoid relying on a numerical score—such as a 1-to-5 rating—to convey to the employee what you've learned. People would rather hear, "You're meeting, not exceeding, expectations," than, "You're a 3 on a 5-point scale." In our work across industries, everyone from senior executives to recent graduates tells us that being reduced to a single number is demeaning and demoralizing. Even worse is the old-fashioned device of forced-curve benchmarking against peers. Extensive research shows that this system is collaboration-destroying because it is a zero-sum game: you can't expect coworkers who are pitted against each other in such a fashion to work together collaboratively. Rather than accentuating a person's performance relative to peers, focus both their monthly and year-end development discussions on their performance trajectory: Are they growing, working effectively across silos, and increasing their impact—not just individually but also as a contributor to the broader organization?

## The Compensation Element

The annual discussion is your chance to use compensation as a strong shaper of a collaborative culture. Because the recap of their performance against targets (*what* they achieved) should be relatively uncontroversial, your efforts should be directed at explaining your assessment of their behaviors (the *how* part of their overall rating).

As obvious as it sounds, what you pay people has to be directly linked to what and how they delivered against their goals. We have worked with a range of organizations to review their compensation outcomes. Many have a compensation policy that includes up to twenty factors they claim to value. When we run a statistical model, however, we find that they are really paying for performance on just two or three metrics. More often than not, the ones that they actually pay for are the highly individualistic goals, such as hitting personal sales targets. This is why rigorously applying weightings to each goal is key.

Adjusting compensation for *how* people deliver their numbers, however, requires some managerial discretion. At one financial institution, for example, 80 percent of an employee's bonus was driven by achievement against the quantitative metrics. The other 20 percent was based on the manager's assessment of how well the employee lived the organization's values, including collaboration.

More than just communicating *what* a person gets paid, a crucial part of this discussion is explaining how the subjective *how* element was assessed and exactly what behaviors informed the assessment. Two people can deliver the same output in very different ways: one might be constructive, inclusive, and collaborative, whereas the other might do it in a "me-first" and sharp-elbowed manner. In the short term, the second person may hit their targets, but the collateral damage can be real. How often have you been in an organization where

## COMMON FLAW #4: AD HOC BONUSES FOR SMALL ACTS OF COLLABORATION

In one consulting firm we advise, the CEO set aside $80,000 for executives to give quarterly rewards to team leaders who worked across service lines. After three quarters, less than 10 percent of this pot had been given away, and he abandoned the project. This firm's mistake is common: rewards for collaboration are added on to the incentive system as an afterthought and not integrated into it. They are not tied directly to the achievement of major strategic objectives. As a result, employees consider them to be peripheral to their main responsibilities and view them with cynicism. "It's total BS," a consulting manager at the firm confided to us. "The whole system is designed to make us focus on hitting our individual numbers, and then a couple times a year they come out pretending that collaboration is really important."

---

you ask, "How can a person like that get ahead?" Frequently, it's because the organization only values the *what* and not the *how*. Leave room in your compensation model for managerial discretion to reward the people who deliver in line with the organization's values and to penalize people who don't. These aren't easy conversations, so make sure those values are well understood and managers are trained to deliver tough messages.

For most people, money isn't everything, so also incorporate creative rewards. No matter how rich or successful people are, they crave recognition for their good work. The NASA@Work program, for example, encourages innovators across the federal government to generate ideas and solve important problems. Winners are rewarded not with money but with other incentives, including recognition—a personalized astronaut autograph, a visit to the employee's department by NASA top brass, or external recognition on NASA's Twitter account. Take this a step further by recognizing team-level outcomes to promote collective working. The more that leaders can embed symbolic rewards for great collaboration, the more that the system fosters a collaborative culture.

## The Role of Culture

If paying people to collaborate worked, this chapter—and even this book—could be quite short. You'd just have to point people in a collaborative direction, put money on the table, and wait for things to sort themselves out.

Unfortunately, it doesn't work that way. Multiple studies have shown that financial incentive systems alone fail to motivate people, at least to the extent that leaders hope and expect.[20] This is especially true when the hoped-for outcomes go beyond incremental, near-term financial rewards into more complex realms. An organization whose members share a strong sense of mission and an accompanying value system can accomplish the near impossible. Culture achieves things that money cannot.

Building a culture is a tricky challenge. You want people to behave in certain ways. Seen in that light, a performance management system is an indispensable tool in the manager's toolkit. And yet, you can't—and wouldn't want to—measure, assess, and control each person's daily actions and decisions. In fact, especially in an environment that will depend increasingly on collaboration, you want people to make the right choices even in the absence of specific metrics.

Culture closes that gap and makes effective measurement, monitoring, and compensation possible. Investing in culture is an investment in your people—and vice versa.

$$\begin{bmatrix} 7 \end{bmatrix}$$

# Collaborating through
# a Sector Lens

P eople, we have a problem."

The executives participating in GlobalTech's monthly Zoom call sat up a little straighter. David Garcia, the company's chief operating officer, was usually pretty upbeat and unflappable. Today, though, he didn't look happy.

"We've had a sector-based sales team in place for three years," Garcia continued, "and they're supposed to really understand the customers and create holistic solutions using more of our offerings. But that effort still isn't delivering the growth we expect. Look at our commercial businesses sector. At least ten customers are using our cloud product—which by most accounts is the best on the market— but *not one of them* is using our analytics or data products, right?

"And commercial's only the most glaring example. The fact is, we're not growing our share of wallet in any of our other three sectors either. Can anyone offer an explanation? Sarah?"

Sarah Fitzpatrick, executive vice president and head of the sector sales team, felt all the virtual eyes on her. Garcia's shot across her bow wasn't a surprise; he had called her the day before to give her a heads-up and to encourage her to speak her mind on the upcoming call. So she plunged in. "Happy to kick off the discussion, Dave. As you all know, I've hired industry experts to lead sales for all four of our sector groups. They're all hotshots. But how are we supposed to win when the rest of the company doesn't support us?"

GlobalTech had reorganized its sales teams along four sector lines (commercial business, public sector, small and midsize companies, and retail consumer) several years earlier, in response to customers' increasing demands that their providers deeply understand the nuances of their market, speak the language of their business, and deliver industry-tailored insights. Garcia was correct in saying that the sector-based sales strategy wasn't delivering the growth that the tech provider had hoped for. But Fitzpatrick had a point, too. At a company like GlobalTech, people had to collaborate across functions—sales, marketing, product management, client services, IT, operations, even finance and HR—to develop the kinds of insights and innovative solutions that could differentiate them from the competition. It wasn't happening.

We call that level of internal collaboration—focused on smart collaborative practices in its sector-based approach—Sector 1.0. GlobalTech wasn't yet succeeding at Sector 1.0–level collaboration. As a result, Fitzpatrick's sales team wasn't wowing its customers, and the sector-based strategy wasn't delivering its potential.

We'll return to GlobalTech several times in this chapter. Meanwhile, let's generalize. No matter what industry you're in, you've almost certainly heard similar demands from your own customers, right? According to our research, most executives cite "industry-specific insights" as the single most important way that their vendors can add value (see Figure 7-1).

As GlobalTech was discovering, this is far from easy. But the truth is that the *real* hard work—for GlobalTech and many other companies like it—is still in the future. In some segments, Sector 1.0 has already become table stakes, and what's needed now is what we'll call Sector 2.0. At this more sophisticated level of smart collaboration, your business collaborates *across* sectors to help clients solve their most complex issues.

For example, at the outset of the Covid-19 crisis, Joan Cisco—a partner in her law firm's automotive practice—began considering the

FIGURE 7-1

**"What is the best way for external advisors to help you add strategic value?"**

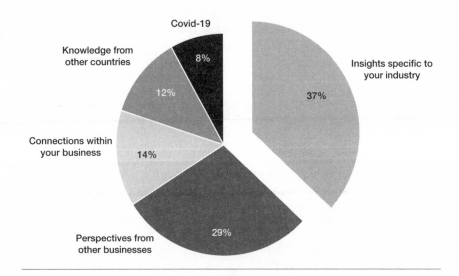

implications of a regulatory change that would massively affect her client. The US government was considering invoking the Defense Production Act to force automakers to manufacture ventilators for use in hospital emergency departments. Cisco immediately spotted the risks associated with manufacturing these products, including a completely new regulatory regime and new product testing requirements. She arranged two quick phone conferences with colleagues in the firm's life-sciences practice to discuss these risks and their possible mitigation. Together, they called the client with observations and recommendations. As a result, the automaker was able to get ahead of the looming government mandate, tool up to produce the ventilators that were desperately needed, and do it in compliance with a completely different and highly controlled set of regulations.

That level of cross-industry collaboration is what we call Sector 2.0.

And this brings us to Sector 3.0. Organizations that deliver at this top level not only understand industry trends and competitive dynamics and integrate thinking across sectors but also collectively help *shape* the industries their customers work in. Operating at this level of sector-based collaboration truly differentiates your company from competitors who merely respond to industry trends; they (and their customers) will be playing catch-up while you are helping your customers on the cutting edge.

This chapter focuses on creating the foundation for a sector strategy and how to take that strategy to the next level.

## Sector 1.0: The Sector-Specialization Imperative

Many companies' websites suggest that they are already well positioned to deliver sector insights. Often, though, the reality is quite different—a case of good marketing verging on wishful thinking. Just because your company has served an airline, you don't necessarily have a "transportation sector group" with deep domain expertise that is able to deliver the full breadth of your organization's capability and the resulting differentiated insights. The fact is, *turning experience into insights requires a collective effort*. It takes intention, resources, energy, and commitment to integrate the perspectives of multiple contributors into a nuanced, customized point of view.

Let's look at it from the customer's perspective (always a good idea!). Why do customers want a sector-focused approach? The answers range from the substantive to the symbolic, as shown in Figure 7-2.

The left side of Figure 7-2 begins with the most substantive reason: customers need *a product or service that is customized* enough to meet their specific requirements. When it comes to consumer sentiment about climate change, for instance, the ramifications are obviously very different for companies in the fashion business versus those in the dairy sector. You need to provide a strong evidence- or experience-backed point of view on what it means for your customer's specific industry.

What else? Customers, like GlobalTech's, expect their vendors to be a source of *market intelligence* and specialized know-how. They ask, *How are data privacy laws in Europe or Asia going to affect US retailers? How can cloud technology better secure data in government agencies and small companies?* Your customer knows that you have experts who are picking up sector-level intelligence. Well,

FIGURE 7-2

## Why do customers want a sector-focused approach?

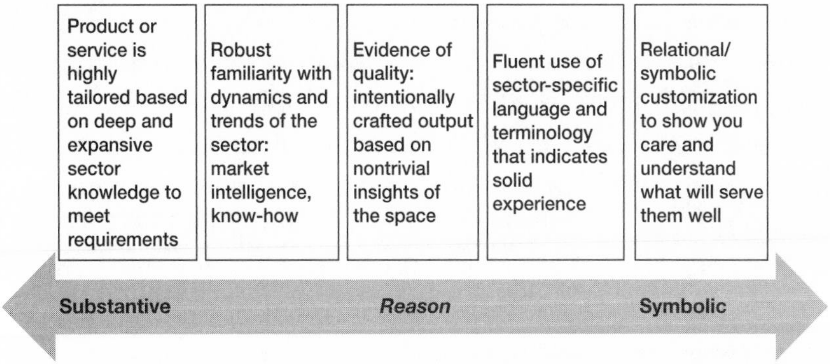

| Product or service is highly tailored based on deep and expansive sector knowledge to meet requirements | Robust familiarity with dynamics and trends of the sector: market intelligence, know-how | Evidence of quality: intentionally crafted output based on nontrivial insights of the space | Fluent use of sector-specific language and terminology that indicates solid experience | Relational/ symbolic customization to show you care and understand what will serve them well |

**Substantive**                    *Reason*                    **Symbolic**

no surprise: they expect you to bring that intelligence to bear—proactively—to help them succeed.

Customers also value sector customization because it *signals quality*. Generally speaking, the more intangible your company's output, the more you should tailor that output. Research shows that the harder it is for buyers to understand the inherent quality of your service, the more likely they are to make judgments based on customization.[1] In professional services, for example, it's often hard to project an initiative's exact value—because it's hard to quantify the "what would have happened otherwise" scenarios.[2] Customers therefore assess a proposal based on the perceived quality—partly as a function of it customization.

*Language and terminology* also matter. If one of your salespeople meets a hospital executive and talks about "customer satisfaction" rather than "patient outcomes," they will instantly lose credibility. "You need to know the lexicon, or you're dead," as the global head of sectors at a Big Four accounting firm recently told us. And this isn't merely good etiquette. Being fluent in their language means you really understand their business and what's important to them. It also means you can deliver insights in a way that they will understand. The general counsel at a pharma company elaborated: "Nine of ten of our ExCo members are MDs; you have to be able to speak 'doctorish,' not 'lawyerish,' to them. If you deliver your inputs to me in legal jargon, then I have to do the translation."

Finally, out on the symbolic end of Figure 7.2's spectrum, we arrive at *relationship-building*. An architect with a thriving practice built his business serving tech companies looking for a completely new work environment. "I'm always watching how people interact with their environment—in the park, on the train, and in the office," he told us. But that's only one small part of his market research. For example, he also subscribes to *Warehouse*, *Wired*, and *MIT Technology Review*. Why? "Clients are thrilled when I can talk about tech trends in their industry. I can point to several commissions we've won because we understood how future technology translates into spaces that would excite them."

## Barriers to Sector Specialization

In Chapter 3, we discussed some of the typical barriers to collaboration in the corporate setting, including a lack of shared knowledge across a complex organization, a lack of competence trust or interpersonal trust, and an unsupportive incentive structure. Of course, all of those challenges still pertain within the Sector 1.0 challenge, but the sectoral focus adds new complexities.

One collaboration challenge arises with tension around *sectors*, *geographic structures*, and *functional departments* within a typical company. The matrix may present a confusing and overlapping customer-engagement model. Who "owns" the customer—the country head, sector lead (e.g., automotive), functional head (e.g., sales), or division or product head (e.g., risk-analytics software)?

This leads to the challenge of *turf wars*. Suppose Amazon is a valued client of your company. Amazon started life as an online retailer and, over time, morphed into also being a leading provider of technology services. So which of your sectoral teams leads the Amazon relationship—retail or technology?

Let's return to the GlobalTech executive call introduced earlier. When no one responded immediately to executive vice president Sarah Fitzpatrick's implied criticism of a lack of collaboration across functions, she plunged ahead: "As Dave pointed out, our US *sales* team is aligned to four sectors, but the other functions aren't structured around customer sectors.

"Our divisional heads are responsible for our four product areas," Fitzpatrick continued. "Each is stand-alone, so clients that buy our devices get no benefit from buying cloud services, analytics, or data from us versus from a competitor. And because the marketing team is organized by product, they create generic product materials. So our sales guy Mike shows up at the Pentagon with the same marketing materials that Eileen takes to WalMart. True, Mike has trained his team to start using public-sector jargon, especially for the military, in their pitches—and by the way, Mike and Eileen are *really good*—but we're gonna need way more than window dressing to make this work."

Again, a long pause. Finally, Garcia responded. "All right, Sarah," he said. "I take your point. Let's pilot something different with public sector. I want sales, product, marketing, and tech development to come back in two weeks with an approach to get better aligned with the actual world of our customers."

## A Holistic and Aligned Approach to Sectors

What's the appropriate response to these challenges? As Garcia's comments suggest, companies need to develop a *clear sector-based engagement strategy*, and then assess their structure, culture, and leadership to see if they are fostering or impeding collaborative customer service. Alignment across these elements is key. See Figure 7-3.[3]

Not surprisingly, strategy is at the top of the pyramid, because everything else flows from that strategy. The next layer consists of the supporting structures: processes and organizational design that provide the scaffolding to support the strategy. But you can't simply structure your way into day-to-day behaviors; people's ongoing decisions and actions have to be shaped by a collaborative culture. And finally, the whole edifice rests on collaborative leadership. After all, the leaders set the tone at the top, role-model collaboration through their own behaviors, determine which stories to tell—collaborative success stories, or the same old individual-hero yarns?—and, ideally, lead at the client coalface.

FIGURE 7-3

## Organizational alignment for sector-based success

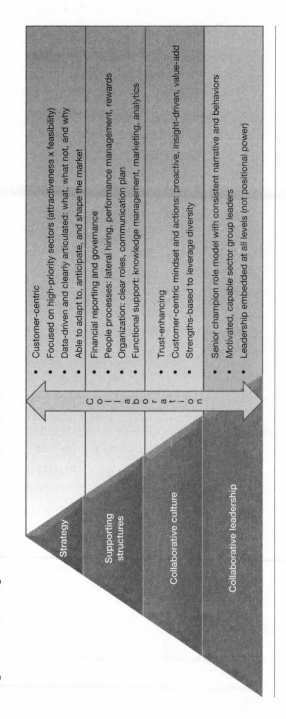

# Building a Sector Strategy

How do you build a sector strategy that will necessarily draw in business units across silos? Start by adopting *a relentless focus on the client*. After all, they consider themselves not as a "purchaser of accounting software" or a "consumer of PR services" but rather as a manager in a financial institution or a hospitality group. It bears repeating here: the *industry sector* is a key driver for collaboration, because it allows your leaders from different parts of your business to integrate their diverse expertise to collectively solve your customers' most complex, cross-disciplinary problems.

Analyze and prioritize the customer segments where collaboration will have the biggest bang for the buck:

- **Size versus growth.** For example, software may be the largest segment within the technology sector, but is it fast growing? Consider the emerging verticals that have the fastest projected growth rates over the next five years. Your firm may be working with only a couple of autonomous vehicle startups, for example, but collaboration across your business lines could generate the sort of novel insights that give you a toehold in the fast-growth sector.

- **Will to win.** How hard will you fight to prevail in a given sector? For example, geography matters: you can't be a legitimate player in certain sectors unless you're part of that sector's hubs—meaning, for example, Boston for biotech and Paris or New York City for fashion. Hubs tend to be expensive and hyper-competitive. Will you commit to that level of investment, and can you sustain collaboration across a wider footprint?

- **Competitive dynamics.** How strong are your competitors in each industry sector? How do they differentiate themselves? Where can you create a competitive advantage? A fintech leader explained his company's rapid growth: "We ended up calling it the Seven Dwarfs Strategy. We started with Sleepy: the segment that no one was paying attention to, which was treasury departments in the corporate sector. After building our capabilities, we tackled Dopey: the much larger insurance segment that was dominated by a few large competitors who had legacy, uninspiring technology. So far, we're avoiding Bully: the mutual-fund sector, where pricing is aggressive and massive scale is critical."

Ultimately, your sectors need to be focused enough so that customers can credibly see themselves within the grouping, but broad enough that you don't end up with dozens of sector teams. Fostering cross-silo collaboration in any sector grouping takes hard work, so savvy companies limit the number of sectors; a good rule of thumb is somewhere between three and seven—even for very large organizations.

## Supporting Structures

If the top of the pyramid in Figure 7-3 is like the brains of the organization, then the next level down—supporting structures—is its bones: the strong skeleton that supports how you put your strategy into action. In some cases, you may need to completely rethink existing structures or processes, but much of the work is likely to involve shifts to make it easier for people to collaborate across functions, departments, and units along a sector. We'll focus here on financial reporting, governance, organizational design, metrics, and budgets, which are the "big bones" in our metaphorical skeleton. And, of course, we'll be X-raying them through the lens of collaboration.

First, you need a *financial view* of your sectors. We almost always see financial reporting based on division, product, or geography—but surprisingly, the industry segment view is often missing. Unless your customers are tagged to a sector with something like Standard Industrial Classification (SIC) codes, it's impossible to get a clear view of sector performance, which then limits how effectively you can include them in the kind of collaboration-based performance management system we talk about in Chapter 6.

But because sector boundaries tend to evolve, effective *governance* is crucial. Does Tesla belong in automotive or technology? Is Alibaba a retailer, tech company, or financial services company? GlobalTech's leaders experienced continuing tensions when it came to serving a customer that cut across sectors. "In the worst cases," Sarah Fitzpatrick told us ruefully, "we sent competing salespeople." Our best advice: don't split the customer—*collaborate*, relying on good governance to make the tough calls like who's working on each account. If customers want a single point of contact, then one sector has to lead the relationship, but that doesn't mean they "own" it to the exclusion of other groups. Complex customers inevitably present multiple business lines that cut across your sectors. Your teams need to deliver joint insights and solutions, which demands strong governance, most likely involving your executives a level or two up from those teams.

*Communication* is key. The account lead within the sector should set the strategy for the customer by bringing together all the interested parties across sectors. Then, align on the engagement strategy. Consider the Amazon example again. Who is calling on the head of Amazon Web Services? Whole Foods? Audible? PillPack? One person (or a pair) needs to own the most senior Amazon relationship, but it's surely not the same person calling on each highly differentiated sub-business. The others need to communicate, with the account lead and with each other, to identify opportunities and ensure a joined-up face to the customer.

You may not need a wholesale *organizational redesign*. If you have solid governance, clear accountability, and strong leadership, you probably don't need to rearchitect your functional and geographic structure. What matters is that people feel committed both to building their industry-specific expertise and to supporting the sector efforts. Each sector head should be the hub who rallies divisions and functions to come together to support the customers. Don't think of "sector" as simply another dimension of the matrix, because that risks condemning it to the "complicated and bureaucratic" basket. Think of it instead as an agile, dynamic way to coalesce *above the formal hierarchy*. In some very large companies, sector heads do own some resources that are 100 percent allocated, but that's not necessary to make the sector approach work.

The gold standard is having subteams within each support function that are aligned by sector, so they can bring their specialized disciplinary expertise to bear on the unique requirements of a sector. For example, the HR professional who engages with the tough questions—questions like, "What challenges are our tech clients wrestling with as regulators consider whether to classify gig workers as employees?"—can inform the scripts of reps who are out there on the front lines.

As you introduce new expectations for sector leaders, your systems need to keep up so that you can adequately *measure and reward* their success along the new dimensions. If you continue to incentivize the same old behavior, sector leaders won't invest the time and energy it takes to build the sector. There's no way around it: you must align growth targets, team goals, and individual goals to sector performance (again, see Chapter 6 for specific recommendations).

Look for ways to give the sector-focused, go-to-market approach some teeth. For example, consider giving sector leaders the "second pen" in compensation decisions, providing input on a person's contributions to sector efforts such as writing thought-leadership articles and supporting customer events.

In the same spirit, successful firms shift their *budgets* to underpin their sector priorities. They reallocate money from nonstrategic areas so that they can make major investments in the industries where they have placed their bets. As one GlobalTech leader told us,

> We had to totally rethink the conferences we put on. For decades, we'd hosted multiple product-oriented events—one for our risk software, another for research, and so on. We blew that up, which was painful. Now we host a conference for the insurance sector and bring all the products together to showcase our integrated offerings. The customers are far more jazzed to be with their peers and hear about trends and capabilities that are really relevant for them.

Also consider how best to *source experts* from outside. Private equity firms have mastered this approach by cultivating a rich network of senior advisers: highly experienced executives from a specific industry who are looking to move into a "portfolio career." In writing this chapter, we spoke with the retired president of a global life-sciences company, the about-to-step-down CEO of an insurance company, and a very senior regulator, each of whom was in the process of signing a contract with a private equity firm. At the very apex of the gig-worker pyramid, these advisers can bring sophisticated industry understanding and an unparalleled network to mine for potential customers and publicity.

## Leadership and Culture

To revive our "living pyramid" metaphor: collaborative leadership and culture—the bottom levels of Figure 7-3—are like the heart and cardiovascular system that pump life throughout your company. They ensure that the strategy (brain) and supporting structures (skeleton) are nourished and can thrive.

Your senior leaders need to continually endorse the sector strategy, both internally and externally. They also need to actively clear hurdles, allocate and align resources to sectors, and educate themselves to speak with customers this way.

Within that team, you need a sector champion at the highest level of your company who is personally accountable for the success of the sector program. At the global law firm of Orrick, Herrington & Sutcliffe, that champion was Chairman Mitch Zuklie, who posed a three-sector-based strategy: technology, energy, and infrastructure. The firm opened new offices in those sectors' hubs (Silicon Valley for technology and Houston for energy), and closed other offices, even profitable ones, that fell outside those key sector geographies. As Zuklie told us,

> This did not come out of some HBS [Harvard Business School] study or consultation with McKinsey, but from listening to clients. General counsels tell us they really want someone who understands their business, who can speak their parlance. They want to know what other companies in their industry are thinking and what they don't know. The simple act of defining yourself in terms of a client's business orients you

around solving the client's problems rather than staying in the comfort area of your expertise.[4]

The overriding imperative is to choose sector leaders who are respected, capable, and passionate about their sector—not those who simply want a title. This is *not* necessarily the person who generates the most sales. Instead, it might be, for example, a thought leader who can be immediately visible and credible in revamped marketing efforts. And don't underestimate the power of *passion*. One account executive whose biggest client is Starbucks told us, "I wake up every day and smell the coffee! For the last eight years, every one of my vacations has been to a coffee-producing country. I've visited coffee farms in Ethiopia, Colombia—you name it!"

At GlobalTech, significant change began when chief operating officer Garcia took responsibility for bringing the sector program to life. To launch their pilot, Garcia's team hired Linda Wilkins, a government partner in a Big Four firm, as the new global head of their public sector. To signal the importance of her role, GlobalTech created subteams within key functions (product marketing, tech development, and client services) aligned with Wilkins and the public sector. A second tier of functions, including Sarah Fitzpatrick's sector-focused sales force, were wholly aligned to sectors. A third tier (risk and compliance, legal, and HR) were not sector aligned, because their processes were deemed not specialized.

So how did that work? Wilkins's kick-off meeting included all her sector-focused functional colleagues. Everyone had performance goals aligned to the success of the sector, regardless of their reporting line structure. And Wilkins had input on performance and compensation for everyone at the table. It was only a start—but it was a strong start.

Remember that *culture is what ultimately determines whether people behave collaboratively*. Unfortunately, you can't simply "process" your way into collaboration. As one account rep at a global company recounted to us, "Leaders created a RACI chart for each sector saying who was responsible, accountable, consulted, informed—and it turned into a box-ticking exercise. All that happened was a fifteen-minute monthly call with no action afterward."

Sodexo exemplifies the opposite: customer service infused with and informed by long-held corporate values. Denis Machuel, Sodexo's former CEO, told us,

> The company's founder started it [in 1966] as a community of its clients, shareholders, and employees. Still today we have a strongly purpose-driven culture with very clear mission around improving the quality of life for people we serve. We are truly consumer-centric because our purpose is to listen to the clients we serve. Because we have shared values, people feel shared accountability for the clients and collaborate more naturally.[5]

Again, structure alone won't cut it. You need people at all levels to think and act like leaders—regardless of whether they have formal positions or titles. This often takes the shape of getting the company to *quickly pivot to face the market*, turning their attention *outward*, to deliver customer value.

We studied one professional services firm early in the implementation of its sector strategy and again eighteen months later, and found marked differences in the activities of highly successful versus less successful sector leaders (Figure 7-4).

**FIGURE 7-4**

**Sector group evolution: Where to focus and when to pivot?**

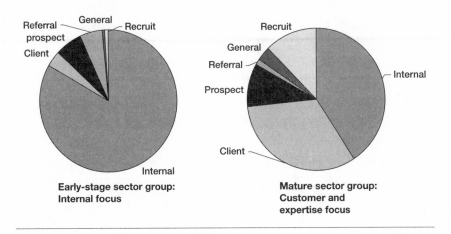

Early-stage sector group:
Internal focus

Mature sector group:
Customer and
expertise focus

In the first six months or so, the startup stage for all sector groups focused heavily on creating a vision for the group, setting strategy, identifying target clients, and bringing people on board. Soon after that, some leaders began pivoting to externally oriented activities: working with clients, pursuing new prospects, and publishing thought-leadership work to enhance credibility and advance their reputation. By the time we analyzed the data, those groups that had made the pivot had won more business from new and existing clients and significantly improved their client-satisfaction scores.

Let's return one last time to the GlobalTech story. Under global public sector head Wilkins's purposeful direction, GlobalTech focused its messaging and picked a few areas where it could significantly integrate its product offerings, specifically tailored to public transportation agencies. Wilkins also launched a public-sector conference, where GlobalTech could showcase its latest thought leadership. The conference gave GlobalTech's divisional heads a concrete effort to collaborate on, then gave them the opportunity to rub elbows with industry leaders.

After racking up early sales wins in the North American public sector, GlobalTech rolled out the pilot to the same sector in Europe, the Middle East, and Africa, then replicated it sector by sector across the company. Ultimately, it put the sector strategy on hold in Asia-Pacific until it had critical mass to launch it there properly— one of a number of strategic decisions governing priorities and resources. But overall, it worked. "One tremendous side benefit is that for people involved in the sector efforts, employee engagement scores have spiked two years in a row," Garcia reported to us. "Now they have much closer links to their clients, and can see tangible results of their efforts."

## Taking It to the Next Level: Sectors 2.0 and 3.0

In Sector 2.0, you work across traditional sectors so that you can integrate expertise from multiple sectors. This is not merely a coordination challenge, where you ensure that multiple sales reps don't call on the same complex customer. Instead, gather market intelligence and other know-how across sectors to generate novel insights, and even truly breakthrough ideas.

When is that required? A common example is when one of your customers launches or buys a business outside its sector. But the need for cross-sector collaboration is not just event-driven: every day, we see a convergence of sectors (fintech, autonomous vehicles, brick-and-mortar retailers to online) that requires integrative, cross-sector thinking. Even more broadly, we see trends that affect multiple sectors—issues like environmental, social, and governance (ESG) ones, where providers can make great strides by taking their learning from one forward-thinking sector to others. For example, one global consultant is working with an energy producer to evolve its business model toward sustainable energy production, and with an investment manager to develop mutual funds focused on ESG themes. Because ESG themes cut across their clients' sectors, the consultants are able to collaborate and reapply insights from one sector to another—like sharing insights with the energy company about what information the fund managers want before investing.

When companies take their approach to the highest level, Sector 3.0, they not only understand industry trends and competitive dynamics and integrate thinking across sectors but also collectively help *shape* the industries their customers work in. That same global consultant also works with government regulators to define ESG reporting requirements in company disclosures, and is able to share insights between the energy company, the fund manager, and the regulator to shape solutions that meet all their needs.

How do you make it happen? Revisit the alignment pyramid we introduced earlier (see Figure 7-3) to make sure that your evolving sector strategy is fully underpinned by the right structures, culture, and leadership.

### Revisit Sector Structures to See If They Support the Sector 2.0 or 3.0 Strategy

Let's start with Sector 2.0. At Sodexo, former CEO Denis Machuel described how they created global teams to facilitate information sharing across sectors—the essence of Sector 2.0. "We created global platforms led by 'offer managers' that cut across our service silos," he told us.

> This small group of global managers liaise across the different sectors to listen to the needs and in a transversal way come up with new solutions or take something that has been created in one sector and apply it to another. During Covid, we launched 'Rise with Sodexo.' Across sectors, our clients were concerned with cleaning protocols. We said, because we are able to clean the rooms of Covid-19 patients in a hospital, with all the safety criteria that you need, then we can go to other areas like offices and schools and use the hospital protocols to clean the desks.

Looking at supporting Sector 3.0, global law firm Hogan Lovells went all in on a sector-based strategy. Its early sector-based approach merely comprised "groups operating more like after-school clubs than professional units," one executive said. To fully achieve Sector 1.0, the firm instituted critical changes, such as appointing a global head of sectors who sat on its international management committee (the highest governing body in the firm), and formalized many other aspects of the structure.

After developing a reputation as a market leader in its individual sectors, Hogan Lovells restructured to embed learning *across* sectors. It created five "super sectors"—clusters of sectors in which cross-cutting trends created ripe opportunities for generating new insights. For example, the mobility super sector brought together automotive, logistics, and other transportation companies to harness knowledge about regulation and other facets of autonomous vehicles—a great example of Sector 2.0. Thinking toward Sector 3.0, the head of the five super sectors, Ina Brock, said, "As the super structures evolve, we will be able to go beyond predicting trends to actually shaping them by working with industry bodies and regulators."

### Enhance Competence and Interpersonal Trust to Support Sectors 2.0 and 3.0

Sodexo's partnership with the international marine contractor Van Oord shows us how both competence and interpersonal trust with the client are essential for Sectors 2.0 and 3.0. To support Van Oord's high-risk business, Sodexo needed to establish interpersonal trust with the ship captains. "Introducing Sodexo was a big change," as one of Van Oord's category procurement managers notes, "especially for our captains who manage the vessels at sea. It was vital that ship captains felt they were heard, therefore we put feedback loops in place to ensure their suggestions were listened to." Toward that end, Sodexo made sure they listened and could "talk the talk," helping to demonstrate that they understood the customer's situation and needs. By establishing that foundation of interpersonal and competence trust, Sodexo was able to expand its work with Van Oord. "Sodexo has gone beyond its remit and now provides great advice for the layout and design of new vessels," confirms Jaap de Jong, Van Oord's staff director in ship management. "They're always willing to cooperate and think for the future of our partnership."[6]

. . .

A migration toward a fully sector-based approach requires considerable change, and as we've seen throughout this chapter, leaders play an outsize role in helping their organizations successfully make that shift. The next chapter helps those leaders—not only people with formal titles but also anyone who steps up to inspire collaboration.

$$\left[\ 8\ \right]$$

# Leading and Sustaining a Collaborative Transformation

O ne day not long ago, the topic under discussion in a Harvard Law School classroom was *leadership*: specifically, how people motivate others to advance a company's strategy. The faculty member leading the discussion was Heidi Gardner, one of this book's coauthors. A student who had previously worked at a prestigious investment bank volunteered some thoughts about leaders there.

"The managing directors," he said, "would come in and sit down with us analysts and talk about the deals that we'd closed—not the size, but the impact. Like, 'You're all aware that we recently helped with the IPO [initial public offering] of a medical-devices company. This was a tough project, and the team really had to pull together to get it done in record time. And thanks to that incredible effort, the company's new heart stent is going to save thousands of lives each year—mostly older patients, maybe including one of your grandparents. And without the IPO, that stent wouldn't have made it to market.' Well, I have to say, that made me *proud* to be a part of that team."

"That's brilliant," Gardner responded, as heads nodded around the room. "Seriously. And how often did they do something like that?"

"Once a year."

*Once a year?* No wonder that student ditched investment banking and headed into law. He was one of those people who really didn't care about doing deals; instead, he was motivated by playing a role, even a *tiny* role, on a team that helped bring life-saving medical devices to the market. One isolated collaboration pep talk was nowhere near enough to sustain his yearning for a sense of higher purpose for the rest of the year.

This chapter is for leaders—not only those with impressive titles. We mean anyone who steps up and inspires a group to collaborate toward a given end.

This often goes as a missed opportunity. Some companies treat collaboration as a thing that is applauded once or twice in the early days of an initiative, and then left to fend for itself. But the truth is that collaboration is a *process*, not an event. It's not just the kickoff, but the whole game. As such, it needs ongoing reinforcement—and lots of it. In fact, it's hard to communicate too much about collaboration, and it's easy to communicate too little. The investment bank discussed that day in the Harvard classroom had decided to treat team-building as an annual event, when what they actually needed was a collaborative culture that was actively supported by ongoing communications.

Why? One reason is recruitment and retention, as illustrated by the law student's example. But another reason grows out of the *timeline* of smart collaboration, and where the associated costs and benefits show up on that timeline. Consider Figure 8-1. Implementing smart collaboration incurs substantial startup costs—for example, the time it takes to build your network of trusted collaborators, or to learn your client's business well enough to tackle VUCA (volatile, uncertain, complex, and ambiguous) problems outside your specialized expertise.

The good news is that these costs drop over time as people gain experience. The less welcome news is that most of the tangible benefits of smarter collaboration—such as increased revenues and profits and higher client satisfaction scores—accrue slowly, which means that in the beginning, the investment can be quite high, in terms of both

**FIGURE 8-1**

## Reaping the collaborative returns

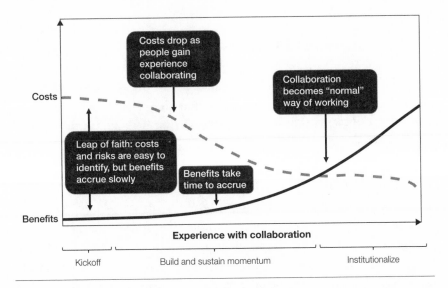

financial and emotional costs. As the organization gains momentum, the lines cross and return on investment turns positive, giving the business a higher chance of continuing a sustained commitment. But what's needed *before* those lines cross—and, to some extent, afterward as well—is strong leadership and communication in support of collaboration.

Our research across industries shows that companies tend to make big mistakes at three critical junctures, which are indicated in Figure 8-1:

- kicking off collaboration, when people need to take a leap of faith

- building early momentum and sustaining it through the periods of investment and negative return on investment

- institutionalizing collaborative practices and embedding them in the broader culture

This chapter lays out a practical and relatively low-cost approach to addressing the challenges posed at each of these junctures, so that collaboration can take root and thrive long term within the organization.

## Sparking Collaboration

One of the most common problems we see in organizations that are trying to implement collaboration is that they treat it as a separate initiative, rather than an ongoing process that is tied directly to their strategic aims. It bears repeating here: *Collaboration is not an end in itself, but a means to an end.*

Your best jumping-off point for sparking collaboration is the evidence and findings from your company diagnostic, as described in Chapter 3. What's the compelling imperative for change? What are the business and talent cases, including the anticipated benefits for the company and individuals within it? Be sure to back up your claims with your quantitative findings, because research shows that when you're trying to change people's perceptions and behaviors, numbers tend to be more convincing than arguments and anecdotes.[1] If possible, anchor your proposed prescriptions in the day-to-day experience of the colleagues you seek to win over.

Let's look at a specific example. Carl Liebert was chief operating officer of USAA, a Texas-based financial services company that provides insurance, banking, investment, and retirement products for US military service members and veterans. USAA is known for its passion and commitment to its customers, whom the company refers to as "members." When meeting people ranging from junior people in USAA's accounting department to the company's most senior executives—many of whom are veterans themselves—a visitor to USAA's San Antonio headquarters quickly picks up on that strong sense of purpose. "It's like a special club with five generations of military families," says Liebert.

But USAA nevertheless has had its challenges, in part due to explosive growth in recent years.[2] From Liebert's perspective, members weren't always satisfied by their interactions with the company. "They experienced USAA in functional silos," he recalls, "which frustrated them. We had no choice but to evolve." As Liebert was well aware, however, many in the organization didn't perceive a problem. So how could Liebert bring people around to his point of view and thereby kick off a journey to transform the way USAA did business? Toward that end, Liebert called together several hundred colleagues for a town hall meeting. As he recalls,

> I wanted an example that would really resonate with the team, so I asked, "Who owns the authentication process?" Four people raised their hands: "I do if they call in." "I do on an iPhone." "I do on Android." "I do from a computer." They could see the silos straight away.

> I reminded them that many of our members live paycheck to paycheck. If they're in line at Walmart, they need to know their account balance quickly—but our authentication was taking up to thirty minutes. They're embarrassed if they ring up all the groceries and then can't pay. That's awful.

> Our younger members are used to instant facial recognition on their phone. They don't understand a thirty-minute wait. Well, it's even worse for our older members. When USAA was small, a ninety-three-year-old admiral would call us, and someone would recognize his voice and know it was him. Now we send a four-digit code to his phone, but he isn't comfortable using his phone that way. The board would get calls from their *admirals* about authentication. Can you imagine their reaction? The user experiences, bogged down in our siloes, weren't working for our members.

You need to *convince* people to go on this journey with you—and with each other. Your challenge as a leader is that not everyone is motivated by the same evidence, so the rousing talk you give to one audience may well fall flat with another. Again, invoking your compelling data will help. So will tailoring your message to a specific listener. Most likely, you'll need to invest in convincing particular influencers through one-on-one conversations, as described shortly; sometimes, you may need to communicate with the entire organization.

Think back to the seven dimensions of smart collaboration described in Chapter 4, and consider what kinds of messages might resonate for those different profiles. For Risk Seekers, for example, winning is a huge motivator. They are quick to see opportunities and are motivated to pursue them. For these people, data and stories about the potential to grow, win new clients, and change the world through collaboration can be powerful. Risk Spotters, by contrast, will be motivated by hearing about how collaboration helps to avoid losses—as in, "Our competition is doing this, and we'll lose market share if we don't keep up."

Along another dimension, Complex thinkers love abstract concepts, innovation, and new ways of working. They will respond if you paint a picture of the intractable problem that no one in the industry has been able to solve, and of the way your team could embrace collaboration to create that elusive solution. If you are trying to motivate people who are Group oriented, think about stories of people coming together as a team to work on a big idea, and the energy created for those involved.

Think about the age cohorts in your audience. Themes of social impact and environmental consciousness may engage the millennial crowd, for example. Ideas about leaving a legacy might resonate more with employees closer to retirement. Whatever your audience—and you probably have multiple audiences in the same group—look for ways to capture the hearts and minds of as many different people as possible.

## Building and Sustaining Momentum

In our experience, this is the most common fizzle-out stage. Why? Most companies fail to persevere through this period—again, as suggested in Figure 8-1, a period of investment—because they *lose focus*. Collaborative transformation requires leaders not only to communicate frequently and consistently in the early and middle phases of the journey but also to structure the work so that they can *capture the power of small, early wins.*

In Chapter 6, we introduced the need to set shorter-term goals, linked to milestones along a journey, so that you capture the motivational benefits associated with what Harvard professor Teresa Amabile calls the "progress principle." Amabile found that when people make even minor steps forward on a project, those successes evoke outsize positive reactions—and the resulting emotions and motivation fuel higher creativity and productivity in the long run.[3]

Here are six additional tactics for building and sustaining momentum:

- **Go where the energy is.** Don't waste a lot of time and effort trying to win over your skeptics in the early stages. In our experience, about a third of the typical organization is highly committed to collaboration after a successful launch; everyone else is noncommittal at best.[4] So in this phase, rely heavily on the core enthusiasts. Nurture their fervor for collaboration— by keeping them in the loop and seeking their advice—so that their excitement has a chance to catch on and spread. Perhaps some will become formal leaders of pilots, as described later.

  In 2019 the oil and gas giant ConocoPhillips confronted the challenge of prompting and sustaining a collaborative approach across a global team of 170 legal and security staff based in nine far-flung offices.[5] Recently arrived senior vice president and general counsel Kelly Rose wanted to create a new mindset within her department. "We need to become both more connected with each other—across domains of expertise and geographies—and more connected to ConocoPhillips," she told a department-wide conference in April, "because forging those connections will make us stronger and better able to serve our clients and bring us more personal satisfaction and fulfillment."

  Through a series of one-on-one and small-group meetings, Rose identified a core group of people who shared her vision. This was time well spent. The so-called OneLegal initiative really took off when an associate general counsel named Suzanna Blades—working with a small group of other enthusiasts—pulled together a cross-functional, collaboratively minded team. They began to make OneLegal a real and compelling activity, focused on changes like introducing short-term rotations, improving social interactions, and revising the performance management system to include collaboration goals. When those efforts began to take root, the team moved on to developing a OneLegal website, creating a Skills and Expertise Directory, organizing a reading and speaking series about collaboration, introducing collaboration training and development, and measuring the larger initiative's success with data and analytics. Rose continued to provide high-level leadership and inspiration, but counted heavily on a broadening circle of collaboration enthusiasts to carry OneLegal forward at ground level.

- **Find and recruit the influencers.** This tactic is related to the energy focus, just described, and is also illustrated by the ConocoPhillips example. In many cases, a company's true influencers aren't its executive-level leaders, who are often perceived as "toeing the party line." In a three-year study of collaborative change that we conducted at a professional service firm, we found that the firm's senior executives actually had very little influence over how people viewed those change efforts. Our findings are consistent with other studies: real influencers are often found several levels down in the organization, where they hold significant sway based on their reputation for speaking the truth, which earns the respect of their peers and helps them build strong relationships.[6] Seek these people out and—if possible—turn them into evangelists for the program.

- **Create shared language.** Shared language helps people connect to new concepts and "import" those ideas into their everyday work.[7] For example, the Smart Collaboration Accelerator uses language like "Risk-Seeking" and "Complex versus Concrete thinkers." These words are sticky. They have residual power. Not long after we start working with teams of executives, we start hearing people saying things like, "Well, I'm a Concrete thinker, so I'm going to focus my energy on the execution plan"—and others immediately get what they're talking about.

For Liebert at USAA, it took time to develop and embed that shared language. "At that kickoff meeting," he recalls, "I started using language like 'experience design' and 'customer journeys.' But people didn't get it. They were asking, 'Wait—*what* are we designing?' So I learned to tell stories like the one about the ninety-three-year-old admiral, and they started to get it. Pretty soon everyone was talking about 'member experiences.'"

- **Carefully pilot some new collaborative approaches.** What's the difference between a "pilot" and just trying out some new approaches? At least three things: *selection*, *criteria*, and *performance data*. In terms of selection, pick one of your collaborative changes and identify a project or business unit in which you can carefully test out that approach. Referring back to the two-by-two matrix introduced in Chapter 3—and keeping in mind Amabile's findings cited earlier—prioritize *feasibility* over the size of the prize.

  As for criteria, be clear about why you are choosing a certain pilot. GlobalTech, mentioned in the last chapter, chose the public-sector team for a pilot because the company had strong penetration with one product line, the team could see a path to creating integration across multiple products, and they perceived little risk in trying something new. Finding a pilot leader who is motivated and has bought into the concepts is also a key factor.

  Finally, data: the sponsors of pilots need to measure inputs, as well as outputs, and have control groups to which they can compare the pilot. For example, how many people teamed up to pitch for new work in one of your core customers? How many pitches were "monoline," as opposed to bringing together multiple capabilities to do something differentiated with the customer? Ideally, you'll also have some results to show, even if they're interim ones, such as press mentions, published articles, inquiries on the website, progress on new cross-silo products in development, and so on. Remember that you may

## WINNING HEARTS AND MINDS AT ØRSTED

What if you wanted to radically reorient your business—betting your future on the part of your business that currently generates only 7 percent of your profit, while deprioritizing the other 93 percent? And what if that would require an unprecedented degree of collaboration across the company?

That was the situation facing Ørsted, Denmark's largest energy producer. "In 2008, we alone were responsible for one-third of all Danish $CO_2$ emissions," says Jakob Boss, former senior vice president of corporate strategy and stakeholder relations. Ørsted's business model was based on fossil fuels, with only 7 percent of operating profit derived from renewable energy. But the company was under increasing pressure—from citizens, governmental bodies, and nongovernmental organizations—to do something about its negative impact on the environment. Ørsted's visionary CEO, Anders Eldrup, made a radical decision: to completely shift Ørsted's core business from fossil fuels to renewable energy.

The resulting collaboration challenge was immense. "It required a complete transformation," Eldrup recalls, "with global infrastructure to be renewed and changed, new technologies to be deployed, and massive investments to be funded. Thousands upon thousands of people had to bring their professional skills and disciplines to bear on making it all happen."

To launch the transformation, Ørsted's leaders focused on winning the hearts and minds of a broad range of stakeholders. They did so by invoking a compelling vision of "a world that runs entirely on green energy."[a] Eldrup wrote an op-ed in the leading Danish newspaper, announcing the vision and laying out the benefits for both the company and the larger society. "[Our] vision," Eldrup wrote, "is to . . . create an energy supply free of pollution."[b] Concurrently, Ørsted aired a TV commercial built around an emotion-laden narrative, and crafted tailored inspirational messages to individual employees to tap into their sense of responsibility and purpose. Across the company, new ways of collaboration ramped up; cross-functional teams were formed to find ways of bringing down costs, and working groups formed to share knowledge about key technology and market challenges.

As usual, the biggest leadership challenges arose during the dreaded middle phase of Ørsted's collaborative transformation. The investments required in renewable energy infrastructure were huge, and by 2012, Ørsted was facing intense financial pressure. To sustain momentum in the face of these headwinds, the company doubled down on its collaborative efforts. "We had started with a vision," recalls CEO Henrik Poulsen, "and then translated it into strategic business ambition: to become a global leader in green energy. We set a handful of targets to guide our vision, and detailed that into a set of action items for each and every employee in the company."

Sustaining momentum on external collaboration was also key: Ørsted needed to team with investors, governments, suppliers, and even competitors to bring down the cost of renewable energy to levels that would ultimately outcompete fossil fuels. Ørsted began partnering with other utilities on a project-by-project-basis, to gather know-how in offshore wind energy projects and share risk.[c]

By 2020, Ørsted had achieved the tipping point, when its investments in collaboration clearly paid off. The company had achieved its goal of transitioning from black to green energy a full *twenty-one years* ahead of its initial 2040 target. Since 2006, its carbon emissions had decreased 87 percent, its operating profit nearly doubled, and the share of that profit coming from renewables increased to 98 percent. Ten years earlier, the company was ranked ninety-fifth out of one hundred Danish companies, in terms of the public's respect; in 2020, Ørsted was ranked the third most respected company in Denmark.

These days, Ørsted's leaders focus on continuing to institutionalize collaboration. The emphasis on vision, sustained by collaboration, has emerged as a way to attract, engage, and retain the kind of people who are passionate about green energy and will operate in ways that promote the collaborative culture. "Most colleagues who join us are motivated by the company's purpose and vision," says Christy Wang, Taiwan general manager. The numbers back this up: employee engagement has increased dramatically over the past five years, with employee satisfaction and engagement up 10 percent and employees' perceptions of Ørsted's image (the second-highest driver of employee engagement) up 50 percent.[9]

Inside and outside the company, the battle for hearts and minds is being won, in large part thanks to the company's extensive and continuing investments in collaboration—and its successful effort to *communicate* the successes growing out of that collaboration.

a. "Our Green Business Transformation: What We Did and Lessons Learned," white paper, Ørsted, April 2021, https://orsted.com/en/about-us/whitepapers/green-transformation-lessons-learned.

b. A. Eldrup, "Mod ren og sikker energie," *Kroniken*, September 18, 2008.

c. "Making Green Energy Affordable," white paper, Ørsted, June 2019, https://orsted.com/en/about-us/whitepapers/making-green-energy-affordable.

need these control cases to convince the skeptics that it wasn't just the market that moved, or some other externality. At GlobalTech, this was a relatively easy challenge: it piloted the change in the public sector and didn't change anything in the other sectors.

- **Gamify the effort to create buzz.** Henry Nassau, the CEO of the Dechert law firm, created a collaboration-focused contest. He identified ten high-potential clients that were then served by only a single practice group, and challenged the sectors to work together to generate a new business. "I dipped into my own pocket to buy the winning team a prize that they would share as a group," he recalls. "Something special, like caviar." Of course, the attention from the CEO was far more motivating than the award itself, and the friendly contest created a real buzz in the firm.[8]

- **Heroize teams.** What stories do you choose to tell? When something good happens in the business, who gets credit? All too often, a company's well-intentioned motivational stories focus on the individual. Liebert recalls,

  > When I started at USAA, we had high [net promoter scores]. Nevertheless, we still lacked consistent processes, which meant we had to rely on individual human heroics—and then we celebrated the lengths that people went to in order to serve our members.
  >
  > But that wasn't sustainable, and over time, our emphasis on the individual completely changed. Instead, we focused on the *teams*, and the impact the teams had. Our communications changed to focus on the experiences of our members and the teams that made those experiences better. And it began to build on itself, with teams functioning in a team-of-teams way, like the Special Forces.

  Liebert's "team of teams" analogy is telling and appropriate. It underscores the power of collaborating on multiple levels simultaneously—and again, nothing succeeds like success in helping to build and sustain momentum.

## Institutionalizing Collaboration

It may seem counterintuitive, but institutionalizing collaboration in the midst of success can represent a true challenge. Even after you've stuck the launch and nailed the pilot, and you're ready to roll out your compelling communications, things can still go off the rails. Psychologists know that under pressure, people tend to revert to their accustomed habits and their comfort zones, which most likely *aren't* the collaborative behaviors you're attempting to embed (for more on this topic, see Chapter 11). The same thing happens at the collective level. If your prior culture celebrated individual heroes at the expense of teams—the USAA example cited earlier—or promoted internal competition, people will find it very easy to revert to those earlier habits and reward systems.

But take heart: culture, if fed and nurtured, is sustainable. When smart collaboration is reinforced by leadership behaviors, performance and reward systems, organization design, communications, and ongoing training—especially of new leaders—organizations can reduce the risk of backsliding.

After multiple successful pilots at USAA, Liebert succeeded in focusing his teams throughout the organization on *member experiences*. First, they identified eleven thousand associated processes. They then created 650 cross-functional teams to work their way through that extensive list and populated those teams with newly titled "experience managers." Knowing that they had to move quickly and empower their change agents, Liebert and other senior managers pushed decision-making down to the lowest possible levels of the organization. "We needed to protect them from meddling," he explains. "In most companies, the CEO calls, and the team says, 'Yessir, right away.' Now, people closest to the process make decisions."

## We Need to Win. *And . . .*

Far too much of contemporary corporate culture can be summed up in the phrase, *We need to win!* And that's not wrong, exactly—but all too often, the competition that this mindset fosters becomes internally focused, pitting individuals and teams against each other.

So this mantra raises the question, *Who are you trying to beat?* Rather than fostering a culture of internal winners and losers, define the competition as the hurdle you are collectively working to overcome. Yes, maybe it's a direct competitor, as in, "We're Coke, let's beat Pepsi." But think back to our law student at the beginning of this chapter. Far more compelling—and purpose enhancing—is, "We're a biotech. Let's beat Alzheimer's disease." If you can cast the mission this way, then everyone is in it together, internally and maybe even externally. Perhaps you now have permission to team up with market competitors, with whom you share the common enemy of Alzheimer's.

This may sound farfetched, but in fact, we see this happening in pharma quite frequently now. The other examples we will mention in Chapter 9—such as the way Natura & Co collaborated with external partners to establish a plan for achieving net-zero carbon emissions by 2030—are only possible when a shared goal has been defined and embraced.

Collaboration has to be embraced as your organization's way of working—from the launch of initiatives, through their associated pilots, and onward. That can only happen through *effective* and *persistent* communication. Very often, this means invoking a shared sense of higher purpose. You need to help the team understand that they are all in it together, helping each other and advancing the organization's mission.

And you can't remind them too often of that reality.

$$\left[\ 9\ \right]$$

# Collaborating with Outside Partners

L et's imagine an investment firm—call it Modern Asset Management—that has decided to take a major position in cryptocurrencies, based on its forecast of near-term market conditions. As it sets out to implement the plan, MAM contacts the outside partner who handles the firm's accounting. *Whoa, slow down,* say the accountants. *It'll take us somewhere between six and nine months to update our software to handle that type of investment.*

MAM realizes too late that it can't go forward with the plan. Within a few months, it becomes clear that it has, indeed, missed a big move in the market. Ouch!

Now imagine those same partners in a different and happier scenario. A year earlier, senior teams from both parties had sat down to talk about their respective strategic road maps. MAM's leaders told their accounting provider that they saw a big opportunity in cryptocurrencies, and that investments in these instruments were likely to take off a year or two down the road. The provider agreed with MAM's assessment and immediately went to work enhancing its software. When MAM decided it was ready to launch, all the necessary tools were in place.

MAM made a *killing* in its first venture into crypto. As we said: a happier scenario!

Every organization above a certain size relies at least somewhat on third parties to accomplish its strategic objectives. Just as professionals must increasingly specialize in their specific domain to develop deep expertise, so too must organizations focus their talent and resources, such as R&D investments, to differentiate themselves from the competition, and to truly excel at their work. It's more or less inevitable: the more complex your challenges, the more strategically focused your company must become—and the more likely it is that you'll need to team up with external partners with complementary expertise and capabilities.

Strategic external partnering can boost your ability to acquire intellectual property, rapidly scale resources, acquire domain-specific knowledge, and access new markets. Biotech and pharma companies partner to develop and distribute drug treatments, pension funds partner with asset managers to run their investments function, law firms outsource back-office operations rather than running them internally, and even NASA works not only with other nationally sponsored counterparts but also with private space companies like SpaceX and Blue Origin.[1]

On the Mars *Ingenuity* helicopter mission, for example, NASA worked closely with numerous partners, including Virginia-based AeroVironment. "Everything we do starts with collaboration," says Wahid Nawabi, president and CEO of AeroVironment. "When you're designing a system-of-systems solution, it is by far one of the most, if not *the* most, important attributes of the team and the entire mission."[2]

The degree of interdependence between partners can range from minimal—such as a referral relationship, where the parties simply introduce potential customers to each other—to significant outsourcing, in which one party depends completely on another to fulfill a function; to transformational, as in the case of the Brazilian cosmetics company Natura & Co, described in the sidebar. But to deliver

## NATURA

In mid-June 2020, Natura & Co—the Brazilian-headquartered parent company of global cosmetics and personal care brands such as the Body Shop, Avon, and Aesop—unveiled an audacious plan.

Recognizing climate change as the largest global crisis of our time, Natura & Co committed to achieving net-zero carbon emissions by 2030: a full twenty years ahead of the goal set by the United Nations. In a comprehensive plan entitled "A Commitment to Life," the company pledged to implement new mechanisms to protect the biodiversity of the Amazon, shift operations toward regenerative business models, and take further steps toward promoting and measuring impact in the areas of inclusion and equality.

It was immediately clear that a plan of this magnitude—calling for what effectively would be a corporate transformation—could be achieved only by developing an ecosystem of strong multistakeholder partnerships. As Roberto Marques, the CEO of Natura & Co, explained, "We absolutely believe that we need to partner with external institutions, academia, science [and] other companies to find the solutions. We're not going to be able to do it by ourselves."[a]

a. B. Gyori et al., *Purpose-Driven Leadership for the 21st Century: Transitioning to a Purpose-First Economy through the New Business Logic* (Leaders on Purpose, 2020), 48.

---

strategic value to the end client, the collaboration usually needs to go deeper than an arm's-length referral relationship.

What are the action implications? Leaders need to conduct a strategic review of how their organization collaborates with external parties, prioritize those relationships based on strategic importance, and determine which ones will benefit from smarter collaboration.

This chapter focuses on how to make those priority relationships truly collaborative. This starts at home: if your own people aren't ready to embrace external relationships, then you will need to shift the culture by helping them understand the benefits of partnering. Next, turning to implementation, we explain how to conduct a diagnostic process to lay the foundation of a new relationship, or to recharge an existing alliance that isn't delivering the strategic value it could. And finally, even the best of starts can weaken over time—as people change and priorities evolve—so we conclude the chapter with a discussion of how to sustain external collaborations.

## Cultural Challenges to Effective Third-Party Collaboration

In previous chapters, we've focused on ways to foster a collaborative culture within your own company—hiring collaborative people, embedding collaborative skills, and so on. That challenge only increases when your company sets out to work in partnership with another company. Any flaws in the "local" collaborative culture will surface and be magnified when you begin working with outsiders.

Transforming a strong, internally focused culture; overcoming resistance to change; and breaking down siloed behaviors are critical steps for forming effective third-party collaborations—and all rely on senior leaders as champions. Larger partnerships or those that touch on mission-critical functions often demand direct executive engagement. But upper-management buy-in is symbolically critical across the board. Leaders who embrace collaboration with third parties define and validate a shared journey. They help make the inherent risks of that journey understandable and manageable. Ultimately, they make it clear how some things will become possible *only* through that journey.

What types of barriers might leaders have to address? We've identified three common cultural challenges that tend to hinder third-party collaboration.

### The "Us versus Them" Culture

Some organizations create such a strong sense of identity that anyone outside is perceived as the enemy. Of course, a healthy rivalry, coupled with a strong dose of self-pride, can help spur people to higher performance.[3] But some organizations and their leaders take it too far. There's a big difference between relishing competition and demonizing your competitors.

One major retailer was notorious, for example, for treating vendors as foes to be conquered. "I dreaded my flight to [that city]," said one technology consultant, "because even the receptionist seemed to regard me as an enemy. It was a constant battle that ended up feeling quite personal. They didn't just want a better price and service; they wanted to score points in arguments."

This wasn't a problem with just that individual consultant, or with the company's IT department. On a fairly regular basis, the company's CEO publicly derided his competitors, suppliers, and regulators—basically, anyone outside the company that his people competed or even interacted with. The tone was set on high, and across the company, people took their cue.

## The "Do It Ourselves" Culture

Organizations pride themselves on the capabilities they've developed and the talent they've recruited. Past a certain point, however, a "do it ourselves" culture inhibits collaboration—either by fostering a fallacy of uniqueness or by fostering risk aversion.

In the latter category, some people may fear losing control of intellectual assets: *They'll just take our intellectual property and build a competitive product.* Managers may not understand the value of a particular alliance, and may feel that their roles are threatened if they give up elements of control to another organization. Comments like, "Our process is unique," and "We are much too complex for someone else to do what we do," are commonly heard.

Similarly, many IT teams prefer to develop capabilities in-house. But that only makes sense for the (relatively rare) capability that is truly a strategic differentiator. By declining to partner with an industry provider, you may end up with a load of custom software that lacks both functionalities and scale.

## The "Laissez-Faire" Culture

Yes, external partnerships can bring enormous value. But if they are managed in a highly decentralized, laissez-faire way, the result may be conflict and wasted effort. For example, in one global technology company, the mergers and acquisitions team, the product teams, and the partnerships team had been left to their own devices. The almost inevitable result? The mergers and acquisitions group was confidentially working on an acquisition that, if successful, would bring in more or less the same capabilities that the IT team was then spending serious money to build. Meanwhile, the partnerships team was out in the marketplace actively wooing potential partners in the same realm.

Inefficient, confusing, and frustrating for all concerned? Yes, especially as all these internal (and potentially external) overlaps began to surface. In this complex realm, laissez-faire doesn't work. Organizations need strong internal alignment around their approach to managing partnerships. In most cases, only the executive team has a clear enough vantage point to see across all of these activities, many of which are necessarily confidential.

## Assessing (and Reinvigorating) Collaborative Third-Party Relationships

How do you set up and manage the working arrangements for a third-party relationship so that truly smarter collaboration can flourish?

Even if you're new to this way of operating, your partner-selection process is almost surely based on robust financial and strategic considerations. The problem we often see, however, even with highly experienced players, is that many companies fail to make collaboration an explicit focus of their evaluation process. We therefore start this section by focusing on how to conduct due diligence on the collaborative potential of a new third-party relationship, and then move on to steps for launching with a strong foundation.

If you've been in this game awhile, chances are high that you're already stuck with some existing relationships that just aren't delivering on their potential. If so, you probably need a top-to-top discussion about whether the relationship still has the potential to deliver the strategic value that you anticipated. This isn't a process of fault-finding or assigning blame; sometimes a relationship goes cold because one party's priorities have evolved in an unexpected direction. If your two leaders (or their teams) agree that the prospect for mutual gain is still there, then you can employ Steps 2 through 5, discussed shortly, to refresh those sleeping winners.

## 1. Smarter Collaboration as Part of Due Diligence

In Chapter 5, we discussed the importance of assessing the degree of smart collaboration in a company you're hoping to acquire. For example, how much cross-silo work is going on? Is it an inclusive organization? Are ideas sourced and used from people across the organization, regardless of their position?

This type of diligence is even more essential in a potential partnership. Why? Because while an acquiring company has a high degree of control over the culture and leadership in its acquired entity, in a partnership that's not the case. In the absence of direct control over each other, the two partners have to rely on a high degree of strategic alignment, organic collaboration among individuals and teams, and strong coordination by the leaders on both sides.

So how do you develop a clear-eyed understanding of the degree of collaborative behaviors in the potential partner? Steve Twait, vice president for alliance and integration management at pharma giant AstraZeneca, explains how he tackles this challenge:

> We conduct a face-to-face diligence as part of our "cultural diligence." I want to know not just how they make decisions, but who makes them? Are they consensus-based? How do they staff their teams? How are people incentivized? How broadly do they communicate across the company? What's their work philosophy? How casual or formal are they? I'm thinking about the corporate culture, as well as the geographic cultural aspects.
>
> What I learn informs AstraZeneca about which leaders to assign to this particular project. I think about the people's styles. We need to understand the human elements of what it takes to work together and how to complement the skills and styles of your counterparts.[4]

These in-depth discussions on strategy, operations, and culture can provide necessary assurances—or they can raise red flags that need to be assessed. Again, in Twait's words,

> I listen for their views on the time horizon. Do they have a long-term commitment and passion, versus just concern about getting to the next important milestone? Some of these collaborations can go on for ten-plus years, so you really have to think about the very long-term potential. I look for warning signs that they may not have a similar level of commitment. I'm also looking for transparency around what a company's strengths are, and areas that they want to grow and develop in.

To dig deeper, particularly on large opportunities, the two potential partners can use a third party to help. This neutral party can run focus groups, interviews, and cultural dynamics surveys—not necessarily with an eye toward surfacing a deal-breaker, but perhaps to provide insights that may help get the relationship off on the right foot. We have played this role, and the smart collaboration diagnostic introduced in Chapter 3 shows how we use surveys and interviews (internal, with clients, and with existing partners) to paint a clear-eyed picture of the degree to which smart collaboration is happening in the organization today, as well as potential barriers to collaboration. This data not only provides an honest assessment of the current state of play; it also provides guideposts regarding constructive steps the two partners might take to set the stage for effective collaboration.

Third parties are only one useful source of information; there are many others. Additional assessment can be conducted through independent research, which might include, for example, a collaboration-focused review of publicly available data (annual reports, LinkedIn, Glassdoor) and targeted interviews with former employees.

## 2. Agreeing on the Goals and Extent of Collaboration

Explicit upfront agreement is critical: Why are we in the relationship, and what are both parties trying to achieve with it? Which teams need to work directly together, and which just need to be informed? For example, in the automotive industry, supplier partnerships often involve joint R&D and product development, but not marketing and sales. In pharma, a partnership may cover every element of the development-through-distribution lifecycle, although the nature of the collaboration is likely to change as the companies evolve over time.

How do you reach this level of agreement right at the beginning, when the two parties are still pretty unfamiliar with each other? Twait explains AstraZeneca's approach:

> At the very beginning of a startup, we conduct what we call the Strategic Futures Exercise. We bring the leaders together and say to them, "Let's fast-forward three, five years, and someone's writing a book about this. What do we want this collaboration known for?" This forces people to be visionary.
>
> I ask each side their ideas ahead of time, and also ask about the obstacles. Because those responses come back to me confidentially, oftentimes you have team members being quite transparent. As in, "I'm not convinced that the other side has the right capabilities." Or even, "I'm not sure my leaders have committed enough resources." During that startup meeting, I play back to them some of what I've heard. "It doesn't matter which side this came from," I say. "Someone in this room thinks this is an obstacle. What do we need to do to overcome that?"

This kind of structured dialogue helps both parties see who needs to be involved, at which stages, and how intensively. From there, the challenge becomes one of establishing the guiding principles for the *ways* to engage.

## 3. Setting Collaboration Ground Rules

A good first step is to hold a workshop solely dedicated to setting (or refreshing) expectations and agreeing on how to address differences in preferred ways of working. By being proactive in this way, partners can help minimize conflicts that might arise along the way.

For example, teams need to agree on a set of specific but simple guidelines, such as, "If I'm upset with you about something, I'll pick up the phone and call you instead of blasting an email to the whole team." Eventually, these conventions can serve as the foundations for a collaboratively built culture. Take, for example, the approach that dominates in the relevant consulting practices at Accenture. As Stuart Henderson, leader of that firm's global Life Sciences practice, explains,

> With some of our clients, we have a joint training program for both Accenture colleagues and clients to talk about the ways of working together, like how we're going to deal with conflicts and issues.
>
> We bring two small model cars—one red and the other green. We explain that the power of positive language, as represented by the green car, always achieves more than the negative. But we also recognize the human need to have a red-car moment, as in, "I'm *angry*. This deliverable was a week late. Unacceptable!"
>
> Meanwhile, everybody knows what's coming next: "Hey, in a second, the green car's coming, and we're going to talk about this rationally." So the group doesn't have to deal with that immediate rush of adrenaline, which gives us a chance to listen and process.
>
> To be honest, by the time I've heard the red-car complaint, I'm often agreeing: "Yeah; this really isn't good enough. How did we let that happen?" But then comes the green car: "OK, how could we make this change?" All of a sudden, you have the power of positivity. It's much more motivating.
>
> If a new person joins the group without training, they may start ranting. And everyone says, "When's the green car coming in?!" Having those metaphors takes the heat out of it.[5]

This approach is consistent with neuroscience, which recognizes that different parts of our brains do different things. The amygdala is a nerve center near the base of the brain that tends to take over when we're under stress, triggering the fight-or-flight response. This is the red-car zone, in the terminology of the preceding anecdote. The frontal lobes of our brains are where more rational thinking goes on. By lowering the heat of the moment, the "green car" allows our frontal lobes to retain control—avoiding what's sometimes called "amygdala hijack"—so that we can choose a more reasoned approach and preserve the relationship.[6]

## 4. Building Sufficient Trust between Organizations

*How do I know I can trust the other party?*

This may be the most commonly asked question in the early stages of a collaborative partnership with an external party. Unfortunately, it's usually the wrong question. Why? Because the only thing that's in *your* control is your own actions. Your job is to work from your side of the partnership to build trust. This entails two kinds of actions: sending loud, clear, consistent signals of your own trustworthiness and making yourself transparent to the point of vulnerability.

AstraZeneca's Twait explains,

> You can build trust by being open and honest—as in, "Hey, this is a particular area where we really need your help." Companies aren't always transparent about their weaknesses, because they see that as a problem when they're trying to get into a new partnership.

> Having a really strong champion involved on both sides who actually shares vulnerabilities really sets the tone for others. If I'm not hearing that from our potential partner, that's a red flag for me.

Trust is *earned*. It's built on a shared understanding of expectations. As a rule, the best way to build trust is through repeated, small, reinforcing steps—in other words, providing recurring evidence. Another way to build trust is to "audition" for it by finding opportunities to work with your counterparts on low-risk tasks, which gives you a chance to demonstrate your organization's competence and integrity.[7]

The alliance management teams need to create a framework to make sure that strategies, goals, and incentives are sufficiently aligned to help the parties avoid misunderstanding, in which trust can erode quickly.

## 5. Communicating the Value

We've already discussed the notion of creating a culture that embraces external relationships. This is a prerequisite, but more is needed. For each alliance, it's important to get everyone on board internally—especially during the prelaunch and launch phases. In particular, you need to take the time early on to identify specific people and departments that could feel exposed by a new external relationship, and keep them apprised.

Leaders need to be especially thoughtful when they set up partnerships with businesses that are thought of as competitors.[8] Iberdrola, Europe's largest private utility, supplies energy to one hundred million people. The company set out to create an ecosystem of employees, technology collaborators, industrial organizations, and public institutions aimed at ensuring universal access to energy services.[9] "Rather than competing against each other, we compete against the issue," says Ignacio Galán, Iberdrola's CEO. "Working in alliances implies a great commitment, and the sharing of results and resources—not an easy task. However, when everyone's investment in time and energy is correct, the added value of these relationships between different actors translates into an exponential increase in the possibilities of producing positive change."[10]

## Creating Sustainably Collaborative Relationships

Most sophisticated corporations enter into outside collaborations on the assumption that there is at least the possibility of long-term value creation. Given the reality of organizational change over time, what are the best practices to sustain partnerships and make them effective in the long run? Here are some practical steps you can take.

## Insulate against Key-Person Risk

An IBM study on partnering in the biotech sector concludes that the biggest contributor to alliance failures is changes in senior management at the companies within an alliance.[11] "A great relationship between two companies typically has two senior executives who are utterly committed to making that happen," says Accenture's Henderson. "And they shake hands on that commitment on a regular basis. So if one of those sponsors leaves, that starts to destroy trust, and the relationship starts to wane."

Organizations change. People get promoted, change roles, leave jobs. If a relationship is centered on one person on either side, that turnover can have immediate consequences for the partnership—interrupting momentum and forcing new leaders to get up to speed with the dynamics of the alliance. At worst, they may even lose sight of the strategic rationale behind it.

To address this challenge of continuity, you need broad-based engagement across multiple functions and areas, rather than a relationship that's single-threaded through the alliance manager of each party. As AstraZeneca's Twait says,

> When we create a governance structure, we normally have people from different silos across the company—commercial, development, operation—all engaged in the relationship to help break down silos and ensure continuity over time.
>
> We're not only trying to build a team with diversity of style and thought, but also a diversity of professional backgrounds. That's important because the issues in a relationship can vary. It could be a human-resources issue today, and then a regulatory one, and the next day a manufacturing snafu.
>
> And finally, it's really valuable to have people who understand the human aspects of a relationship. We can manage the

business risk, the legal risk, the contractual risk. Those are the easy aspects. But understanding and managing the human interaction—that is the real challenge.

It also requires active succession planning. "As an executive, you have to be a steward of a partnering relationship, handing it on to the next person," says Accenture's Henderson. "When I took over a client from my predecessor, who had built this multidecade trust-based relationship, we did a six-month handover. The client wanted to see if I could be trusted the same way my predecessor was, before he was going to trust me to continue the relationship."

## Optimize Structures for Alliance Management

Over time, your organization may need to coordinate across a large number of partnerships. This requires resources dedicated at the right level of seniority. A five-year study of the inner workings of fifteen strategic alliances found that good design—alignment and concrete governance structures—allows those partnerships to reap significant benefits, such as broadening consumer choices and addressing significant gaps in the marketplace.[12]

This is in part a challenge of correctly assigning certain kinds of responsibility, an assignment that often reflects company- and sector-specific issues. In the bio-pharma industry, for example, a centrally run global alliance management department may handle the highest-profile third-party relationships—often in the range of eighty alliances—whereas the R&D function manages myriad academic and research collaborations, which are more focused on the earlier stage of the drug discovery and development process, and typically number in the hundreds.[13]

If your organization operates multiple alliances, you also need a central repository that captures standardized models, process frameworks, procedural documents, the business case for the partnership—the kinds of practices referred to earlier. This not only proves invaluable when you're trying to unearth details about an alliance that may go back a decade or more; it also provides consistency and continuity for this and future alliances going forward.

For example, in a rapidly growing tech company, multiple partnerships had gone stale over the course of a decade—and yet the restrictive agreements underlying those partnerships lived on. When a long-quiet "partner" demanded, more or less out of the blue, that the two companies collaborate on a new opportunity, the tech company had to scramble to find the relevant agreements, and it discovered that it was bound to conform to those standing agreements.

All things considered, the tech company would have been far better served if it had maintained—and regularly consulted!—an institutional memory of its ongoing collaborative relationships.

## Continually Validate Alignment with Your Business Strategy

It's not only people that change over time. So do market dynamics and business strategies. Mergers, acquisitions, and divestitures can all help determine the continuing relevance of a collaboration. What was initially a strong partnership and relationship structure may be inappropriate for the business's objectives five years down the road. Through the alliance management team and top-to-top discussions, the two parties need to communicate their strategic plans and transparently assess whether the partnership—in its current structure or some amended version of it—will remain relevant moving forward.

Earlier we talked about the visioning exercise AstraZeneca uses to kick off its new partnerships. We recommend repeating this exercise every three years to help both parties stay focused on mutual priorities, or to flag early if one side's strategy starts to drift.

## Fix Trust Breaches Fast

Problems will inevitably arise. When they do, you need the wide-open channels of communication described earlier to prevent those issues from lingering and destroying trust.

A divisional manager in a global consumer goods company recently underscored this point. "After a blowup, we held an hour-long debrief between the two teams," he told us, "which turned out to be an immersion in each other's cultures. This person from the Midwest said, 'You know what? When I send you a presentation that I've worked my butt off on, you *never* send me an email thanking me!' And his German counterpart responded, 'Well, that's your *job*. In Germany we don't send emails back and forth thanking people just for doing what they were supposed to do.'"

The manager agreed that this exchange had come too late—but at least it sparked some process improvements. He explained that both teams had put in place a cultural liaison to bring newcomers up to speed on different ways of working and identify the first outlet for voicing (and ideally handling) frustrations before they intensified.

If things *do* go off the rails and trust breaks, you first have to decide if the relationship is worth saving. Assuming it is, you next have to figure out who's committed and capable of doing the hard work of rebuilding trust. As the manager just quoted told us, "The rebuilding process requires serious transparency, honesty, and integrity—and more than a healthy dose of humility on all sides."

## Get Personal

This may be a surprising prescription, but we think it's valid. When the partnership needs help, *get personal*—by which we mean, put yourself in your counterpart's shoes. Imagine what the world looks like from the other side of the table, especially when everyone is away from the table. What are they thinking about? What pressures are they under as a result of their relationship with you?

One of our interviewees—we'll call him Tom—tells of the time when his company's CEO came face-to-face with this challenge. That CEO oversaw a far-flung pharma empire, WorldPharm, which included a number of joint ventures with much smaller companies, in which this CEO didn't seem to have much interest beyond their bottom-line impact. Tom tried a novel way to get the CEO to focus on one of these collaborations. "Let's listen in on that company's quarterly update phone conference," he suggested, "and see what's on their minds."

The CEO didn't look particularly interested, but agreed to go along with it. They dialed in on the public line. The update was just getting started. After that company's leaders made a brief presentation, the floor was opened to questions from investors—and the very first questions had to do with the company's alliance with WorldPharm: "Is it turning out like you hoped it would? Are you going to be able to keep it going? Was this a good bet?"

Tom's summary, after the fact: *You have to seek out ways to see things from your partner company's perspective.* What's keeping them up at night? The answer may not be one to which you can respond effectively—or it may translate into a request that's an easy accommodation for you and your company.

## Health Checks with Senior Leaders

For top leaders to jump in at difficult junctures, as we discussed earlier, they need a good sense of how the partnership is progressing. Moreover, by regularly reviewing key milestones, senior leaders can use those health checks to find opportunities to enhance the relationships between the two parties' upper managements.

## Review and Retreat—or Reinvigorate and Relaunch?

The bottom line? *Things change.*

Strategies evolve. Markets and competitive dynamics shift. People move on. Early enthusiasm lags. Products need a refresh. For all these reasons and more, the partners in a collaborative external venture eventually may need to take time, step back, and reassess the partnership. Part of that assessment needs to be objectively historical, with a minimum of recrimination and finger-pointing. If sales are on the decline, *why?* Are key people in the venture getting burned out? Who, and why? Is one party to this marriage happier than the other—and if so, can the value proposition be adjusted to address that perceived imbalance?

Jointly conducting this kind of assessment is not an admission of failure. In fact, it reflects a relationship that's still *working*, at least to some extent. And in fact, most partnerships eventually face this type of fork in the road: retreat, or reinvigorate?

At some companies, a periodic relaunch is a standard part of their long-term external collaborations. Yes, it's mostly a symbolic gesture.

At the same time, though, it can be a highly significant vote of confidence, as the collaborating companies look forward into a shared future.

This concludes the "how-to" chapters of *Smarter Collaboration*. Now we turn to what might be called the how-*not*-to's: the very real pitfalls that even the best-intentioned collaborators can fall into if they're not careful.

# PART FOUR

# TROUBLESHOOTING COLLABORATION CHALLENGES

$$\left[\begin{array}{c} 10 \end{array}\right]$$

# Watch Out:
# The Illusion of Inclusion

We talked recently with a partner at a large private equity firm who happens to come from a minority background. He was discussing the culture at that firm:

> I'm not a scratch golfer, and I didn't go to Yale or study economics. And I'm not white. For my first several years here, I was pretty much of an outsider. Everyone was nice and polite, but the more archetypal guys were always tapped for the juiciest projects. I eventually did make partner, and we've recently managed to hire just a few other people of color. But now it's the opposite problem: we allocate the "diverse people" [*he used air quotes*] to every single project. They're burning out because they're way overstretched, but they feel like they have to shoulder the burden to prove themselves.

Collaboration, when it is truly smart, is inherently inclusive. Organizations that practice smarter collaboration are more likely to call on the right people at the right time, regardless of their place in any formal hierarchy. They are more likely to encourage diverse inputs, recognize a broader range of potential solutions to challenges, value unorthodox contributions, and give more types of people opportunities to engage in higher-value work.

But as in the private equity firm just mentioned, even the best-intentioned efforts at collaboration can go off the rails. Initiatives that are structured in a way that fail to take diversity, equity, and inclusion (DEI) into account, *explicitly*, can backfire. In this scenario, people become engaged in teamwork that masquerades as smart collaboration but falls short and even undermines DEI efforts. Diversity without inclusion is not enough.[1] In the worst case, bad collaboration sets traps and sets people up for failure.

In this chapter, we look at these kinds of traps—and how to avoid setting them. Or, phrased more positively, we suggest ways that your company can engage in truly smart collaboration that fosters inclusion, which in turn makes collaboration more productive and engaging. It's a virtuous cycle that requires leadership and intentionality.

## How Mismanaged Diversity Undermines Collaboration

Let's start with the basics. Numerous studies purport to show a correlation between companies with diverse leadership and business success.[2] One McKinsey report, for example, suggested that companies in the top quartile for racial or ethnic and gender diversity were respectively 35 percent and 15 percent more likely to have financial returns above their national industry medians.[3] As we've said throughout the book, diversity is essential for collaboration: the power comes through harnessing differing knowledge and experiences.

But some caution is in order here. The fact is, an even greater number of studies show that a nonstrategic approach to diversity can actually have a *negative* effect on performance. Diversity purely by the numbers and token representation without real inclusion, in other words, becomes dysfunctional. Decades of research show us that diversity, unless actively managed, often creates a whole range of dysfunction on teams: as one example, employees become fearful of conflict, so they stop communicating or only talk with others who are similar to them, and the group fractures instead of collaborating.[4] When differences are not skillfully and consistently managed, they can lead to workplace tension, which in turn often inhibits smart collaboration.[5]

Leaders don't always see the chilling effects of mismanaged diversity on collaboration because those effects tend to manifest themselves in day-to-day encounters. One workplace where this phenomenon has been studied is the national parliaments in Australia, the United Kingdom, and Canada, where women members of Parliament are interrupted (mostly by men) more frequently than their male counterparts. The result? Many women stop participating in floor debates: not only those who were interrupted but also their peers who want to avoid getting shut down.[6] The implications are far reaching and serious. Those members who don't participate are less effective at representing their constituents' interests.[7] When this happens in the workplace, some women might opt out of participating in debate and discussion—but as we've seen, smart collaboration hinges on getting people with diverse views to actively contribute. And over the long run, when these types of negative behaviors are not surfaced, discussed, and resolved, they tend to become culturally acceptable.

Negative behaviors and outcomes don't always arise out of ignorance or ill will. Sometimes they crop up in contexts where people have the "best of intentions" about collaboration, and things *still* backfire.

## The Tokenism Trap

Going all the way back to the beginning of the book, we defined smart collaboration as being hyperintentional about who gets involved, and then not just having people on the team, but truly valuing them and drawing out their strengths. When leaders fall into the tokenism trap, they violate both these principles.

For example, our analysis of project databases across several industries shows that even though women may make up at least half of a team, their contributions may not be proportionate. During our research, one leader we talked to, whom we will call Nancy, said, "On a couple of our larger accounts, I would be invited for random meetings with the client, but it was rare that I was asked to dive deep into any of the major tasks. I kind of felt like I was warming up on the sidelines but was never put in the game."

Figure 10.1 illustrates this pattern in two professional firms we worked with. On Team 1, there's a 50/50 gender split, but the firm overall is 17 percent female. We can infer that Team 1's leader must have worked extra hard to achieve gender parity. The problem, though, is that these women contribute only 26 percent of the project's billable value.[8] In another firm, Team 2, also shown in Figure 10-1, the disparity between the proportion of women on the team and their contributions is even starker: the team is 60 percent women, with 22 percent as female partners, and yet women only contribute 18 percent of the project's billable value.

How should we interpret this gap? Simple: women are getting pulled into small pieces of work that don't allow them to develop new skills or build deep relationships with clients and senior team members, as Nancy was suggesting. In addition, those women incur massive switching costs as they attempt to juggle multiple projects at once.[9]

Our interviews with the firms' leaders suggest that they are, indeed, well intentioned: *let's make sure we have enough women on the team*. But without data and a comprehensive view of what happens when all these individual actions converge on the shoulders of individuals, those leaders fail to notice when their good intentions backfire. This, ultimately, is where smart collaboration requires a specific strategy, turning those good intentions into implementation and action.

Tokenism can take other forms, and can conceal significant problems. In the hit musical *Hamilton*, Aaron Burr laments his misfortune at being excluded from "the room where it happens." He is right: if you're not in the room (literal or virtual) where the critical decisions are playing out, you have little hope of exercising influence. This raises the question, Even if you track diversity at the department or team level, how certain are you that diverse people are truly involved in the group's core collaborative activities, where their contributions are welcomed, valued, and used?

FIGURE 10-1

# Firm and team composition vs. contribution by gender

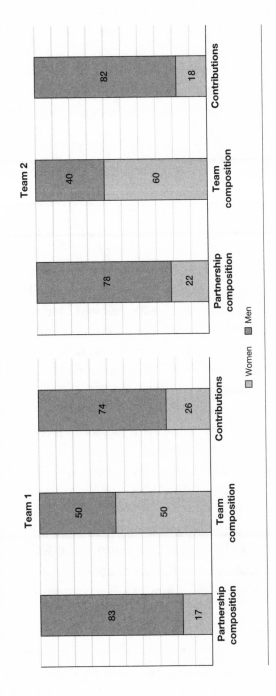

Ben Waber, an MIT scientist, turned up a shocking example—in the context of a well-regarded corporation—of people being excluded from the "room where it happens." Waber examined a combination of email, calendar, and chat data across the company, where about half of the employees were women. He found that in many divisions, both genders were equally likely to be "in the room" for important meetings. But in one division—a unit with more than one thousand employees—women were only invited to 5 percent of the meetings. When Waber and his fellow researchers looked deeper, they discovered that when it was one of several senior people who was booking the meeting, women were *especially* likely to be excluded.[10]

Intentional? Consciously misogynistic? Perhaps not. But the people who are penalized by these kinds of slights and exclusions can be forgiven for believing so.

Here's another way to look at inclusion: Who gets approached to engage in which kinds of collaboration? One of our research partners collected data from more than two thousand workers across industries ranging from dairy farming to university administration to a state transportation agency.[11] Across these industries, women made up 40 percent of workers. The researchers asked people to name others in their own organization to whom they turned for information or help in solving problems. Then they rated how important those interactions were.

When we analyzed this data by gender, we found that across industries, women were more likely to be overtapped (relative to their representation in their company) for lower-value interactions such as providing information, which involves a one-way flow rather than real collaboration. In contrast, for interactions that involved more value-adding exchanges, such as contributing new ideas or engaging in problem-solving discussions, women were more likely to be excluded. These results are summarized in Figure 10-2.

Let's parse this data by the gender of who initiated the collaboration on problem-solving and ideas (see Figure 10-3). The analysis shows that women were equally likely (50/50) to turn to either men or women.[12] And given that women represented only 40 percent of the organization, that means they were highly inclusive of other

FIGURE 10-2

## Who's sought out for which kinds of interactions?

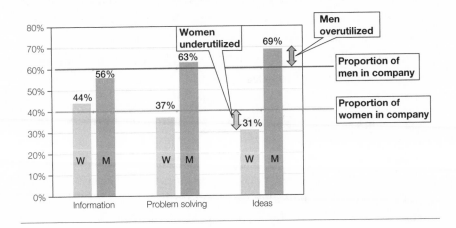

FIGURE 10-3

## Whom do women vs. men seek out for problem solving and idea generation?

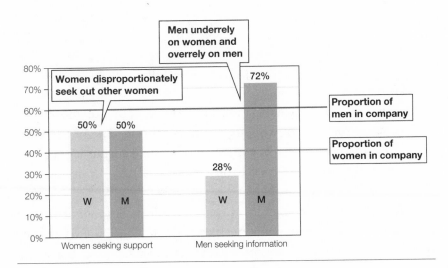

women. In contrast, men underrelied on women, turning to them just 28 percent of the time.

Of course, these kinds of demoralizing patterns aren't universal. But they arise often enough to warrant exploration. Are they happening in your organization? Where and why? Whenever we present our findings to women's groups and other affinity groups in various companies, audience members tell us that they often immediately recognize the problems captured in the data and are relieved to learn that they're not alone. One participant, nearly in tears, said, "I thought it was just me." But it wasn't, and isn't.

Later, we talk about ways to use data and analytics to understand these patterns in your organization and hold people accountable for managing them.

How does all of this come to bear on smart collaboration? Smart collaboration hinges on *inclusivity*, and not just the working processes of a project team. It has to start with scrutiny of the kinds of interactions that occur across the organization, on a daily basis. How are individual decisions made about whom to collaborate with? A laissez-faire approach can actually be damaging to individuals, teams, and the company. Even decisions made by well-intentioned leaders at the team level—people who are convinced that they are acting in ways that support diversity—can lead to counterproductive outcomes.

## The Mini-Me Trap

Now let's look at another potential pitfall, which we call the "Mini-Me" trap.

Imagine you're a woman who's just landed your dream job as a junior professor at a prestigious business school. One of the most senior faculty members pulls you aside to impart some wisdom about how to successfully lead a class of first-year MBAs—a notoriously critical audience.

"When you walk into the classroom," he begins, "let your demeanor say it all: buttoned up, formal, in charge. But at about the six-minute mark, after you've grilled someone and set the tone for a robust discussion, take off your suit jacket and hang it on the back of the chair. After another ten or twelve minutes, roll up your sleeves—and be sure you're not wearing cuff links, so that you can pull this off without a hitch."

Maybe at this point you're thinking about those ninety-four pairs of eyes that are watching you disrobe. "Ummm, *really*?" you ask him.

"Yes," he winks. "Gets 'em every time."

What's tough here is that in all probability, the senior professor really does mean well. He's genuinely trying to collaborate across divides (age, gender, background), share his hard-earned wisdom, and thereby give you an edge. But you also know—or at least hope!—that there's more than one way to succeed, because this one is not right for you. If you get repeated signals that you need to "fit in" in order to succeed, you are probably less likely to contribute the unique perspectives that would make collaboration truly valuable. Over time, you may withdraw entirely.

Maybe this scenario sounds extreme. Maybe you doubt that, in this day and age, someone would step forward with this kind of antiquated and counterproductive advice. But our research across many dozens of companies shows that, in fact, this type of thing happens all too frequently. And it's not a trivial concern. The small decisions about collaboration—whom the leaders choose to invest in, how they choose to coach them, what they hold up on a day-to-day basis as indicators of "success"—inevitably lead to bigger choices like promotion outcomes and career progression.

Let's take just one example: succession planning. We studied this empirically in a set of four professional service firms and have observed similar patterns with account leaders in other organizations such as financial services and software. Our findings, summarized in Figure 10-4, show how an unfair pattern of leadership-succession decisions emerges. In the year after promotion, a man's "book of business" (revenue from the clients he leads) is already close to double that of his female peers. The gap widens, often very significantly, in the following year or two, and then persists. So what's going on here?

The answer is painful but simple: men are *far more likely* to be selected as the lead partner for the firm's existing clients, essentially handing them a book of business, whereas women need to build their revenue by attracting new clients. This finding holds true even when controlling for other variables that are likely to predict who "inherits" the client relationship, such as client-specific experiences, length of relationship with the existing leaders, and a host of other variables. Further analyses show that the bigger the client, the more likely it is that a man becomes the next leader.

FIGURE 10-4

## Gender discrepancy in business development outcomes

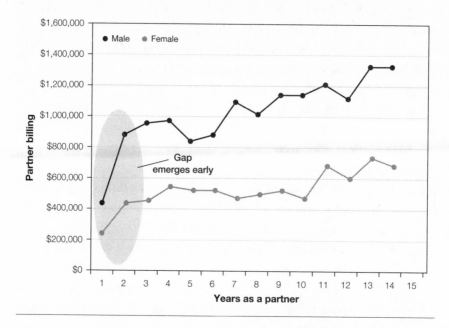

When we interviewed professionals about their choices for a successor, existing-client lead partners tended to say things like, "Well, my client is happy and well served, and it's critical that we appoint as my successor someone whom they'll trust as much as they trust me." Subconsciously—and sometimes *not* so subconsciously—this search for a "trustworthy" successor causes the leader to appoint a Mini-Me, who is very often a white male of a certain age who dresses and comports himself in a certain way.

The foundations for this kind of biased succession planning tend to get laid early, as leaders choose which younger staff to collaborate with, to bring into their clients, and to invest in through coaching. Data shows that they tend to groom the people who are like them—or try to mold them into their own image. This is the problem posed by the professor in the earlier vignette. Yes, he gets credit for reaching out to a woman—not an obvious Mini-Me. But he earns an F for trying to turn her into him.

Why do well-meaning people fall into the Mini-Me trap? As we explained in Chapter 2, homophily is the basic human tendency to form connections with people who are like them (age, gender, ethnicity, socioeconomic status, personal beliefs, and so on), which ends up undermining the inclusion of others. So far, we've been examining the trap in the context of succession planning, where homophily quietly influences many points of the process, such as choosing whom to mentor, coach, and sponsor. And of course, it doesn't only play out in the context of gender. Scholars such as Harvard Law School professor David Wilkins have decades of research showing similar patterns for people of color in professional workplaces.[13]

But smarter collaboration involves the integration of diverse views, not the imposition of one dominant perspective on others. In the short term, when people feel pressured to conform, they suppress their personal values, views, and attributes to fit in with organizational ones.[14] Smarter collaboration simply cannot play out without diverse inputs. And in the longer term, assuming the constraints are uncomfortable enough, those people under constant pressure to conform tend to opt out of the company.

So clearly, the traps are in place, and it's the job of company leaders to keep their good people out of them.

## How to Promote Inclusion

What steps can senior leaders take to make sure that collaboration from the grassroots level on up is truly inclusive? How can they be sure that *inclusion* is being defined as broadly as possible—encompassing not just gender and race but also socioeconomic background, disabilities, and diversity of professional experience?

We group our answers to these questions into two categories. The first focuses on ways for a company to *measure and monitor effects* across the organization, to ensure that local actions—even the well-intentioned ones!—aren't backfiring, and to help prevent misfires before they happen. As in most of business, accountability is the means to the desired end.

The second category includes activities aimed at *building a learning culture*. A learning culture encourages curiosity, exploration, and a genuine interest in other points of view. An organization with this orientation seeks out diverse viewpoints and, in the process, naturally avoids elevating Mini-Mes with similar experiences, reduces tokenism, and embraces differences.

Let's look at some specifics in these two categories.

## Measuring and Accountability

Succeeding at inclusion requires you to measure results. It's less about making the business case for inclusion, and more about setting targets for the specific goals you are trying to reach.[15] For most organizations, *inclusion* is key not only to smart collaboration but also to overall organizational health and effectiveness. A recent Gartner survey found that 85 percent of DEI leaders cited "organizational inclusion"—meaning integrating their diverse talent into the "deal stream" of the organization—as the most important talent outcome of their DEI efforts. Strangely enough, though, only 57 percent of organizations are currently using an inclusion metric to track their DEI progress—and to make matters worse, even many of *those* organizations don't express a lot of confidence in their ability to measure it.

At the risk of stating the obvious, achieving diversity through successful recruitment is only a point of departure. Of *course* you need to bring diverse people into your organization so that you can begin the process of including them. But it's a *cycle* of success, or failure. Without inclusivity, you won't get the best out of that new talent, and you won't retain them. And eventually, the word will get out, and you'll no longer be able to attract diverse talent in the first place.

How do you use metrics to foster inclusion? A good and necessary foundation is the smart collaboration diagnostic discussed in Chapter 3. Here are four additional suggestions.

### *Measure Inclusion, Not Just Diversity*

Can we presuppose that you are already measuring diversity effectively? Check this assumption: scholars like Harvard Kennedy School's Iris Bohnet and Siri Chilazi show that, beyond merely collecting the data, you need to ensure that it is accessible, legible, easily understood by the intended audience (like a scorecard or dashboard), and preferably collected and owned by the group that is going to use it.[16]

Beyond tracking the representation of various groups within the workforce, measure whether the people in those groups are actively engaged in the core work of the organization. We introduced this idea in Chapter 5, which focused on getting newly hired people involved in this work *quickly*. What types of work are different kinds of people spending time on? How many of our people are included in core work, and are thereby in a position to make real contributions going forward? Look back to the examples earlier in this chapter, in which women—although reasonably well represented, in terms of raw numbers—were contributing a disproportionately small part of the project and were engaged in less valuable kinds of work.

The data doesn't need to be perfect, but it should provide broad-brush, orders-of-magnitude depictions of inclusion.

Many of the emerging tech-based approaches for capturing and analyzing data on workplace interactions can be mined for insights about inclusion. Digital workplace platforms (Microsoft Teams, Slack, Symphony), email, and calendars contain extensive data on who is communicating or meeting with whom, and how often. We can see how many "communities" a person is engaged in. Who is reaching out to the broader organization, and how extensively do their peers respond? Not only is this data powerful for analyzing inclusivity, it can also be used for integrating new hires, as discussed in Chapter 5, and for monitoring overcommitment, covered in the next chapter.

That said, not every organization has the resources or the appetite to use a technology-based approach. Several more manual approaches exist. If you're in a billable-hours environment, these inputs can be directly measured from timesheet records. Otherwise, look for proxies. For example, in research-driven companies or other organizations (such as nonprofits) that depend partially on grants, funders may require certain metrics that are captured in project management databases. In one biotech we worked with, project rosters and HR databases allowed us to piece together a picture of individual members' work patterns and analyze them by demographic categories.

Our experience suggests that the best data for analyzing DEI outcomes will not be collected specifically for this purpose but rather from existing records or "data exhaust." This approach avoids two problems: first, the kind of extra work that makes inclusion efforts burdensome; and second, the kinds of positive bias that direct measurement tends to create, and which—although perhaps encouraging in the short term—won't be sustained.

## Set Goals

We can't make blanket statements here about the exact goals for your organization. Those goals need to be tightly aligned to your organization's current state and aspirations, and should represent a mix of the objective and subjective factors cited earlier.

Think about what we've discussed thus far in this chapter. If hiring patterns are skewed, does a new metric need to be put in place in that area? If significant work that results in real contributions to the company is reserved for a small minority, what goal can be put in place that will address that organizational shortcoming?

## Create Scorecards and Dashboards

Scorecards and dashboards are powerful tools for several reasons. First, they allow you to measure progress against the goals you've set. Second, when shared publicly, they create a sense of peer pressure, because they allow the outcomes of leaders to be compared to those generated by their peers. Third, they make critical information accessible, and thereby make the process of inclusion more transparent.

If you follow the first three prescriptions listed in this section, you will generate some robust data streams. Revisit the question we raised previously: Which data should be shared, and when, and how? The point is not to hide data, but rather to make it accessible and useful to specific audiences. A good rule of thumb: err on the side of oversharing.

## Track Subjective Experience

Tracking the objective data on representation and contributions is necessary, but alone it is not sufficient. To truly understand their degree of inclusion, organizations need to assess people's subjective experiences: Do they *feel* they belong and are valued, respected, and listened to?

Tools can help with this assessment. Gartner's Inclusion Index, for example, provides organizations with a way to measure inclusion through a seven-question survey covering the more subjective elements of inclusion, including fair treatment, decision-making, and trust.[17] With this knowledge in hand, leaders can develop and implement the strategies that are likely to have the most impact.

Pulse surveys can generate volumes of data, especially in larger organizations. Sentiment analysis uses technology to identify and characterize opinions expressed in text or phone calls to understand the respondent's attitude toward a particular topic. This kind of analysis is widely used to analyze customer feedback—for example in online reviews. The technology can also help leaders efficiently parse and interpret the information from internal surveys, identifying trends or parts of the organization that they should look further into.

## Building and Nurturing a Learning Culture

A learning culture encourages curiosity: exploring ideas from multiple angles and seeking out different views and new perspectives. Pioneering research by Harvard professors Robin Ely and David Thomas shows that a learning culture directly promotes inclusivity.[18] Organizations with this orientation tend to avoid the Mini-Me and tokenism traps because people within those organizations genuinely value different experiences. In fact, recent research confirms that it may be the *only* common denominator that ties together truly inclusive organizations.[19]

If this is true, how do you encourage a learning culture? How do you create a workplace that provides the psychological safety people need to make creative contributions that may be "risky"?

### Emphasize the Importance of Open and Curious Leaders

In a survey of nineteen thousand business leaders, 30 percent of respondents reported that their leaders were ineffective at role-modeling and

building an inclusive culture.[20] This suggests that at many companies, creating a learning culture is an uphill slog, at best. What's the
remedy?

First, look to your leaders. Research by Francesca Gino at Harvard Business School found that only one-quarter of people at
work reported feeling curious about their work, and 70 percent said
they faced barriers to asking more questions at work.[21] Are your
leaders encouraging the curiosity that underpins a learning culture?
Do they give and receive constructive feedback? Are they open and
approachable?

This is key. When leaders open up about their experiences—for
example, involving race, disability, or gender identity—it makes
the topic "discussable." Microsoft, for example, runs stories in its
newsletters featuring employees, including senior managers, who "go
public" about their nonapparent disabilities. Colleagues with similar experiences are far more likely to open up, ask for what they
need at work to thrive, and have more confidence in their own
futures.

Set up mechanisms that will enable you to ask these kinds of "curiosity questions" *over time*. Do Manager X's thinking and views
evolve? Does he change directions in response to evolving circumstances? Does she recognize and support those who take risks and
think outside the box?

## *Promote Psychological Safety*

Creating a learning culture that supports inclusion—and, by extension, collaboration—is challenging, and in some cases it generates
conflict, as people are encouraged to share their unique perspectives
and challenge others. Given that reality, you need to create a zone of
psychological safety in which people feel free to admit mistakes, challenge each other, and talk about unique perspectives that they bring
to the table. This is an extension to the broader base of the Microsoft
story mentioned earlier. Make it safe for people to talk about their
lived experiences, which could enrich your culture but might not feel
"okay" to reveal. The goal is to shift diversity from being perceived
as a weakness to being perceived as a strength.

Would someone on your staff feel comfortable revealing that they had experienced homelessness—for example—or spent time in the foster-care system? Don't be too quick to answer that question with a "yes." If you're a leader, the chances are that you radically overestimate how safe your organization feels. A recent global survey by the consulting firm Accenture found that 84 percent of executives believe that employees in their organization feel safe to disclose physical disabilities, but only 65 percent of employees with disabilities agreed. The same survey reported that 80 percent—four out of five!—of chief-level execs and their direct reports with disabilities don't disclose them, suggesting that there are a *lot* of companies that don't feel safe even to their leaders.[22]

As noted, creating a learning culture, especially when that involves bringing in new and diverse skills, can lead to conflict. It's not unusual for managers to try to sweep this kind of conflict under the rug, or at least make it less visible. "I'm open to challenge," as one manager phrased it to us, "but do it with me one-to-one, not in the team meetings." But going down that road fails to encourage collaboration in groups and risks creating a back-room culture, in which side deals get cut: in other words, the *opposite* of inclusive participation. Far better to acknowledge that challenges exist, and hammer away at why creating and responding to those challenges is worth it.

### Support Collaboration through Mentoring and Reverse Mentoring

Your company probably conducts a formal mentoring survey, presumably on an annual basis. If it doesn't, consider implementing one. Most such programs ask people, *Whom do you mentor?* This enables the organization to spot gaps, which of course is a good thing. Less common is a second question: *Who are your mentors?*

This second question allows a company to detect much more nuanced challenges. In one company we studied, senior employees—who happened to be mostly straight white men—tended to list between six and eight juniors as mentees. But an analysis showed that only one or two of those juniors, on average, listed the senior as a mentor. Usually, these "confirming mentees" were young white men. Why this imbalance? Because for women and people of color, the way those seniors were trying mentor them was perceived as monitoring or some other unhelpful intervention.

At the risk of stating the obvious, mentors need to know how to mentor across differences. To do so, they need to understand *specific* issues faced by underrepresented minorities—for example, Asians getting "talked over" by white colleagues. This may require holding discussions on a smaller community level, followed by focused discussion at multiple levels of the organization to promote inclusivity.

Some companies engage in formal "reverse-mentoring" programs, in which junior people are invited to offer advice to senior leaders in the company. The benefits can be many: increasing the retention of juniors, sharing technology expertise, driving cultural change, and—most interesting for our purposes—promoting inclusion.[23] In 2013, for example, BNY Mellon's Pershing affiliate launched a reverse mentoring program, CONNECT, to provide the organization with generational perspectives that bring divergent ideas, challenge strategic-tactical mindsets, and retain top talent. Within four years, the community involved 150 supporters and participants.[24] If you undertake to set up or expand a reverse-mentoring program, consider broadening it beyond the traditional concept ("young mentoring old") to include older people who are not highly positioned in the hierarchy, but who have valuable experience to share.[25]

. . .

Even as we explore these individual trees, let's keep our eyes on the collaborative forest. In all of the efforts described in this chapter, the goal is to create and support a learning culture: a critical underpinning for a *collaborative* culture.

# [ 11 ]

# Watch Out: Pressure Undermines Collaboration

Imagine that you're the CEO of Raytheon, the $29 billion defense contractor. The US State Department has just informed you that your company is out of compliance with both the Arms Export Control Act and the International Traffic in Arms Regulations. You've also been told that you have only seventeen weeks to meet the relevant export-import control obligations—or else lose your right to sell defense products internationally.[1] At the risk of understatement, this is a *huge deal*.

What do you do?

The simple answer is, you turn to your team of in-house experts and external advisers to get you out of trouble—in a hurry! But when it comes to collaboration, high-pressure situations can be a double-edged sword. On the positive side, a strong sense of urgency and an external enemy can galvanize action and inspire people to pull out the stops. We all can recite stories about teams that, when faced with a clear threat, sprang into action—throwing themselves into the breach and working against long odds to make it through the crisis at hand.

This is the stuff of corporate myth-making, and we don't diminish the importance of such heroics. But very often, there's another side to the story. The actions those heroes actually take—the ways they go about responding to their challenge—aren't necessarily the most effective responses. In other words, even the most determined and courageous of heroes are not necessarily working *smart*.

Maybe the team helps the company wriggle its way out of this particular crisis—but they don't seize the moment to create breakthrough solutions or sustainable change. Research across a range of companies in a wide variety of contexts shows that under pressure, people often resort to siloed behaviors that feel safe in the moment but actually squash the innovation and perspective-taking needed in a crisis. Or worse, maybe the toxic dynamics of this episode weaken the team in the longer run, damaging interpersonal trust and establishing counterproductive norms that undermine the team's effectiveness. Counterproductive behaviors at the local level, especially if seemingly endorsed by senior leaders, can radiate across the culture and warp it.

In this chapter, we explore the factors that spark this kind of downward spiral, and provide ways to counteract it. These are important lessons not only in moments of existential crisis—such as the Raytheon example—but in a whole host of less dramatic circumstances. Senior leaders need to proactively manage collaboration under pressure. They have to plan for how smarter collaboration will play out when people are in the heat of the battle—and look for ways to turn crisis into opportunity. Let's dive into some ways you can do that, and then we'll return to Raytheon.

## The Psychology of Performance Pressure

When people refer to "pressure," what usually comes to mind is *time* pressure—that is, deadlines. But that's not always the underlying issue. There are plenty of circumstances in which a team has most or all of the time and resources it needs, and still faces unrelenting pressure from one or more directions—including from within. And when pressure is not well managed, it usually puts team dynamics at risk.

It's not just the pressures growing out of a dramatic turn of events that can lead to dysfunctional behaviors. So too can the performance pressures that arise in everyday work—for example, when the team is working on an important project, with lots of people inside and outside the company watching and counting on a great outcome. Or how about that situation in which an anxious new boss is scrutinizing the team's every move and effectively transmitting that anxiety to the team? Or those times when a key client is demanding an immediate fix to a defective product?

If even one person on the team feels like the project may be make-or-break for them, *personally*—a team leader coming up for promotion, or a sales director who absolutely needs to *close that deal*—that individual's behaviors can destabilize the team and destroy the prospects for smart collaboration. True, people may be operating with the best of intentions, trying to help the team through this difficult pressure point. But good intentions aren't enough, and the siloed behaviors that emerge under pressure can be poisonous for collaboration, both in the short term and longer term.

How so? Research shows that the anxiety that tends to be inherent in a high-stakes situation makes people more risk averse, which means that they are less likely to seek out differing perspectives and rely on others.[2] They tend to fall back on actions and solutions that have worked in the past—a psychological stance that researchers call "threat rigidity."[3] The desire to try to bring things under control can also lead to a go-it-alone mentality. As a result, collaboration across an organization can break down.

It's worth underscoring here that while situational pressure often creates dysfunctions on the individual level—as we'll detail in the following pages—what we're really talking about is how excessive pressure comes to bear on the larger collaborative process. When individuals hurt, so do their teams, and so does collaboration.

With that said, let's look at the four faces of threat rigidity:

- **Conformity.** Research has long shown that when a group is stressed, its members exert subtle and not-so-subtle pressure on each other to *conform*, and thereby get to a resolution.[4] Of course, every project has to get completed, sooner or later,

so it's natural for teams to push for consensus at some point.
But threat rigidity tends to short-circuit the kinds of debate
that still need to take place. In extreme cases, the group's
majority—once it has agreed on a plan—may start pressuring
dissenters to fall into line with the consensus view. Even when
the pressures to go along aren't this intense, conformist cues
can emerge in subtle but still powerful ways: a well-timed
eyeroll or sigh of impatience, or a snippy ("Hey, Joe, let's cut
to the chase") text message. And even without these cues,
people may be inclined to self-censor, not wanting to be the
loner standing in the way of what most people seem to think is
the best way to resolve the crisis. But this willingness to go
along may mean that the group fails to explore better options.

- **Safe (but generic) solutions.** As pressure increases, people
  become more and more aware of the consequences of failure,
  and therefore become more conservative in their decision-
  making. There's no nice way to say it: when people are
  selecting a path forward based on a set of options—say, brand
  managers choosing a social media campaign for a new product
  launch—they show a *bias against creativity*, even under the
  best of circumstances. Novel ideas are, by definition, uncertain. They haven't been tested—and therefore are more difficult to embrace.[5] Overall, pressure to perform drives people
  toward safe, generic solutions and encourages them to fall
  back on existing remedies: *You know—the stuff we do well
  most of the time.*

- **Deference to hierarchy.** As pressure mounts, teams stop making
  the effort to sound everyone out and instead default to their
  traditional hierarchical roles. Team experts willingly cede
  authority to team leaders, and dissenters are chided by their
  colleagues for "forgetting their place." Another wrinkle: this
  stove-piping can stifle team leaders' willingness to empower
  others. Maybe in the crush of the crisis they stop calling on
  junior members with specialized knowledge. Maybe they start
  taking on more work themselves—even relatively humble tasks
  like generating new statistical models or copyediting a report.

In other words, just when the team is looking to the leader for inspiration, insight, and strength, he or she goes micro, or hides in the herd.

- **Narrowing voices.** In times of stress, the team risks losing the voices that can bring in outside perspectives and bold new ideas. Why? As noted in Chapter 2, people under pressure tend to turn to others who are most like themselves—the phenomenon known as homophily. This is a comforting form of retreat from a challenging reality, but it is one of the more insidious forms of threat rigidity. Without realizing it, the group excludes the kinds of diverse voices that previously might have been welcomed. In extreme cases, only an informal "inner circle" even learns about, and gets to weigh in on, the problem at hand, almost guaranteeing a narrow range of opinions.

Let's underscore the fact that the problems that arise when people must collaborate under pressure are not limited to the ranks of middle managers or lower-level employees. It's true: even senior executives and board members—some of whom may have no direct responsibility for responding to the crisis at hand—are susceptible to these pressures.[6]

## Adverse Effects on Individual-Level Collaboration

As we've seen, people under pressure tend to revert to their fundamental tendencies. This may sound like a safe enough strategy, but there's a hidden paradox in this kind of reversion: these stressed people may actually move toward *more extreme positions*, in terms of the behavioral dimensions of collaboration that we addressed in Chapter 4. This, in turn, may decrease the prospect of smart collaboration, affecting not only the actor's own performance but that of the entire team—which, again, is our larger focus and concern.

What does that look like? A Group-oriented person may well seek out others to collaborate with—but because of homophily, described earlier, the members of that newly constituted group are likely to share similar views that will limit conflict and reduce stress within the team.

It's only a short step to ignoring—or even excluding—those with dissenting views.

A person with an "Individual" profile, by contrast, is likely to shift into an even more extreme go-it-alone mode. The person in this intensifying mindset may feel performance pressure acutely, and—increasingly convinced that working with others is a less efficient and effective approach—may just decide to "solve the problem" on his or her own.

Our research into the 2008 financial crisis surfaced precisely these kinds of effects, and their consequences. We collected a decade's worth of data on collaboration and financial performance across dozens of organizations, including professional service firms, financial institutions, and health-care organizations. In interviews with some of the subjects, we asked open-ended questions about how they handled work during the crisis. Very different collaboration patterns became obvious. Figure 11-1 shows the outcomes for one law firm: patterns that were typical across many of the companies we studied.

Records from project and financial databases showed how partners worked before, during, and after the crisis, tracking their relative performance outcomes. To control for outliers, we excluded the partners with the highest and lowest performance historically, and also those in groups that were likely to flourish during a downturn, such as the bankruptcy and restructuring practices. We separated the remaining four-hundred-plus partners into deciles based on the proportion of their work conducted with other partners versus work conducted on their own. Then we plotted their respective revenues generated during the period.

The results were stark and compelling. The most highly collaborative workers—the top 10 percent—*grew* their business during the crisis, and they continued that upward trajectory afterward (the black line in Figure 11-1). The performance of the middle group (the second and third deciles) declined slightly during the crisis, but their revenues started to recover within a year (the light gray line). People in the third group (the bottom 70 percent, in dark gray) hunkered down and dramatically reduced their collaboration with others. They guarded their clients and hoarded work. But did that strategy work? No. The revenue generated by this group shrank during the crisis, and

FIGURE 11-1

# The benefits of collaboration during crisis

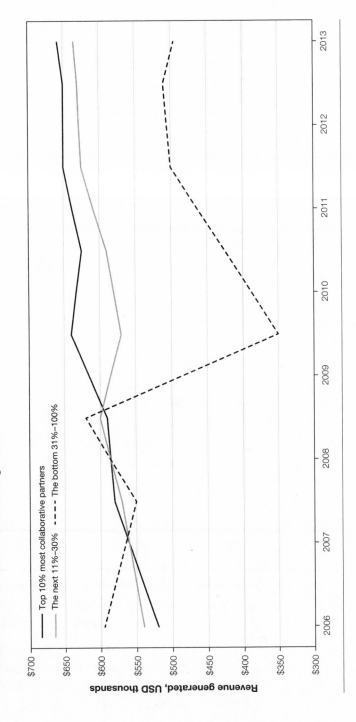

it still had not recovered five years after the recession had ended. Again, we saw similar patterns in other organizations.

You can make an analogy to the benefits of a diversified stock portfolio. As uncertainty and stress increased in the early phase of the crisis, the highly collaborative people adapted their approach to developing business and executing work. They expanded their network across functional and industry silos and increased the number and kinds of colleagues they worked with. They demonstrated their willingness to pitch in on projects led by others, in addition to their own work. As the crisis evolved and pressure rose, they teamed up with trusted colleagues to identify and pursue new opportunities, even when it meant getting less personal glory on a project-by-project basis. As a result, they ended up working with a wide variety of clients, essentially spreading their bets across different kinds of opportunities. They *diversified*. Or—switching to a soccer metaphor—they played different positions to fit changing circumstances, and thereby earned themselves more shots on goal.

The self-focused, uncollaborative people took a wholly different approach. As noted, they erected walls around their projects, pushed colleagues away, held their business and clients closely, and hoarded work. As a result of their self-interested behavior, their network diminished. They had no "tribe" to bring them into existing opportunities or to help identify new ones. In one health-care organization, for example, when grant funding started to dry up, the loners suffered because they weren't involved in enough research initiatives to keep money flowing into their labs.

As described in Chapter 1, when experts collaborate, they are able to address more complex and higher-value problems. The inverse is true for those people who decide to go it alone. By focusing more narrowly on their personal areas of expertise, they provide narrower solutions, which are therefore less valuable. And their ability to solve those problems is impaired, because they lack the diversity of experiences and new perspectives needed to generate innovative insights. Not only do they reduce their access to a broader range of projects, the work they *are* engaged in tends to be of lower value, which may put them on a "double-down" escalator: fewer projects and more commoditized projects.

The effects of reducing your network go far beyond the strictly commercial. Going it alone during a crisis leads to increased isolation and loneliness, at exactly the time when you most need social support. In Chapter 2 we discussed the detrimental effects of loneliness, including health implications.[7]

The obvious conclusion: the degree of collaboration during a crisis has a huge impact on whether people thrive, both professionally and personally. Researchers from the Center for Creative Leadership have studied tens of thousands of leaders from around the world to understand factors that make some executives' careers go off the rails while others keep forging ahead. They found that the most frequent and detrimental cause for derailment under stress is insensitivity to others. Under pressure, those leaders become abrasive and intimidating. Yes, their subordinates suffer in real time, but those intimidating bosses are the ones who suffer in the long run, because their careers dead-end.[8]

## Adverse Effects on Group-and Organization-Level Collaboration

As we've seen, group members who are feeling anxious typically race toward a conclusion. They land early on a plausible solution, then exert subtle and not-so-subtle pressure on one another to conform to that emerging view. The drive for consensus shuts down paths to further exploration.

The usual meetings may still get held, but fewer and fewer people participate. When they do, they tend to seek reassurance that the emerging plan is safe—asking questions like, "How does this usually play out?" or, "Where else has this worked?" Enthusiasm for innovation and improvisation gives way to covering all the bases.

To the participants, this may still seem like a discussion, but in reality, it's an effort to get everyone to agree that the best choice on the table is the Less Risky Plan A rather than the More Optimized Plan B. The warning signs are there to see, for those who are still paying attention to such signs. People endorse plan A by asking for more details, favoring positive comments with encouraging nods, and capturing those comments on flip charts. They discourage plan B by rolling their eyes, checking their phones mid-discussion, leaving the white board untouched, and even turning their backs on those colleagues offering alternate views.

When those colleagues realize that their observations or objections are meeting resistance—often embedded in humor—they back down. They stop offering up perspectives that are not "with the program." Even senior team members are vulnerable to these pressures.

Though premature consensus-seeking may be unwitting, its consequences can still be far reaching. That's what a trustee of a major museum found, to his regret, when he reviewed transcripts of trustee meetings held during a financial downturn. "One of my fellow directors repeatedly tried to raise different options," he recalls, "but we completely steamrolled him. We got set on a course of action, and it seemed like any new views were threats to our very survival."

As a result, the group not only failed to explore alternatives to the drastic staff cuts that were proposed—and subsequently enacted—but the board member who was steamrolled resigned in frustration. "In the end," the trustee concludes, "we lost more than just a set of ideas. We lost a key *source* of ideas. And at the time, we didn't even realize it was happening."

As explained earlier, the phenomenon of homophily reduces a team's access to new ideas. Under pressure, that tendency intensifies. You start to hear leaders saying things like, *When the stakes are high, Paul is my go-to guy.* As a result, some members of the group become increasingly marginalized, putting real diversity and inclusion at risk. During the Covid-19 crisis, for example, women were hit disproportionately hard with outside responsibilities. One McKinsey study suggested that one in four women in corporate jobs in the United States was considering "downshifting" her job or leaving the workforce entirely—a trend that, if realized, will have dire consequences for diversity in the workplace.[9]

This kind of marginalization is unfair, of course, but it's also bad business. It not only reduces the company's ability to position itself for renewal and growth down the line, but it also risks sparking backlash from customers who remain committed to their own DEI initiatives.

When these bad habits return, and dysfunctional processes spring up, they tend to work their toxic magic at the group and local levels, which often means that they're hard to observe in real time. But even though their effects may be muted in the short term, when they unfold over time and build across the organization, the effects can be dire. And again, what may seem like an individual's optimal decision—for example, *I'm going to keep my head down and focus on getting work out the door!*—with only minor individual consequences can actually lead to broader organizational malfunctions.

## Collaborating under Pressure: Tools and Practices

As we saw underscored in our analyses of the 2008 financial crisis, pressure on individuals and teams can threaten collaboration and thereby lead to disastrous outcomes for the business. Your first job as a leader is to reduce the unnecessary pressures and unhealthy fears that tend to undermine collaboration.[10] How is that done? The answers fall into three groups of prescriptions: *planning for the onslaught, avoiding the avoidable*, and *managing pressure in real time*.

### Planning for the Onslaught

Some pressure is inevitable. So how do you prepare yourself and your teams to handle that pressure when it comes, allowing you to collaborate effectively when you most need to?

The first step is to *understand your behavioral tendencies*. As noted earlier, people under pressure tend to revert to their central tendencies. With pressure increasing, those tendencies typically become self-reinforcing: risk aversion or extreme risk seeking, individualism, over-communicating or undercommunicating, micromanagement, trust where it isn't warranted, and so on. Reflect on your behavioral tendencies and how they've manifested themselves in the past when you've been under pressure. With these patterns in mind, you'll be more alert to the kinds of reactions on your part that could unintentionally undermine collaboration.

Encourage the team to do the same. A lot of people have blind spots, so use a psychometric tool for your group to unveil those foibles. Talk openly with your team about these possible pitfalls, so that people can help each other when crises do hit.

Meanwhile, *make a plan for how your cross-silo work will play out in a crisis*. Put structures in place that will facilitate communication, as needed. For example, are you convening people across departments? Remembering that the go-it-alone urge tends to arise under pressure, you need to identify specific ways that people, departments, and even the board will be able to tap into resources to help them navigate.

## Avoiding the Avoidable

Our first prescription here is to *manage yourself*. We observed a senior manager at a prominent consulting firm who was on track for promotion to partner. This was his big client project and—at least in his mind—the outcome would make or break his promotion prospects. His resulting anxiety and stress were translated directly to the team through his behavior in multiple meetings: a raised voice, unconstructive criticism, demands that the team work extreme hours, and so on. Constructive? Definitely not. Not only was the team starting to crack, but the client also saw these behaviors.

What's our prescription for this collaboration-blocking manager? First, *get some sleep.*[11] The prefrontal cortex in our brains is in charge of what psychologists call executive functioning. These are the higher-order cognitive processes—such as reasoning, organizing, and managing one's inhibitions—that are at the core of collaborative leadership. Although other brain areas can cope relatively well despite too little sleep, the prefrontal cortex cannot.[12] So when leaders are tired, collaboration suffers, because those leaders tend to seek fewer different perspectives and are less capable of weighing the relative significance of different inputs accurately.

They're also inclined to succumb to bias, which dampens smart collaboration. In a sleep-deprived state, your brain is more likely to misinterpret contextual cues and to overreact to emotional events, and you tend to express your feelings in a more negative manner and tone of voice.[13] Recent studies have shown that people who have not had enough sleep are less likely to fully trust someone else. Another experiment has demonstrated that employees feel less engaged with their work when their leaders haven't gotten enough sleep.[14]

At the same time, *manage others*. This starts inside the organization. Identify those around you who are mishandling the pressures you're facing collectively. (See the symptoms just listed: overreacting, being consistently negative, and so on.) Most organizations today run engagement surveys or use 360 feedback tools to identify teams that need help. It's a short step from there to finding the individuals on those teams who need help. Give them that help. Provide them with professional coaching, which is often the best way for people in trouble to hear that their behavior is counterproductive.

Pay particular attention to your remote staff and distributed teams. Geographic differences (the London office versus the Tokyo office) create natural fault lines that become accentuated in times of heightened pressure. Make sure your teams are aware of the underlying issues that can create these fault lines and watch for them to emerge. The isolation and loneliness we referred to earlier in the chapter may be further compounded when people work remotely. Increase the frequency of communication around goals, expectations, the responsibilities of team members, and deadlines to lower the anxiety that naturally arises when people feel isolated.

Also look outside the organization. Take a hard look at your clients. Yes, the customer is always right—until they start mistreating your employees. If that's happening, you need to make it clear that abusive pressure will only make existing problems worse. If it comes down to it, you may need to fire that client. A consulting firm that we worked with recently stopped doing business with a regional public transportation agency. The publicly stated reason was "creative differences," but privately, our clients told us they could no longer live with the agency's efforts to reach into their firm and divide and conquer—that is, playing one employee off another, in a context where collaboration within the firm and between the firm and the agency was critically important.

## Managing Pressure in Real Time

Lightning will strike. When it does, great teams rise to the occasion and get the best from their people. Conversely, failed teams make bad situations worse.

Reducing this challenge to its essence, you need to *strike the right balance*. The worst leaders we've seen take a small problem and magnify it, turning an X-size problem into a 10X-size one. Yes, you have to communicate a sense of urgency. (Shielding your team from legitimate pressure is ineffective and unsustainable.) But you need to do so in a way that creates positive energy. Set the bar high. Push the team to deliver their best—which of course they are helping to define— but give them the support they need to get there. Talk less about stress, and talk more about reaching for a higher purpose.

This may take several forms. For example, you need to *avoid narrow thinking*. All the experts will see the problem at hand through their own specialized lenses. Is the team getting all those different perspectives out on the table? If there are weak signals, do they need to be strengthened?

Has everyone received the full set of information and been given a chance to form his or her own opinion before hearing others? Does everyone fully understand and appreciate the problems and have an opportunity to ask questions before they are presented with any proposed solution? Have directors been given access to relevant executives outside the C-suite whose knowledge is essential in addressing the crisis—perhaps including (for example) functional heads who normally don't have board access? Make sure that people are confident about speaking truth to power.[15]

In the same spirit, *look outside*. What are other organizations doing—particularly new entrants, who may have novel approaches to the business? Are the experiences and expertise represented on the team diverse enough? If not, could outside advisers (lawyers, consultants, auditors, etc.) help the team think more expansively about the problem and its potential solutions?

At the same time, *head off undue deference to the leader*. Is the team becoming overly reliant on the leader to make decisions? For all the reasons stated earlier, that won't work. The entire team has to be involved in inventing solutions and communicating what is happening throughout the invention process.

Finally, *make sure that everyone is doing his or her part*. Don't let anxiety turn into incomplete engagement. Has the team simply accepted the first plausible solution, or does it continue to search for alternative and potentially superior solutions? The group should strive to come up with a range of possible futures and different options for each scenario.

## Raytheon's Crisis

Let's turn back and look at what happened at Raytheon. The company's senior leaders made it clear that its days of ignoring compliance issues were done—and that employees from across the sprawling organization were now expected to pitch in and resolve the crisis, *in a hurry*. As Raytheon's general counsel Frank Jimenez put it, "Our days of putting global trade compliance on the back burner, separate from our day-to-day business practices, are over—and every employee of the company needs to be part of the solution."[16]

With this sweeping mandate in hand, Raytheon's vice president of legal operations, Sol Brody, assembled a cross-functional team from a wide range of departments to shape a new compliance strategy. That team worked collaboratively to overcome a host of technical, cultural, and institutional challenges as they hammered out a new compliance framework.

"As it turned out," recalls Brody, "it really wasn't a compliance challenge; it was a collaboration challenge. The idea was to make the right way the easy way, with the global-trade requirements baked into how our units operated going forward. Of course, we had to build trust among ourselves. But being part of an incredible cross-functional team actually made working together easier. So did the burning platform, of course. People got behind a common vision, without the pushbacks you might otherwise expect to see."[17]

In less than a month, the team developed a scalable and sustainable world-trade framework that not only brought aboard all the key internal constituencies but also satisfied the US State Department.

Raytheon agreed to pay a civil penalty of $8 million and change its ways, going forward; the federal government agreed—in its own bureaucratic language—that "an administrative debarment of Raytheon is not appropriate at this time."[18] And beyond the resolution of the crisis at hand, the collaborative exercise at Raytheon also paved the way for a far more effective working relationship with the Directorate of Defense Trade Controls—the regulatory body within the State Department that monitors defense-related exports.

Raytheon rose to the collaborative occasion—and thereby saved itself. Your company, under pressure, can and should do the same.

## From under Pressure to Overcommitted

We opened this chapter by noting that crises sometimes—but not always—reflect time pressures. We've stressed the negative impact of those pressures on teams and, by extension, on the whole organization. Finally, we've suggested ways that teams and their leaders can head off and work through the pressures that grow out of crisis.

In the next chapter, which is the third and last of our "Watch Out!" chapters, we examine some of these same issues that are caused by another common collaboration misfire: the overcommitted organization. How can a company get the advantages of multiteaming—assigning talented people to a number of concurrent teams and projects—without burning out those people and putting them and their teams under undue pressure?

# [ 12 ]

# Watch Out:
# The Overcommitted
# Organization

D r. Mark Warner was ready to pull his hair out. He had been yanked off his regular job to run Project Tsunami. This was no regular task force; it was commissioned by the chief operating officer to bring control to its R&D programs. BioNext, a leading global life-sciences company with more than $1 billion in annual revenues and extensive research centers spread across five countries around the world, had just missed its financial targets, and the stock price had tumbled.

A problem that started as a small tremor in one project had rippled across the organization, eventually creating a tsunami that swamped one of BioNext's most critical initiatives and caused the earnings miss. When a long-running project began to blow up, the members of the extended project team swarmed to the rescue—a seemingly reasonable reaction in the moment, right? Not if they had the big picture. When the key scientists on that team diverted their attention to the project in crisis, their other projects suffered. Even worse, the project in crisis was a lower strategic priority. People ran to the problem without a view of the systemic impact.

The upshot? A small crisis was averted. Meanwhile, though, a lucrative new product that was just about out of the pipeline in another part of the company was delayed, and this caused BioNext to miss its financial targets for the year. In short, what seemed like a series of sensible decisions at the team level added up to board-level problems.

Smart collaboration requires people to work across teams, but unfettered collaboration can lead to many people—and often *essential* people—becoming stretched too thin across multiple teams. Just as in the examples we discussed in Chapters 10 and 11, decisions that look sensible, even optimal, at the team level can add up to problems at the company level.

When team leaders lack the big picture of how things fit together and allow their teams to get overcommitted—basically, an amped-up form of "collaboration"—to solve a near-term problem, the result can be a series of unintended consequences. We saw a similar pattern of unwelcome outcomes in Chapter 11, where it became clear how even the best-intentioned collaborative efforts can pose challenges to corporate commitments to diversity and inclusion.

"I needed to quickly understand what was going on in the company," Warner recalls. "We knew we needed our scientists working on multiple projects, but how did a major project get derailed by a much smaller one?" To get at the root causes, he asked us to conduct a smart collaboration diagnostic.[1] Analyses revealed that the overcommitment that caused the meltdown was far from unusual at BioNext. Why was that? Why hadn't senior leadership already spotted and tackled the problem of overcommitment?

Digging into the data at the company-wide level showed how the pattern of overcommitment was nearly imperceptible until it was too late. What emerged was a clear case of multiteaming—that is, assigning valuable employees to multiple projects simultaneously—run amok. Ultimately, the company had to embrace a holistic, top-down and bottom-up set of interventions to dig itself out of its hole and get its culture back on track—a story to which we'll return later.

In many cases, multiteaming lies at the heart of smart collaboration. So when does multiteaming (often a good thing) turn into overcommitment (almost always a bad thing)? What perils does that unhealthy transformation pose to a company, its teams, and the people on those teams? In this chapter, we explore these questions on each of those three levels and prescribe practical remedies.[2]

## The Roots of Overcommitment

Multiteaming has compelling advantages. Businesses today must draw on their expertise to solve complex problems that span multiple departments. And as we've argued in earlier chapters, this end is best achieved through smart collaboration. It's often multiteaming that makes smart collaboration possible, by making both skilled generalists and "deep-knowledge" experts available to a range of teams across the business. This is a choice, but it may also be a necessity. Few organizations can justify having their most valuable talents engaged in only one project at a time, especially if that project involves intermittent downtime. As one BioNext executive told us, "We can't afford to have one of our leading experts focused entirely on one project for twelve months when that project really only needs him or her intensively at three points during the project, and other projects also need that expert help." So it makes sense, at least on paper, to share these kinds of specialized talents across functional and departmental lines—most often, through participation on multiple teams.

Sharing resources across multiple teams is becoming commonplace across most industries as they shift away from hierarchical, centralized staffing toward dynamic project teams. This shift not only increases access to scarce resources, as suggested earlier, but also gives employees exposure to more projects and people across the organization. According to one BioNext division head, "Our people expect variety in order to grow. They don't want to be trapped only in their functional or department silos. They want to constantly see and learn—and be *seen* to be learning."

Beyond learning, many people find it highly satisfying to work on teams. At BioNext, people are passionate about the company's mission of curing deadly diseases, and they genuinely want to contribute as much as possible, wherever possible. But for some people, this can be the gateway to overcommitment. Looking back to Chapter 4, some talented contributors who are highly Trusting and thrive on group work may well say yes to each promising-looking team that asks for help. And while those individuals may well be helpful across multiple team settings, they may also put themselves at risk of overcollaboration through multiteaming.

Misguided or just plain bad leadership plays a role too. The proactive manager can gradually turn into a hoarder of resources, especially after his or her project gets deprioritized. Conflict avoidance also enters into the picture: the most aggressive team leader may succeed in bullying shared experts into overcommitting time to the bully's project.

Over the longer term, organizational priorities can get lost or skewed. At BioNext, one executive admitted, "Nothing ever gets cut. Projects just get 'deprioritized,' but that means people are still partly staffed on them until eventually they sort of wither away." In a bank, an accounting firm, and a government agency we worked with, leaders fell prey to the same psychological trap: escalation of commitment.[3] When people are personally invested in a project, either emotionally or because their reputation is at stake, they are likely to keep "throwing good money after bad" even when the project is obviously a dud.[4] Coauthor Matviak, formerly chairman of several subsidiary software companies at State Street, was stunned when the chief operating officer praised him for being "the only person he'd ever seen actually shut down an underperforming business."

Corporate leaders often tell us that they are doing everything they can to combat overcommitment. They point to their efforts to create a culture that's safe for people to raise the alarm if they're feeling at risk of burnout, for example. Yes, these kinds of cultural fixes are important, but the remedy is flawed in two ways: it puts the onus on individuals to deal with overcommitment, and it's reactive—waiting till overcommitment is a problem, rather than preventing it in the first place. We argue that nothing will really change unless leaders proactively address the root cause at the organizational level: *Why are people getting overcommitted in the first place?*

This is key. The failure to tackle the root causes of overcommitment is one of the reasons why collaboration sometimes gets a bad rap. As recounted in the next section, BioNext undertook just this kind of root-cause analysis and, in the process, made some interesting discoveries.

## Uncovering the Perils of Overcommitment

Going into the smart collaboration diagnostic at BioNext, leaders were well aware that the company's biggest strategic threat came from nimbler competitors that could innovate faster. In the biotech ecosystem, collaboration among industry players—the biotech companies themselves, their pharma counterparts, and the distributors—is essential. BioNext's leaders knew that competitors were doing it better. But it now emerged that for BioNext, one of the biggest problems stemming from overcommitment was that the company spent so much time fighting internal fires that it couldn't spend enough time looking outside. Said one surveyed exec, "We're too internally focused. We not only miss good ideas, but also good acquisition opportunities. External conversations would put us in position to innovate faster."

What else goes wrong when an organization becomes overcommitted? Very often, it fails to allocate resources in ways that are aligned with strategy and priorities. Fewer than half of the BioNext employees surveyed agreed with the statement that "project teams have the resources they need to achieve their goals." While a typical reaction is to think, *We need to hire more people*, often the problem isn't too few resources but how the resources you have are distributed.

Even worse, as the BioNext case illustrates, balls get dropped on high-priority initiatives. That, in turn, can lead to a cascade of problems at the organizational level. Organizational researcher Mark Mortensen describes what he calls "shocks and ripples," whereby an unexpected event blasts one project off kilter and the ripples are felt across many other projects.[5] Consider a situation in which people are multiteaming on (only) two projects. A shock to one of them can have a major impact on the other, but those impacts are likely to be visible and traceable. On the other hand, if people are multiteaming on many projects, a shock can ripple across several of those, and it

FIGURE 12-1

## Shocks and ripples

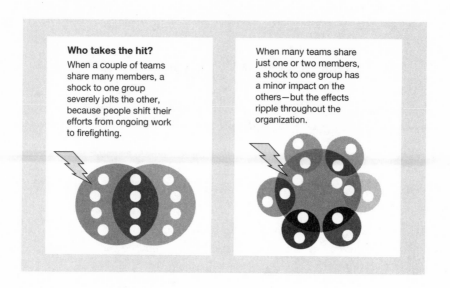

**Who takes the hit?**
When a couple of teams share many members, a shock to one group severely jolts the other, because people shift their efforts from ongoing work to firefighting.

When many teams share just one or two members, a shock to one group has a minor impact on the others—but the effects ripple throughout the organization.

*Source*: M. Mortensen and H. K. Gardner, "The Overcommitted Organization," *Harvard Business Review*, September–October 2017, p. 65. Originally titled "Who Takes the Hit?"

may become far harder to trace the impacts. Smaller problems at the team level start to push their way up to organization-level problems—and unless the organization has controls in place, these ripples may quickly add up to a tsunami (Figure 12-1).

This onrushing tsunami is not always easy to see, even when you're looking for it. At BioNext, while it was true that not everyone was being stretched across a crazy number of projects, the hidden problem was the *pattern* of overcommitment. The data showed that certain kinds of people—in particular, the MD-PhDs and the regulatory lawyers—were stretched incredibly thin. Their input was essential for each project they touched, so when one of their assignments "got shocked," it did indeed ripple across the company.

If your people are stretched thin, they can't engage deeply with each other. The result? The team lacks the spark that comes from batting around ideas and building off each other in real time. Without time for co-creation, team-level innovation suffers. The team also incurs too many *coordination costs*, such as constantly needing to bring

**FIGURE 12-2**

## Multiteaming burnout by role

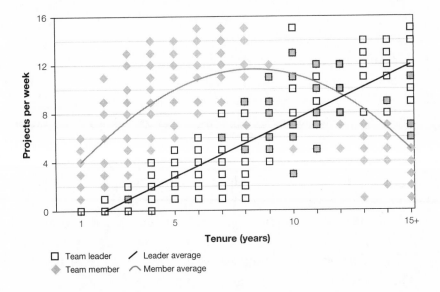

Source: M. Mortensen and H. K. Gardner, "The Overcommitted Organization," *Harvard Business Review*, September–October 2017, p. 63. Originally titled "Who's Feeling the Pain?"

people up to speed on what's happening. Surely you've felt the frustration of team members dipping in and out, disrupting the flow and pulling the team back to issues that were already resolved.

At a law firm we studied, first-year associates worked on as many as six projects in a week, which at a glance seemed like a lot. But we also found that that number rose steeply with tenure, and employees who had reached the six-year mark were working on as many as *fifteen projects a week* (Figure 12-2). True, more-experienced people were members of fewer concurrent teams—but the more senior they got, the more likely they were to be *leading* many projects at the same time. This level of stretch means it's often the leader who's dipping in and out, requiring updates, losing the thread—which can be exceedingly frustrating for the team.

Nearly all of us have personally felt the human toll of overcommitment, but unless we unpack the problems in a more nuanced way than "burnout," we can't address them. Having all your time booked is hard enough, but excessive multiteaming imposes unreasonable switching costs of at least three kinds. First, bouncing from one project to the next, constantly pushing the mental "reset" button, leaves you little time to prepare for meetings, let alone reflect and learn afterward. One researcher found that "attention residue," the way our brain sticks to an unfinished task, makes it difficult for people to shift their focus and perform well on a new task.[6]

Second, it's not easy to fit into multiple team cultures at once, especially when you can only make a limited time commitment to any of them. At one semiconductor company we work with, people routinely work on four or five major projects at any given time. One of them told us, "I have to be two different people one moment to the next. One team is high stress with a hypersensitive manager on the verge of promotion where I have to be totally buttoned up and think through every comment before I say it. The other is much looser and people are batting around ideas, debating, and actually laughing. It's hard to be Jekyll and Hyde—and sometimes I don't make the switch well."

Third, moving between teams probably compels you to adjust to different roles—you might be the boss on one but a junior member of another, for example—which changes not only your level of accountability but also your ability to juggle resources when a crunch time hits. You might need to play the Hands-on, roll-up-your-sleeves doer on one team if everyone else has a Hands-off preference (see Chapter 4), but you might be able to be much more Hands-off on another team. Dealing with these three types of switching is hard across two teams; doing it well across many teams is incredibly difficult, and stressful.

Other problems surfaced as well at BioNext—problems that were hard to quantify but nevertheless posed real challenges. For example, the so-called 10 percenters—people who were involved in close to a dozen projects—very often found themselves doing smaller and more marginal tasks, rather than being in the thick of things. Accordingly, they were less likely to perceive the benefits of their efforts, or to feel really engaged with others on the team. And unless you carefully plan and negotiate your contribution on each team, you may end up doing repetitive work on areas where you are already the expert instead of supporting your own development and advancing your career. This negative dynamic reinforced the one described in Chapter 11, in which certain groups at the margins, including women and minorities, were unintentionally denied adequate development and advancement opportunities. One pernicious result (of these several problems, among others) was increased attrition, especially among some groups that BioNext was working very hard to recruit and retain.

Overcommitment affects your people, the teams they work in, and ultimately the entire organization. Back in Chapter 2 we talked about the importance of engagement and noted that it stems from having a chance to contribute, a sense of belonging, and opportunities to learn and grow. Stretching people too thinly across many teams, and allowing them to become overcommitted, undermines engagement. This was a fundamental issue at BioNext, and it's no surprise that attrition was too high. In exit interviews, some people revealed that they'd felt badgered to live up to unrealistic competing deadlines, they didn't feel in control, and they hadn't felt free to raise the issue. Others wound up feeling inadequate, convinced that it was their fault that they hadn't been able to juggle the workload. Stretched across too many projects, people struggle to fully contribute, feel disconnected from their peers, and can't develop new, deeper expertise if they are dipping in and out work.

In the next several sections, we suggest actions that the key players should take at the organization, team, and individual levels. As you'll see, responsibility for managing overcommitment mainly falls on the shoulders of the organization's senior leaders and team leaders. But if you find that you're the one who's being stretched thin across many projects, you too can help manage that challenge.

## Actions for Senior Leaders

If an organization is serious about rooting out overcommitment and the problems it creates, its senior leaders have to generate a new vision of the organization. One approach that BioNext used is a "from-to" message (Figure 12-3); the contrast between current and desired states is a clear, powerful way to communicate your vision.

Look at the top bullet in each column. You see a call to move from a function-dominated mindset to a team-dominated one—which is

**FIGURE 12-3**

## Transformation requires changes across three dimensions

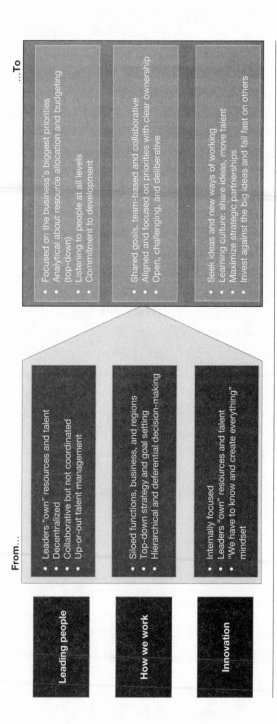

From…

**Leading people**
- Leaders "own" resources and talent
- Decentralized
- Collaborative but not coordinated
- Up-or-out talent management

**How we work**
- Siloed functions, business, and regions
- Top-down strategy and goal setting
- Hierarchical and deferential decision-making

**Innovation**
- Internally focused
- Leaders "own" resources and talent
- "We have to know and create everything" mindset

…To

- Focused on the business's biggest priorities
- Analytical about resource allocation and budgeting (top-down)
- Listening to people at all levels
- Commitment to development

- Shared goals, team-based and collaborative
- Aligned and focused on priorities with clear ownership
- Open, challenging, and deliberative

- Seek ideas and new ways of working
- Learning culture: share ideas, move talent
- Maximize strategic partnerships
- Invest against the big ideas and fail fast on others

an important way to emphasize cross-silo working. Note that the bullet in the lower right-hand corner talks about making trade-offs across the portfolio. This puts the spotlight on the root causes of overcommitment *across* teams. The business's senior leaders have to map and analyze the patterns of multiteaming, as suggested earlier. Which teams are *overly interconnected* (with an eye toward managing the risk of shocks)?

To create this from-to vision and then implement and sustain it, you need to conduct an initial diagnostic and some ongoing data collection and communication. This means that you have to look at both quantitative and qualitative measures—taking a first pass at assessing where and how much overcommitment is a problem, and generating hypotheses that can be tested against the emerging data.

- **Quantitative measures.** How many teams is each employee working on? (Take into account not only formal work projects but also committees, task forces, and other activities that eat up people's time and attention.) How much does overcommitment vary by function, level, role, or organizational tenure? How much overlap is there across teams? We've described in several previous chapters how leaders can use technology like Microsoft Teams and Slack to analyze workplace interactions. Similarly, data from these platforms can help leaders analyze overcommitment.

  Remember that this is where averages can lie to you. At BioNext, leaders had assumed that people were generally on two or three projects at once—and on average, that was true. But certain key people were very stretched. In one early workshop, we looked at the graph shown in Figure 12-4. "Wait! Who's that person on the far right with ten projects?!" A quick search showed it was Julie Davis . . . and nobody knew who she was. Turns out Julie had joined BioNext just nine months earlier. When we started digging into Julie's story, it showed a common problem: from the moment she started, she faced a massive backlog across multiple projects, where work had been building up since her predecessor left. "I had

FIGURE 12-4

## Multiteaming across programs

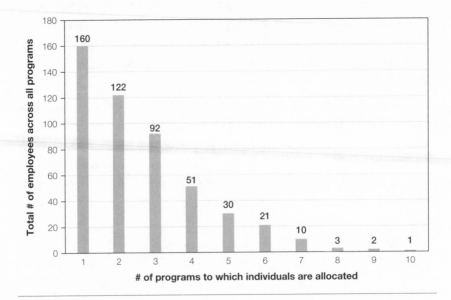

no idea what was a normal workload, and so I tried to tackle them all," Julie told us in an interview. "It was insane and I nearly quit." Digging into this single data point revealed three major, ongoing pain points at BioNext: new hires were poorly onboarded, managers often didn't have a clue how many projects their people were assigned to, and individuals themselves didn't feel comfortable speaking up.

- **Qualitative measures.** How stressed are people? Do functional heads and project leaders negotiate resources and give people guidance as to how to prioritize, or do they just let employees juggle competing demands and suffer the consequences? Many companies already gather data about employee engagement, but few succeed in tracing burnout back to its root cause: overcommitment. One useful tool here is a "heat map," as depicted in Figure 12-5. The hot zones tend to highlight areas of both low engagement and overcommitment.

If you don't have this data (maybe certain business units or functions don't track time this way), consider polling the

FIGURE 12-5

## Heat map of engagement and workload

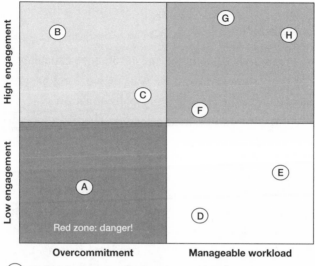

= individual employee position based on survey results.

organization on a periodic basis. Capture the data at a granular enough level (by department, function, title, etc.) that you can slice it, pinpoint potential problems, and dig further into those areas.

After you have developed a baseline understanding of the root causes of overcommitment and where it is happening, you need to create a culture that can manage it over time. The following steps can help:

- **Communicate the priorities.** Do your people know where to focus and, as important, areas that are no longer a priority? If people understand the organization's priorities and what's changed, self-governance is far easier.

- **Create a "speak-up" culture.** Make it an expectation that people will discuss what they are asked to work on, ensure it is aligned with the organization's priorities, and raise their hands when they are overcommitted, and then make it safe and normal to do so by equipping them with the necessary data. (The person who is speaking up isn't just whining; he or she is underscoring a reality that the company needs to know about.) Knowing that she was a true outlier would have helped Julie, the new joiner in Figure 12-4, escape from her whirlpool of overcommitment.

- **Create a data-driven monitoring and governance capability.** At BioNext, projects are the core way of working and usually involve heavy multiteaming and collaboration with third parties. The company's senior leaders therefore decided to create a centralized team to manage prioritization and resourcing.

- **Crowdsource.** Give people a way to learn and contribute without having to be part of every team—our research shows that a desire to learn is a frequent driver of "voluntary" overcommitment. "Communities of practice" (which can be created through Slack and similar messaging tools) are a great way to spur virtual forms of collaboration, knowledge sharing, and knowledge distribution.

- **Generate "vicarious involvement."** Share the success stories and energy of what's happening across the organization. Again, give people the thrill of participating, and even contributing, without actually having to be a team member. "At every town hall," said one executive at an automotive parts manufacturer, "I try to share a story of something exciting happening in the company. These stories generate great feedback and a little bit of positive competition."

## Actions for Team Leaders

While a company's senior leaders need to develop an organization-wide understanding of multiteaming and overcommitment, the day-to-day management happens at the team level—and the team leader is usually in the best position to address it. Launching the team, and relaunching it when things change, is key to managing overcommitment. To keep the team on track and manage the risk of overcommitment, take these actions:

- **Figure out overcommitment.** How many projects are people on your team working on? What's the distribution of effort—do you have people highly dependent on one another with very different time allocations? How are people feeling? If any of these are out of whack, deal with it early.

- **Map and handle crunch times.** As you form a team, explicitly talk about everyone's competing priorities up front. By preemptively identifying crunch periods across projects, you can revamp deadlines or plan on spending more hands-on time yourself at certain points. Making the topic "discussable" so that people won't feel guilty about conflicts allows the team to openly and productively handle these issues when they come up later.

- **Get personal.** A robust team launch helps to establish trust and familiarity. When people learn about their teammates' outside lives—family, hobbies, life events—they can coordinate better (they know, for example, that one teammate is offline during kids' bedtimes or that another routinely hits the gym during lunch). They know better how to seek and offer constructive feedback, introduce one another to valuable network connections, and rely on one another's technical expertise.

  When multiteaming, people tend to be hyperfocused on efficiency and are less inclined to share personal information. If you don't engineer personal interactions for them, therefore, chances are good they'll be left with only an anemic picture of their teammates, which can breed suspicion about why others fail to respond promptly, how committed they are to team outcomes, and so on. This is especially true in distributed teams. So make sure team members spend some time in the beginning getting to know their colleagues. This will also help far-flung contributors give one another the benefit of the doubt later on.

You may be tempted to skip these discussions about personal preferences if many members of your team have worked together before. But we've found that even familiar teams are likely to hold incomplete or outdated assumptions about individuals' potential contributions and often disagree about their teammates' expertise. As a result, they may argue about which roles members should play or bristle at assignments, thinking they're unfair or a bad fit. People may also waste time seeking outside resources when a teammate already has the needed knowledge, which demotivates those whose skills have been overlooked.

- **Use technology.** Although technology doesn't replace face-to-face interaction, it can give you efficient alternatives. And be creative: younger team members are more likely to watch a thirty-second video update than to read a two-page memo. Brief, spontaneous check-ins with team members over Zoom, Teams, or similar virtual-meeting tools can keep you updated on their competing deadlines; this visual interaction makes it more likely that you'll pick up cues about their stress and motivation levels too. And "communities" in Teams or Slack make it much easier for people to follow the thread of a conversation versus searching for emails.

- **Manage the "10 percenters."** Many organizations have subject-matter experts whose role demands that they work across many projects at once. At a global engineering firm, we spoke with Martin, the so-called Tremors Expert. "On every project," he said, "I analyze earthquake activity in the area and advise on structural requirements. It's a short and critical piece of work—these can be billion-dollar projects—but I don't stay on for the duration." It is every team leader's job to make sure such experts are as engaged as possible. "I love it, but you don't really feel like you are part of the core team. . . . When the projects are done I rarely get invited to the opening or the team celebration drinks."

On traditional, fixed teams, a strong sense of cohesion and group identity motivates members. But leaders in multiteaming environments need to leverage more of an exchange relationship. The ability to get jazzed about a project naturally flags when members spend only a small amount of time on it. Their inner accountant starts to ask questions like, "If I'll get only a small share of the credit, how much time and effort should I devote to this?" Figure out what your 10 percenters really value and frame the work in terms of those rewards. For example, if you have a millennial who is eager to develop transferable skills, you might occasionally take time during meetings to have team members share and learn something new, or commit yourself to holding one or more workshops— midstream or at the end of the project—whereby members will be able to cross-train.

At BioNext, a task force developed a set of guiding principles for the project leaders across the company that helped them focus on outcomes that previously had been neglected, such as "team learning and health." To put those guidelines into action, BioNext developed toolkits that included exercises and best-practice examples, then ran multiple pilots to test their effectiveness and develop a framework that teams could customize to their own needs.

Ultimately, BioNext implemented a holistic approach for managing teams that included leadership skills training for both existing and potential project leads, a revamp of the performance management system to reinforce team-based behaviors, and stronger project governance to support project leaders.

## Actions for Individuals

People who are being pulled in multiple directions have to develop a sense of the big picture, prioritize their competing tasks strategically, and set and communicate expectations and progress carefully—a tall order!

A first step toward developing the big picture is to map the interdependencies in which you are personally involved, including the key knowledge flows. How do things get decided, and how are those decisions coordinated and communicated across teams—if indeed they are? The answers to these questions create a context within which you can chart your personal course, because you're better able to manage your time and set expectations. To succeed at this, you will need to do the following:

- **Sequence strategically.** Sequence your investments of time strategically. Decide on a distinct set of must-achieve outcomes, figure out which actions you can take to achieve those results, and then *focus intensely on those actions.* Research shows that attention residue—thoughts held over from a project you're transitioning from—takes up valuable mental space, so the fewer switches you can make in a given day, the better.

    If you must multitask, then coordinate and group any compatible duties. For example, if you know you are going to need to answer phone calls at random intervals, work on another task that can be interrupted at any time.

- **Communicate selectively and effectively.** You don't have to be available to everyone all the time, but you do have to make it clear when you'll be available to take a call, answer a text, or participate in a virtual meeting. One seasoned team member we talked with during our research said that many of his responses to team requests consist of only two words: "On it." Even this super-brief response tells colleagues that he received their request and that he'll follow up on it. Another tended to put "out of office" on during the day when they needed to focus—"I'm focused on a key project this morning and will respond to emails after 3 p.m."

    The other side of this coin, of course, is telling people what they need to know ahead of time—even if it's bad news. Be up front when problems arise. The earlier you say, "I've got a conflict and might have trouble delivering 100 percent," the more leaders and teammates will trust you.

- **Key an eye on your own development.** We've made reference to how team leaders have to invest in creating a learning environment. As the potential beneficiary of those investments, you need to be clear on what *you* need. After identifying and communicating your development goals, block out time for actual learning.

Research shows that a critical determinant of learning is time spent reflecting on and integrating new information. This is a challenge, because multiteaming forces people to jump between projects with the express goal of reducing downtime. Therefore, you need to intentionally and explicitly schedule time for reflection. At BioNext, one team member pushed the group to shorten hour-long meetings to forty-five minutes and blocked "thinking time" in her own calendar. "If I didn't," she said, "I'd never have time to reflect on anything I had just learned."

## Ongoing Vigilance against Overcommitment

While the practical steps described in this chapter can be very helpful in untangling an overcommitment mess after the fact, they also can serve to insulate the company and its teams against other kinds of derailers.

For example, toward the end of the organizational "fix" described earlier, BioNext hired a new head of R&D. Not surprisingly, that individual arrived with strong ideas about organizational priorities and launched a series of new projects. The cultural, systemic, and structural steps that the company had already taken to avoid over-commitments allowed BioNext to manage the new priorities without sliding back into chaos. Ultimately, the new R&D head's vision was successful.[7]

That's a dramatic example, but in most corporate settings, erosion is a bigger danger than revolution. It requires vigilance to make sure that smart collaboration and its associated multiteaming don't degenerate into overcommitment—and the rewards more than justify that vigilance.

$$\begin{bmatrix} 13 \end{bmatrix}$$

# The Next Frontiers of Smarter Collaboration

L
et's imagine that you've assigned yourself a truly ambitious goal: *to save the world's oceans.* What kinds of collaboration might improve your chances of getting there?

This was a core question faced by the father-and-son team of Ray and Mark Dalio. Ray founded Bridgewater Associates, an investment firm that grew into the world's largest hedge fund, along the way making Ray a multibillionaire and giving him the resources needed to support selected philanthropic causes. One of those causes is oceanographic exploration, research, and conservation—a passion shared by his son Mark.

Together, in the spring of 2018, the Dalios launched an initiative called OceanX.[1] Their goal was "to explore the ocean and bring it back to the world."[2] But beyond pure scientific exploration, their project has a second, equally important aspect: to raise public awareness of the importance of the oceans to the global ecosystem, and to make people fall in love with this critical habitat and ultimately want to protect it.

Toward those ends, they purchased a former oil-support ship and retrofitted it to conduct serious scientific work.[3] Meanwhile, they entered into a series of partnerships with established and respected oceanographic research groups, such as the National Oceanic and Atmospheric Administration (NOAA) and the Woods Hole Oceanographic Institute, to define and pursue their scientific goals. And only a few years into its work, OceanX has already racked up some impressive successes. The team was the first to explore the deep seafloor of Antarctica, the first to tag a deep-sea shark from a sub, and the first to film a giant squid in the deep. They have discovered 180 new species of biofluorescent fish and have worked with NASA's Jet Propulsion Laboratory to test equipment that one day may be used to study ocean worlds beyond our planet.

OceanX's second goal—advancing public awareness and education—argued for a collaboration between scientists and members of the media and creative community, including filmmakers, videographers, and social media content generators. The BBC shot *Blue Planet II* aboard OceanX's first ship, *Alucia*.[4] Leonardo DiCaprio made a dive in one of OceanX's Triton submersibles for his documentary film *Before the Flood*. James Cameron—the celebrated director of *Avatar* and *Titanic*, as well as an avid diver—is coproducing an ocean-focused documentary series with OceanX, BBC Studios Natural History Unit, and National Geographic.[5]

OceanX employs advanced technology to accelerate collaboration between people with such different backgrounds. Dalio describes,

> One challenge is that we generate a lot of data from different exploration technologies aboard our vessel. We want teams to interact with the data in their own way so they can use their specialized knowledge, see and understand it differently, and then bring those insights back together. We use Microsoft's augmented reality Mesh technology to visualize all this data in a virtual environment on board OceanXplorer. We're seeing the positions of the remote vehicles and subs, live feeds from cameras, and bathymetry of the seafloor all coming together in our holographic laboratory. This way the scientists, the ship crew, and the media people all participate by visualizing data in their own ways.

Ranging even farther afield, the collaboration has expanded to include companies like Crayola, the iconic maker of crayons. "Crayola and OceanX are two organizations both dedicated to pushing creative boundaries and expanding the collective imagination," Dalio explains. The two organizations share a common goal "to educate young leaders through imagination, wonder, and exploration," and they partnered to create cobranded products and experiences like home adventure kits, creative products, educational content, and events.

What does this brief account illustrate? Like the other initiatives we will encounter in this chapter, OceanX pushes the frontiers of smarter collaboration. It is building and leading an ecosystem of players with radically different expertise who are joined by a common passion. Why? Because as the world becomes ever more complex, addressing issues that fundamentally affect humankind requires unprecedented levels of commitment and investment, over ever-longer time horizons. Collaboration is already evolving and adapting to meet these needs.

## Fighting the Tides

In the same spirit, let's look at another global challenge related to the oceans: sea-level rise. This is one of the more visible threats arising from global warming, posing an existential challenge to low-lying coastal regions around the world and threatening the very existence of dozens of small island nations.[6]

This very real threat is prompting initiatives based on smart collaboration at both the local and regional levels. A case in point comes from southeast Florida, where sea-level rise is already disrupting entire communities. Several vital roads in the Florida Keys, for example, are expected to be underwater by 2025. "Without a change in strategy," commented one environmental planner, "parts of the Keys will become accessible only by boat."[7]

Anticipating this mounting challenge, local leaders in 2010 established the Southeast Florida Regional Climate Change Compact (SFRCCC), which is aimed at supporting collaborative efforts across county lines to reduce greenhouse gas emissions, implement adaptation strategies, and build climate resilience across the region.[8] Those collaborative partnerships include a wide range of businesses, government agencies, and nonprofits.[9] One example is the Nature Conservancy (TNC), which works with SFRCCC to catalog, track, and implement coastal defense pilot projects that are "nature-based"—that is, not predominantly dependent on man-made structures—and at the same time are based on a combination of cutting-edge science and local knowledge.[10]

The Florida Keys Coral Restoration Project is one such project. A TNC global study showed that coral reefs that crest at the surface are a natural barrier to beach-eroding ocean waves. These reefs can absorb up to 97 percent of a wave's energy—and natural reef enhancements are cost effective when compared with man-made breakwaters and seawalls.[11]

With these arguments in hand, TNC launched a collaborative effort with NOAA and other partners to develop breeding populations of threatened staghorn and elkhorn corals and transplant them to degraded reefs along Monroe County's oceanfront. To date, some ten thousand of these colonies have been established, with first-year survival rates above 80 percent.[12]

Of course, one revived coral reef is a mere start. But the success of the TNC-NOAA collaboration led to a new partnership in 2019 between the Florida Keys National Marine Sanctuary and the NOAA Restoration Center, which aims to rebuild seven reefs in the sanctuary within twenty years.[13] And each success helps TNC and others make the case to the Florida legislature for increased support for environmental conservation. Last year, that support amounted to nearly $1 billion, in part because conservation is now seen by many as a shared responsibility requiring collaborative effort.

Over time, the SFRCCC communities recognized that the climate-change challenges that initially brought them together were interlocked with a host of other systemic issues, including a range of fairness and equity concerns:

> Equity should be an integral part of policy making at every
> level of government within Southeast Florida, and should be

understood as a policy objective in developing plans, budgets, and in prioritizing and designing climate projects. Historically disadvantaged communities will continue to be the most vulnerable to climate change threats, unless action is taken to create targeted policies and resources. In addition, efforts to create more resilient and sustainable communities, if not designed thoughtfully, can benefit some residents while harming others.[14]

In other words, sustainable coasts can't be built on injustice. If rising sea levels force changes in zoning regulations or transportation grids, for example, those changes have to be conceived and implemented in consultation with vulnerable populations. And a focus on these populations reinforces sustainability by generating commitment from those groups' political representatives. In other words, smarter collaboration evolves toward a broader systems perspective. Collaborators who consider the wider context become aware of adjacent issues affecting the original problem, and of the interactions among these different components.[15]

Of course, reframing a problem with a wider lens is not an entirely new angle on smart collaboration. In Chapter 6, for example, we advocated using end-to-end metrics that capture outcomes for an entire process, not just one department's inputs. Our point here is that the next frontiers will deepen this way of thinking: applying smarter collaboration to tackle multiple, interconnected problems to create a stronger, more holistic, and sustainable solution.

## Collaboration at Broad

Cambridge, Massachusetts-based Broad Institute traces its roots to the successful mapping of the human genome, achieved by several teams of scientists back in 2003. A year later, Broad (rhymes with *toad*)—a collaboration among MIT, Harvard, and a community of researchers across many institutions—was founded. Its mission, stemming directly from the Human Genome Project, is to use genetic research to better understand the roots of disease and narrow the gap between new biological insights and impact for patients.[16]

Today, Broad works to accelerate biomedical research and improve human health through a number of distinctive kinds of collaboration. First, it partners with scientists and institutions around the world to make discoveries and engage in genomic data sharing, which can speed the pace of scientific discoveries, enable new insights into disease, and advance precision medicine (i.e., medical treatments tailored to an individual) in the clinic. These efforts currently add up to more than one hundred projects in some forty countries.[17]

To deliver on that mission, however, the institute has had to help those researchers and overcome a major barrier: mountains of disease-related data that was trapped in virtual silos—separated by disease area, institution, or country—which made that data extremely difficult to combine and analyze. In 2014 Broad scientists helped launch the Global Alliance for Genomics and Health as a coordinated effort to help scientists access and share their scientific data. Collaborating with teams around the world, the alliance creates standards and policy frameworks for data representation, storage, analysis, security, and more. Such standards allow researchers and clinicians to analyze massive amounts of disparate genomic information simultaneously, advancing the study of disease biology.[18]

In other words, smarter collaboration relies increasingly on *capacity building*: enabling broader communities to solve the problem. Human health is obviously far bigger than any institution can tackle on its own; therefore, Broad purposefully strengthens other organizations' ability to work on these highly complex problems. The next frontiers of smarter collaboration will harness the efficiency and power of distributed groups to make progress independently—but in a collaborative, not siloed, way.

Collaboration at Broad also involves broadening the lens—that is, stretching the definition of the medical ecosystem much further than the community of traditional biotech researchers. By harnessing the power of crowdsourcing, for example, the institute captures insights from people with no prior biotech experience. In one recent case, Broad partnered with Topcoder in a competition to drive rapid enhancements in precision medicine. The goal was to crowdsource new and faster algorithms crucial to accelerating this burgeoning field of study. Over one thousand members of the Topcoder community registered for the competition, and seventy-two members submitted 410 unique algorithms over its three weeks. The top solution performed as accurately as the existing algorithm—but *fourteen times faster.*[19]

"I should say that this was the first time I have approached a computational biology problem," said the winner of the competition, a Polish computer scientist named Marek Cygan. "I have no prior knowledge whatsoever about DNA sequencing. I decided to enter this challenge as it appeared to me as a nice mix of algorithm design, code optimization and possibly machine learning."[20]

What does the Broad-Topcoder example show us about the future of smarter collaboration? It suggests strongly that this kind of collaboration will hinge increasingly on diversity. According to its website, "Accelerating biomedical research and improving human health require diversity of all kinds in our community—in education, training, background, perspectives, interests, and identity—because it expands our creativity in how we approach problems and find solutions. Broad aims to ensure that the benefits of genomic medicine are shared by all."[21]

Broad's results with Topcoder weren't a fluke. A study involving twelve thousand people participating in innovation contests to solve 166 different real-world problems, for example, demonstrated that "unconventional individuals win innovation contests."[22]

And finally, smarter collaboration grows out of *inclusivity.* To that end, the institute collaborates with patients, who share their data, samples, and perspectives with Broad to advance research related to their disease or condition. This involves work with both patient advocacy groups and individual patients, through custom-built websites and social media channels. The Rare Genomes Project is a case in point. "We believe that families should be at the center of research involving their diseases," says the project website, "and encourage the involvement of families and the advocacy groups that support them throughout the study." At the same time, genetic information generated through the project is shared with scientists around the world, to "ensure that it has the widest possible impact."[23]

Another take on inclusivity involves not just experts handing down their wisdom to the so-called less informed masses, but truly involving people who are experiencing the issues; this inclusivity helps to build solutions are more well rounded, innovative, and useful. Broad accomplished that by including patients in its research, and we see glimmers of this inclusivity across health care. Emerging research by New York University professor Pat Satterstrom and Harvard School of Public Health professor Michaela Kerrissey shows that multidisciplinary health-care teams' decisions reflect a more comprehensive set of priorities when they rely on inputs from a diverse set of constituents, ranging from front-desk staff to patients.[24] Looking forward, collaborators will insist that inclusivity be adopted more widely and effectively.

## Collaboration in Space Exploration

International collaboration in space is not new, certainly. For example, the International Space Station has been operating for two decades, hosting astronauts from eighteen countries and serving as the base for experiments designed by scientists from a total of ninety-three countries.

But the stakes and the payoffs keep going up and up. One celebrated and massively complex collaborative challenge that was recently completed—flying a helicopter remotely on a planet millions of miles from Earth—drew on the talents of multiple disciplines, including mechanical and systems engineers, robotics experts, pilots, physicists, chemists, microwave experts, thermal fluid system engineers, guidance and control experts, geologists, and visual strategists, among others.[25] Participating institutions included NASA's Ames Research Center, Langley Research Center, and Jet Propulsion Laboratory (managed by Cal Tech); AeroVironment; SolAero Technologies; Lockheed Martin Space; and many others.

By any measure, it was a delicate operation. The *Perseverance* rover landed on Jezero Crater on the surface of Mars on February 18, 2021. Strapped underneath it was a tiny four-pound helicopter called *Ingenuity*, aimed at determining whether powered and controlled flight is possible in the extremely thin atmosphere of Mars.[26] On its first flight—on April 19, 2021—*Ingenuity* took off, climbed about ten feet above the ground, hovered, turned, and landed safely: an astounding accomplishment.

Implicit in the *Perseverance* rover story is the importance of a new collaborator: artificial intelligence (AI). Massive problems require the engagement of massive brainpower, which sometimes exceeds the capacity of the humans collaborating on the project. Remote space exploration, in particular, increasingly calls for a combination of AI and sophisticated robotic technologies. The *Curiosity* rover that rolled across the Martian surface a decade ago had to "call home" for instructions if it encountered a boulder in its path. *Perseverance* is smart enough to get around obstacles on its own. In another ten years, thanks to AI, remote probes should be able not only to steer around a boulder but also to recommend to Earth-bound scientists which boulders to study.[27]

The larger impact of AI will lie in complementing and augmenting human capabilities—that is, technology truly working in collaboration with humans. "In our research involving 1,500 companies," wrote two researchers, "we found that firms achieve the most significant performance improvements when humans and machines work together. Through such collaborative intelligence, humans and AI actively enhance each other's complementary strengths: the leadership, teamwork, creativity, and social skills of the former, and the speed, scalability, and quantitative capabilities of the latter."[28]

Are you thinking that maybe this isn't "real" collaboration? If so, think again. Humans engage *deeply* with these machines—for example, by teaching them how to interact with people in ways that mimic human emotions like sympathy. In turn, AI can help augment truly human capabilities such as creativity. For instance, one program allows designers and machines to actively iterate to reach a new, optimized product concept. The designer uploads specs defining critical constraints (such as weight and strength), the machine generates thousands of designs, and the designer "teaches" the software through a succession of selections and refinements. Through these iterations, their collaboration leads to a better outcome than either could have achieved on their own.

An unconventional kind of collaboration, to be sure—but very likely to be a dominant thread in smart collaboration going forward.

## From the Cutting Edge to the Everyday

OK; let's get back down to Earth.

We assume that our readers are mainly interested in practical challenges—the kinds of things they might encounter in their own workplace. So why indulge in stories about the deep oceans and deep space, with shorelines and precision medicine in between?

To us, the answer is clear and compelling. The success of ideas explored at the cutting edge inspire us to apply those ideas to our everyday work. Thinking about the next frontiers of collaboration forces us to deepen the concepts of smarter collaboration that we've talked about throughout this book. We are reminded that we collaborators need to engage with those directly affected by our work and those who bring different perspectives. We need to build a global community of groups that make progress independently but in a way that harnesses their learning and builds on each other's knowledge for collective advancement. We need to involve people beyond the traditional definitions of *expertise*. We need to ensure that capacity building is at the heart of the mission. Throughout the book, we highlighted the learning and personal development of core collaborators, and now we are pushing this perspective out to the broader community. We need to take a systems view, thereby creating more holistic solutions that also tackle adjacent issues, as well as the problem at hand. We need to embrace and collaborate with emerging technologies. We need to use collaboration as a means to a higher end and a more profound purpose.

All of this adds up to one imperative: as smart collaborators, we need to *lead*.

In the collaborative space, leaders aren't just those with formal titles; leaders are those who step up to move the collaboration journey ahead. They are people who actively include and amplify voices that might otherwise go unheard. They are people who empathize and share credit easily. They are capacity builders. They are people who help others understand why collaboration is essential for achieving their goals, both collective and individual: the *why* of smart collaboration.

We'll say it once again: smarter collaboration is the means to an end. That end is your strategy. Implementation—the *who* and *how* of smart collaboration—is *key*. Think of smart collaboration as a touchstone that you go back to constantly, end to end, across your business processes. How can we use collaboration at this point in the evolution of our product, or of our larger portfolio, or of the company itself, to be more effective and efficient?

Let's conclude on the individual level. This may seem like a strange choice for wrapping up a book on collaboration. Clearly, you can't collaborate alone. But as just suggested, each of us, individually, has a crucial role to play. Each of us is a culture builder. We meet that obligation through the stories we tell, how we engage with each other day-to-day, and the people and accomplishments we decide to celebrate.

So on the most fundamental level, smart collaboration begins with you. Your choices *matter*—and we encourage you to choose to be a smarter collaborator.

# ACKNOWLEDGMENTS

This book is a testament to the value of smarter collaboration. As coauthors, we drew on our very different professional experiences to enrich the ideas and challenge each other. But far more than that, we were blessed with an enormously diverse, generous community of people who really, really believe in the power of collaborating across silos to generate more innovative, inspiring, and productive outcomes. These are people—probably just like you—who have seen that we can achieve so much more, in such better ways, when we value the inputs of a highly diverse set of people, bring in those voices at just the right time, and throw ourselves into the sometimes vulnerable space of smarter collaboration. We can only begin to thank those contributors here.

Let's start with some people whose unique inputs made a big difference to our research. We are grateful to Christa Gyori for her keen insights and generosity in making introductions. Heidi's colleagues at Harvard Business School and Harvard Law School provided valuable insights and challenge throughout our research process, as did all the members of our ongoing research symposium GroupsGroup. Special thanks to Dr. Ruth Wageman for continuing that forum, which was begun by our revered, late mentor Dr. J. Richard Hackman. Professor Rob Cross and Dr. Mark Mortensen, who coauthored prior *HBR* articles with Heidi, continue to be important sources of ideas and inspiration. Major thanks go to Claudio Fernández-Aráoz, Steve Immelt, and Laura Melchor McCanlies for providing valuable feedback on an early version of our manuscript.

Our deep thanks go to the people who directly worked with us on the manuscript and all its iterations. The indomitable Gardner & Co. team includes Cheryl Caruolo, Christine Dunne, Esteban Guijarro,

Lea Haggarty, Csilla Ilkei, and Geoff Watkinson, supported by our fabulous interns Justin McMahon, Ana Sofia Moraskie, Allison Puglisi, and Mohammed Siraje. We also thank Joanna Wozniak for superb data crunching and Stephanie Bennaugh for expert research assistance. Steve Prokesch edited multiple *HBR* articles that underpin ideas in this book, and challenged us to sharpen our thinking at each stage. To Jeff Cruikshank, our developmental editor: thank you for your creativity, humor, patience—and pushing us to use the occasional exclamation point! Jeff Kehoe and the amazing team at HBR Press provided the perfect level of input to help us refine our ideas.

We are indebted to the many interviewees and others who directly added your ideas, data, experiences and network to this book. Whether we quote you by name or simply drew on your inspiring stories, you have been invaluable: Jennifer Artly, Diane August, Nitesh Banga, Ester Banque, Paul Barnett, Prof. Iris Bohnet, Jakob Bohnet, Ben Christensen, Tom Comery, Mark Dalio, Dr. Aaron Deykin, Leslie Dory, Philip Goodstone, Jason Hardgrave, Stuart Henderson, Portia Hickey, Donna Hicks, Dan Hoffman, Ambassador Stuart Holliday, Perry Hooks, Lisa Inserra, Michael Jackson, Michelle Jubelirer, Roberto Junguito, Ged Keogh-Peters, Martin Kingston, Denise Kruger, Helene Kubon Skulstad, James Lam, Eric Lee, Andrea Legnani, Carl Liebert, Tammy Lowry, Karen Lynch, Denis Machuel, Karn Manhas, Daniel Mauro, Dan Mearls, Kathryn Metcalfe, Matt Meyer, Jesper Michaelsen, Tangy Morgan, Tom Moriarty, Dr. Rebecca Newton, Rebecca Normand-Hochmann, Rob Ollander-Krane, Yvette Ostolaza, Nicole Petrie, Alex Poniewierski, Sharon Price, Steve Rader, Dr. Amrit Ray, Darrell Rigby, Mark Rivera, Tom Ruderman, Maria Salinas, Chris Shaida, John Shiel, Julie Thomas, Puru Trivedi, Jennifer Trosper, Steve Twait, Tamsin Vine, Dr. Ben Waber, Micah Waldman, Janet Woods, and Mitch Zuklie. We also appreciate all the coaches, facilitators, and consultants who became Accredited Partners in the Smart Collaboration Accelerator tool; your work in spreading and expertly applying these ideas is a vital part of our journey.

Writing this book would have been impossible without the unwavering love and support of our friends and family. Forgive us, dear friends, for not giving you individual shout-outs; we will continue to thank you in person. Our parents—Phyllis and Bill Gardner, and

Carla and Greg Matviak—have encouraged and helped us over the years in too many ways to mention. Thank you for being our role models over the decades. Finally, our daughters Zoë and Anya have inspired, bolstered, tolerated, and sustained us as we started working on this book during Covid lock-down and continued since. A project of this magnitude has required some sacrifices on everyone's part; we hope that the laughs along the way and knowing that this book pushes forward our shared passion for diversity and inclusivity make it all worthwhile.

In closing, we return (no surprise) to the theme of smarter collaboration. In the years since the initial book, *Smart Collaboration*, was published, literally thousands of people have helped us to understand the power of applying these principles. Across the planet, leaders of major companies, professional firms, and nonprofit organizations seized the ideas, found ways to activate them, and deepened our know-how along with them. Moreover, people at all levels of seniority wrote and called us, offering their own insights, queries, and tips. With this new book, we hope to supercharge this smarter collaboration movement. We invite you into our smarter collaboration community!

# NOTES

## Introduction

1. H. K. Gardner, E. Bedzra, and S. M. Elnahal, "Ganging Up on Cancer: Integrative Research Centers at the Dana-Farber Cancer Institute (A)," Case 412-029 (Boston: Harvard Business School, September 2011; revised October 2012); J. T. Polzer and H. K. Gardner, "Bridgewater Associates," Multimedia/Video Case 413-702 (Boston: Harvard Business School, May 2013); H. K. Gardner, "Getting Your Stars to Collaborate: How Dana-Farber Turns Rival Experts into Problem-Solving Partners," *Harvard Business Review*, January–February 2017, 100–108; H. K. Gardner, "PwC's Performance Pilot Transforming Compensation and Leadership," Case HLS22-64 (Boston: Harvard Law School, March 2022).

2. Heidi K. Gardner and Ivan A. Matviak, "Smarter Collaboration Toolkit: Conducting a Data-Driven Diagnostic to Boost Collaborative Outcomes" (Boston: Harvard Business Review Press, forthcoming), hbr.org.

## Chapter 1

1. We have worked directly with clients ranging in size from a sixteen-partner boutique economic advisory firm to highly diversified companies with more than 250,000 employees and measured the revenue uplift from enhanced collaboration across that whole spectrum. Naturally, the shape of the curve—that is, how much each additional business line adds to the average annual revenue—depends in large part on how narrowly or broadly the firm defines a business line. Nevertheless, cross-business, multiexpert, integrated services consistently bring value to the client or customer—and therefore increase revenues for the provider.

2. With apologies to McDonald's, customers hate to be cross-sold. Why? Cross-selling is vendor-focused, while collaboration is client-focused.

3. K. M. McDonald et al., *Care Coordination*, vol. 7 of *Closing the Quality Gap: A Critical Analysis of Quality Improvement Strategies* (Rockville, MD: Agency for Healthcare Research and Quality, June 2007).

4. "Continuum Health Coordinated Care: Key to Successful Outcomes—Best Practices in Care Coordination Improve Health, Lower Costs and Increase Patient Satisfaction," Continuum Health, 2015, https://www.continuumhealth.net/coordinated-care-key-successful-outcomes/.

5. M. K. Bailey et al., *Characteristics of 30-Day All-Cause Hospital Read-missions, 2010–2016*, Healthcare Cost and Utilization Project Statistical Brief #248 (Rockville, MD: Agency for Healthcare Research and Quality, 2019).

6. For the best chance at remission, chronic myeloid leukemia patients need to maintain greater than 90 percent adherence in the first year after diagnosis.

7. C. Sawicki et al., "Two-Way Clinical Messaging in a CML Specialty Pharmacy Service Model," *Journal of Managed Care and Specialty Pharmacy* 25, no. 11 (2019): 1290–1296.

8. D. Crouch, "Teams of Inventors: Trends in Patenting," Patently-O, January 30, 2019, https://patentlyo.com/patent/2019/01/inventors-trends-patenting.html.

9. Innovation requires both novelty and usefulness. Creativity and innovation are related, but separate. Creativity is often *the big idea*, and innovation occurs when the team *applies* that big idea to improve products, services, methods, or ideas. See D. K. Rigby, J. Sutherland, and A. Noble, "Agile at Scale," *Harvard Business Review*, May–June 2018, 88–96.

10. B. Gyori et al., *Purpose-Driven Leadership for the 21st Century: Transitioning to a Purpose-First Economy through the New Business Logic* (Leaders on Purpose, 2020).

11. C. E. LaCanne and J. G. Lundgren, "Regenerative Agriculture: Merging Farming and Natural Resource Conservation Profitably," *PeerJ* 6 (2018): e4428, https://doi.org/10.7717/peerj.4428.

12. L. Bryant, "Organic Matter Can Improve Your Soil's Water Holding Capacity," May 27, 2015, NRDC, https://www.nrdc.org/experts/lara-bryant/organic-matter-can-improve-your-soils-water-holding-capacity.

13. J. Gelski, "Study Shows Nutritional Benefits in Regenerative Agriculture Crops," World Grain, February 28, 2022, https://www.world-grain.com/articles/16547-study-shows-nutritional-benefits-in-regenerative-agriculture-crops.

14. See the company's website at https://www.terramera.com/company/about-us.

15. C. Metz, "This Company Believes You Should Never Hack Alone," *Wired*, November 12, 2013, https://www.wired.com/2013/11/pivotal-one/.

16. Research interview with authors; permission granted for publication.

17. See, for example, the kinds of metrics that are emphasized by Candid (formerly GuideStar) at https://candid.org/.

18. "Gates Foundation Focuses on Efficiency," *Financial Times*, October 10, 2011, video, 5:30, https://www.ft.com/video/6f43dc89-ae24-3906-b808-2d50e6a6f95c.

19. M. A. Valentine and A. C. Edmondson, "Team Scaffolds: How Mesolevel Structures Enable Role-Based Coordination in Temporary Groups," *Organization Science* 26, no. 2 (2015): 405–422.

20. This is why the US Securities and Exchange Commission mandates time off for executives in sensitive positions: it creates transparency for the organization by giving others access to the vacationing executive's accounts.

21. Research interview with authors; quote approved for publication. Also see James Lam, *Enterprise Risk Management: From Incentives to Controls*, 2nd ed. (Hoboken, NJ: Wiley, 2014).

22. "Business Roundtable Redefines the Purpose of a Corporation to Promote 'an Economy That Serves All Americans,'" Business Roundtable, August 19, 2019, https://www.businessroundtable.org/business-roundtable-redefines-the-purpose-of -a-corporation-to-promote-an-economy-that-serves-all-americans.

## Chapter 2

1. W. A. Kahn, "Psychological Conditions of Personal Engagement and Disengagement at Work," *Academy of Management Journal* 33 (1990): 692–724; B. L. Rich, J. A. Lepine, and E. R. Crawford, "Job Engagement: Antecedents and Effects on Job Performance," *Academy of Management Journal* 53, no. 3 (2010): 617–635; W. Macey et al., *Employee Engagement: Tools for Analysis, Practice, and Competitive Advantage* (Malden, MA: Wiley-Blackwell, 2009).

2. Rich, Lepine, and Crawford, "Job Engagement."

3. J. S. House, K. R. Landis, and D. Umberson, "Social Relationships and Health," *Science* 241, no. 4865 (1988): 540–545; P. B. Carr and G. M. Walton, "Cues of Working Together Fuel Intrinsic Motivation," *Journal of Experimental Social Psychology* 53 (2014): 169–184.

4. J. K. Harter et al., *Q12 Meta-analysis: The Relationship between Engagement at Work and Organizational Outcomes*, 10th ed. (Omaha: Gallup, 2009).

5. *State of the American Workplace* (Gallup, 2020), https://www.gallup.com /workplace/285818/state-american-workplace-report.aspx

6. T. Neeley, *Remote Work Revolution: Succeeding from Anywhere* (New York: HarperCollins, 2021).

7. Harter et al., *Q12 Meta-analysis*. Other researchers have reached similar conclusions. See A. Grant, "When Strength Becomes Weakness," April 2019, in *WorkLife with Adam Grant*, TED podcast, 36:43, https://www.ted.com/talks /worklife_with_adam_grant_when_strength_becomes_weakness/transcript ?language=en; and B. Gleeson, "5 Powerful Steps to Improve Employee Engagement," *Forbes*, October 15, 2017, https://www.forbes.com/sites/brentgleeson /2017/10/15/5-powerful-steps-to-improve-employee-engagement.

8. Those studies, although conducted long before we coined the term *smart collaboration*, underpin much of our current work.

9. Project launches are a remarkably powerful but underused way to improve performance. M. Haas and M. Mortensen, "The Secrets of Great Teamwork," *Harvard Business Review*, June 2016, https://hbr.org/2016/06/the-secrets-of -great-teamwork.

10. M. Mortensen and H. K. Gardner, "WFH Is Corroding Our Trust in Each Other," hbr.org, February 10, 2021, https://hbr.org/2021/02/wfh-is-corroding -our-trust-in-each-other; H. Hickock, "Why Remote Work Has Eroded Trust among Colleagues," BBC Worklife, March 18, 2021, https://www.bbc.com /worklife/article/20210315-why-remote-work-has-eroded-trust-among-colleagues. For advice on building trust in distributed teams, see Neeley, *Remote Work Revolution*.

11. B. Nelson, "The Data on Diversity," *Communications of the ACM* 57, no. 11 (2014): 86–95.

12. T. A. Voelker, W. C. McDowell, and M. L. Harris, "Collaborative Preference: The Role of Homophily, Multiplexity, and Advantageous Network Position across Small and Medium-Sized Organizations," *Administrative Issues Journal* 3, no. 2 (2013): 11.

13. House, Landis, and Umberson, "Social Relationships and Health"; J. Holt-Lunstad, "Why Social Relationships Are Important for Physical Health: A Systems Approach to Understanding and Modifying Risk and Protection," *Annual Review of Psychology* 69 (2018): 437–458.

14. C. Orchard, "The Business Benefits of a Healthy Workforce," Harvard School of Public Health, June 1, 2015, https://www.hsph.harvard.edu/ecpe/the-business-benefits-of-a-healthy-workforce/.

15. N. Eisenberger et al., "Does Rejection Hurt? An fMRI Study of Social Exclusion," *Science* 302 (2003): 290–292.

16. Ethan Kross et al., "Social Rejection Shares Somatosensory Representations with Physical Pain," *PNAS* 108, no. 15 (2011): 6270–6275.

17. S. Cohen et al., "Sociability and Susceptibility to the Common Cold," *Psychological Science* 14, no. 5 (2003): 389–395.

18. J. Holt-Lunstad, T. B. Smith, and J. B. Layton, "Social Relationships and Mortality Risk: A Meta-analytic Review," *PLoS Medicine* 7, no. 7 (2010): e1000316.

19. "Why New Hires Fail," Leadership IQ, accessed April 21, 2022, https://www.leadershipiq.com/blogs/leadershipiq/35354241-why-new-hires-fail-emotional-intelligence-vs-skills.

20. M. Bidwell, "Paying More to Get Less: The Effects of External Hiring versus Internal Mobility," *Administrative Science Quarterly* 56, no. 3 (2011): 369–407.

21. R. Cross and I. Carboni, "When Collaboration Fails and How to Fix It," *MIT Sloan Management Review* 62, no. 2 (2021): 24–34.

22. H. Boushey and S. J. Glynn, *Cost of Losing Talent* (Center for American Progress, 2012).

23. "Lateral Damage: Failed Hires Cost London Dear," *Lawyer*, February 2012.

24. B. Groysberg, *Chasing Stars: The Myth of Talent and the Portability of Performance* (Princeton, NJ: Princeton University Press, 2011); B. Groysberg, A. Nanda, and N. Nohria, "The Risky Business of Hiring Stars," *Harvard Business Review*, May 2004, 92–101.

25. K. Rollag, S. Parise, and R. Cross, "Getting New Hires Up to Speed Quickly," *MIT Sloan Management Review* 46, no. 2 (2005): 35.

26. Interview with authors.

## Chapter 3

1. TechStar and Rick Jones are pseudonyms, but their circumstances are very real, and typical of companies we have worked with.

2. G. Van Kleef et al., "Power, Distress, and Compassion: Turning a Blind Eye to the Suffering of Others," *Psychological Science* 19, no. 12 (2008): 1315–1322.

3. Ineffective teamwork exhausts employees and can cripple productivity. For more information on how to avoid it, see R. L. Cross, *Beyond Collaboration Overload: How to Work Smarter, Get Ahead, and Restore Your Well-Being* (Boston: Harvard Business Review Press, 2021); M. Mortensen and H. K. Gardner, "The Overcommitted Organization," *Harvard Business Review*, September–October 2017, 58–65; and R. Cross, R. Rebele, and A. Grant, "Collaborative Overload," *Harvard Business Review*, January–February 2016, 74–79.

4. Heidi K. Gardner and Ivan A. Matviak, "Smarter Collaboration Toolkit: Conducting a Data-Driven Diagnostic to Boost Collaborative Outcomes" (Boston: Harvard Business Review Press, forthcoming), hbr.org.

5. R. Lines, "Influence of Participation in Strategic Change: Resistance, Organizational Commitment and Change Goal Achievement," *Journal of Change Management* 4, no. 3 (2004): 193–215.

6. M. Niederle and L. Vesterlund, "Explaining the Gender Gap in Math Test Scores: The Role of Competition," *Journal of Economic Perspectives* 24, no. 2 (2010): 129–144.

7. M. B. Miles, A. M. Huberman, and J. Saldana, *Qualitative Data Analysis: A Methods Sourcebook*, 3rd ed. (Thousand Oaks, CA: SAGE, 2014).

8. Some assume that this barrier only exists in huge companies, but it's prevalent in nearly all rapidly growing companies and those with dispersed offices. We have worked with many small organizations, such as a sixteen-partner consulting firm and a twelve-person tech startup, where people don't know about their colleagues' true capabilities.

9. For more on this topic, see H. K. Gardner, "Collaboration for Ringmasters," chap. 6 in *Smart Collaboration: How Professionals and Their Firms Succeed by Breaking Down Silos* (Boston: Harvard Business Review Press, 2017).

10. H. K. Gardner, "By Failing to Collaborate, Law Firms Are Leaving Money on the Table," *American Lawyer*, October 2018.

11. Historically, research has shown that some people are more swayed by explanations of "why change," whereas others are influenced by "how it will work." We categorize these two groups as Complex and Concrete thinkers, respectively, as we describe in Chapter 4.

## Chapter 4

1. Talks at Google, "Quiet | Susan Cain | Talks at Google," YouTube, February 8, 2012, video, 43:48, https://www.youtube.com/watch?v=AzlCIS072_Y.

2. Psychometrics is the theory and technique of psychological measurement.

3. For more information, see "Smart Collaboration Accelerator," Gardner & Co., accessed April 22, 2022, https://www.gardnerandco.co/services/accelerator/; and Smart Collaboration Accelerator homepage, accessed May 25, 2022, https://smartcollaborationaccelerator.com/.

4. H. K. Gardner and L. Kwan, "Expertise Dissensus: A Multi-level Model of Teams' Differing Perceptions about Member Expertise" (Working Paper 12-070, Harvard Business School, 2012).

5. One somewhat indirect, and therefore less threatening, way to encourage this kind of discussion is to focus it on another company's experience, perhaps

through a case discussion. See, for example, H. K. Gardner, "Coming through When It Matters Most," *Harvard Business Review*, April 2012.

6. S. Dixon-Fyle et al., *Diversity Wins: How Inclusion Matters* (McKinsey & Company, 2020); T. L. Dumas, K. W. Phillips, and N. P. Rothbard, "Getting Closer at the Company Party: Integration Experiences, Racial Dissimilarity, and Workplace Relationships," *Organization Science* 24, no. 5 (2013): 1377–1401.

## Chapter 5

1. Quotes in this chapter from CVS Health executives are based on research interviews with authors; case and quotes cleared for publication.

2. See B. Groysberg, *Chasing Stars: The Myth of Talent and the Portability of Performance* (Princeton, NJ: Princeton University Press, 2012).

3. See Groysberg, *Chasing Stars*.

4. T. N. Bauer et al., "Newcomer Adjustment during Organizational Social-ization: A Meta-analytic Review of Antecedents, Outcomes and Methods," *Journal of Applied Psychology* 92 (2007): 707–721.

5. Gallup, *State of the Global Workplace* (Gallup, 2017), https://www.gallup .com/workplace/238085/state-american-workplace-report-2017.aspx.

6. For practical, research-backed advice on actions the new hires can take on their own, see R. Cross, "New Role? Learn What Top Performers Do," accessed April 22, 2022, https://www.robcross.org/new-role-learn-what-top-performers -do/.

7. T. Neeley, *Remote Work Revolution: Succeeding from Anywhere* (New York: HarperCollins, 2021).

8. B. Kaetzler, K. Kordestani, and A. MacLean, "The Secret Ingredient of Successful Big Deals: Organizational Health," *McKinsey Quarterly*, July 2019, 3, https://www.mckinsey.com/~/media/McKinsey/Business%20Functions /Organization/Our%20Insights/The%20secret%20ingredient%20of%20 successful%20big%20deals%20Organizational%20health/The-secret -ingredient-of-successful-big-deals-organizational-health-VF2.pdf.

9. E. K. Thompson and C. Kim, "Post-M&A Performance and Failure: Implications of Time until Deal Completion," *Sustainability* 12, no. 7 (2020): 2999.

10. "CVS Health Opens COVID-19 Testing Site in Massachusetts," press release, CVS Health, March 19, 2020, https://shrewsburyma.gov/Document Center/View/7270/CVS-Health-opens-first-COVID-19-testing-site-in-Shrewsbury -Massachusetts-_-CVS-Health_March-19-2020.

11. "COVID-19 Testing Information," CVS Health, accessed April 22, 2022, https://cvshealth.com/covid-19/testing-information.

## Chapter 6

1. For more information, including example scorecards, see H. Gardner and I. Matviak, "Performance Management Shouldn't Kill Collaboration: How to Align Goals Across Functions," *Harvard Business Review*, September–October 2022.

2. Scholars Deci and Ryan argue that the more we experience this control, the more we are likely to lose interest in what we are doing. E. L. Deci and R. M. Ryan, *Intrinsic Motivation and Self-Determination in Human Behavior* (New York: Springer Science and Business Media, 2013).

3. Freedman and colleagues found that the effect of the value of the reward devaluates the means. They studied activities ranging from a medical experiment to eating unfamiliar foods, and in each case the activities themselves didn't seem to matter. J. L. Freedman, J. A. Cunningham, and K. Krismer, "Inferred Values and the Reverse-Incentive Effect in Induced Compliance," *Journal of Personality and Social Psychology* 62, no. 3 (1992): 357–368.

4. J. Condry, "Enemies of Exploration: Self-Initiated versus Other-Initiated Learning," *Journal of Personality and Social Psychology* 35, no. 7 (1977): 459.

5. J. Margolis, P. McKinnon, and M. Norris, "Gap Inc: Refashioning Performance Management," case study 416-019 (Boston: Harvard Business School, September 2015, revised September 2020).

6. S. Garr and L. Barry, "Performance Management Is Broken," *Deloitte Insights*, March 5, 2014, https://www2.deloitte.com/us/en/insights/focus/human -capital-trends/2014/hc-trends-2014-performance-management.html.

7. Personal communications to authors; quote approved for publication.

8. P. C. Earley, T. Connolly, and G. Ekegren, "Goals, Strategy Development, and Task Performance: Some Limits on the Efficacy of Goal Setting," *Journal of Applied Psychology* 74, no. 1 (1989): 24.

9. P. B. Carr and G. M. Walton, "Cues of Working Together Fuel Intrinsic Motivation," *Journal of Experimental Social Psychology* 53 (2014): 169–184.

10. A. G. Dittmann, N. M. Stephens, and S. S. M. Townsend, "Research: How Our Class Background Affects the Way We Collaborate," hbr.org, July 20, 2021, https://hbr.org/2021/07/how-our-class-background-affects-the-way-we -collaborate; A. G. Dittmann, N. M. Stephens, and S. S. Townsend, "Achieve- ment Is Not Class-Neutral: Working Together Benefits People from Working- Class Contexts," *Journal of Personality and Social Psychology* 119, no. 3 (2020): 517.

11. Dittmann, Stephens, and Townsend, "Research"; Dittmann, Stephens, and Townsend, "Achievement Is Not Class-Neutral," 517.

12. T. M. Amabile, "The Power of Small Wins," *Harvard Business Review*, May 2021.

13. "Women in the Workplace 2021," McKinsey & Company, September 27, 2021, https://www.mckinsey.com/featured-insights/diversity-and-inclusion /women-in-the-workplace.

14. J. Bersin, "The New Organization: Different by Design," Josh Bersin Company, last updated May 1, 2016, https://joshbersin.com/2016/03/the-new -organization-different-by-design/.

15. P. Cappelli and A. Tavis, "The Performance Management Revolution," *Harvard Business Review*, October 2016. For more information about GE's shift from a formal annual review structure to a less regimented system for more frequent feedback, see M. Nisen, "How Millennials Forced GE to Scrap Perfor- mance Reviews," *Atlantic*, August 18, 2015, https://www.theatlantic.com/politics

/archive/2015/08/how-millennials-forced-ge-to-scrap-performance-reviews
/432585/.

16. T. Chamorro-Premuzic and J. Bersin, "4 Ways to Create a Learning Culture on Your Team," hbr.org, July 12, 2018, https://hbr.org/2018/07/4-ways-to-create -a-learning-culture-on-your-team.

17. S. Harrison, "Curiosity Adapted the Cat: The Role of Trait Curiosity in Newcomer Adaptation," *Journal of Applied Psychology* 96, no. 1 (2011): 211–220.

18. P. Zak, "Measurement Myopia," Drucker Institute, July 4, 2013, https:// www.drucker.institute/thedx/measurement-myopia/.

19. D. A. Garvin, "How Google Sold Its Engineers on Management," *Harvard Business Review*, December 2013.

20. A. Kohn, "Why Incentive Plans Cannot Work," *Harvard Business Review*, September–October 1993.

## Chapter 7

1. B. C. Skaggs and C. C. Snow, "The Strategic Signaling of Capabilities by Service Firms in Different Information Asymmetry Environments," *Strategic Organization* 2, no. 3 (2004): 271–291; K. S. Coulter and R. A. Coulter, "The Effects of Industry Knowledge on the Development of Trust in Service Relationships," *International Journal of Research in Marketing* 20, no. 1 (2003): 31–43.

2. Thus arises "information asymmetry": providers know but buyers do not know the extent and nature of the efforts a provider intends to make in completing a service transaction. P. R. Nayyar and P. L. Templeton, "Seller Beware: Information Asymmetry and the Choice of Generic Competitive Strategies for Service Businesses," in *Advances in Services Marketing and Management*, ed. T. A. Swartz, D. E. Bowen, and S. W. Brown (Greenwich, CT: JAI, 1994), 95–126.

3. This figure, and the ensuing discussion, builds on the "alignment pyramid" from J. W. Lorsch and T. J. Tierney, *Aligning the Stars: How to Succeed When Professionals Drive Results* (Boston: Harvard Business Review Press, 2002).

4. H. K. Gardner and R. Sine, "Supporting a Sector Strategy at Orrick," case study HLS20-55 (Harvard Law School, November 2020).

5. Research interview with authors; quote approved for publication.

6. From a published summary of the relationship between Sodexo and Van Oord, comprising some seventy ships: J. de Jong et al., *Partnering for Success: The Van Oord/Sodexo Story, 2010–2019* (Sodexo, n.d.), https://tracks.sodexonet .com/files/live/sites/com-nl/files/2_PDF/2020/Case%20studies/Partnering_for _success.pdf.

## Chapter 8

1. For a readable summary, see H. Villarica, "Professional Help: 5 Ways You're Influenced by Numbers Psychology," *Atlantic*, February 3, 2012. For more research,

see C. K. Hsee, Y. Rottenstreich, and Z. Xiao, "When Is More Better? On the Relationship between Magnitude and Subjective Value," *Current Directions in Psychological Science* 14, no. 5 (2005): 234–237; and J. Ye, K. Zhou, and R. Chen, "Numerical or Verbal Information: The Effect of Comparative Information in Social Comparison on Prosocial Behavior," *Journal of Business Research* 124 (2021): 198–211.

2. Between 2011 and 2020, for example, the company's net worth increased from $19.3 billion to approximately $40 billion. See "USAA History," Zippia, accessed April 26, 2022, https://www.zippia.com/usaa-careers-42941/history/; and USAA, *Demonstrating Resilience When We Need It Most: 2020 Annual Report for Members*, accessed May 11, 2022, https://content.usaa.com/mcontent /static_assets/Media/report-to-members-2020.pdf?cacheid=2827458110.

3. T. M. Amabile and S. J. Kramer, "The Power of Small Wins," *Harvard Business Review*, May 2011; T. M. Amabile and S. Kramer, *The Progress Principle: Using Small Wins to Ignite Joy, Engagement, and Creativity at Work* (Boston: Harvard Business Review Press, 2011).

4. This means that a significant launch has doubled the number of committed people: If prelaunch commitment levels were normally distributed (68 percent of people within one standard deviation of the mean), only 16 percent of people were highly committed. The launch should have shifted the bell curve to the right, mostly by moving people from the middle to highly committed, and perhaps a smaller number from highly skeptical to average.

5. This example is distilled from R. Gordon and H. K. Gardner, "OneLegal: A Legal Department's Quest for Collaboration," case study 20-60 (Harvard Law School, November 23, 2020).

6. M. Arena et al., "How to Catalyze Innovation in Your Organization," *MIT Sloan Management Review* 58, no. 4 (2017): 38–48. See also D. Brownlee, "The Five Levels of Organizational Influence: Where Are You?," *Forbes*, March 21, 2019, https://www.forbes.com/sites/danabrownlee/2019/03/21/the-five-levels-of -organizational-influence-where-are-you/?sh=29f461a217b8.

7. Social science shows that developing a shared vocabulary helps improve coordination, resulting in better outcomes ranging from patient care to race equity to strategy implementation. See, for example, "Equity in the Center Expands beyond ProInspire," accessed April 26, 2022, https://www.proinspire .org/equity-in-the-center-expands-beyond-proinspire/; and M. Stühlinger, J. B. Schmutz, and G. Grote, "I Hear You, but Do I Understand? The Relationship of a Shared Professional Language with Quality of Care and Job Satisfaction," *Frontiers in Psychology* 10 (2019): 1310.

8. A word of caution: although many managers try to stoke "healthy competition," research shows that collaboration is undermined by incentive systems that pit teams against each other for financial rewards. Note that the example we use is a short-term contest for a symbolic prize. See De Matteo et al.; and K. Murayama and A. J. Elliot, "The Competition-Performance Relation: A Meta-analytic Review and Test of the Opposing Processes Model of Competition and Performance," *Psychological Bulletin* 138 (2012): 1035–1070.

9. Ørsted internal research, shared with the authors and approved for publication.

## Chapter 9

1. M. Sheetz, "How NASA Is Evolving through Partnerships with Private Space Companies," CNBC, November 30, 2019, https://www.cnbc.com/2019/11/30/how -nasa-is-evolving-through-partnerships-with-private-space-companies.html.

2. A. Cameron, "JPL: Autonomously Alone on the Red Planet," *Inside Unmanned Systems*, June/July 2021; Abe Peck, "Inside Ingenuity with Aero-Vironment," *Inside Unmanned Systems*, June/July 2021, 49.

3. C. To, G. J. Kilduff, and B. L. Rosikiewicz, "When Interpersonal Competition Helps and When It Harms: An Integration via Challenge and Threat," *Academy of Management Annals* 14, no. 2 (2020): 908–934.

4. Research interview with authors; permission granted for publication.

5. Research interview with authors; permission granted for publication.

6. For a colorful discussion of the amygdala hijack, see K. Holland, "Amygdala Hijack: When Emotion Takes Over," Healthline, updated September 17, 2021, https://www.healthline.com/health/stress/amygdala-hijack.

7. See M. Mortensen and H. K. Gardner, "WFH Is Corroding Our Trust in Each Other," *Harvard Business Review*, February 10, 2021.

8. N. Watenpaugh, "How to Create a Successful Partnership with Your Competition," *Forbes*, July 29, 2019, https://www.forbes.com/sites/forbessan franciscocouncil/2019/07/29/how-to-create-a-successful-partnership-with-your -competition.

9. For the company's explanation of the initiative, see "Open Innovation and Partnerships," Iberdrola, accessed April 26, 2022, https://www.iberdrola.com /innovation/open-innovation-partnerships.

10. B. Gyori et al., *Purpose-Driven Leadership for the 21st Century: Transitioning to a Purpose-First Economy through the New Business Logic* (Leaders on Purpose, 2020): 48.

11. S. Buffier, V. Deshors, and C. Enriquez, "7 Best Practices for Building a Successful Alliance Management Function in the Biopharma Industry," white paper, Inova, 2021, https://go.inova.io/7-best-practices-for-building-a-successful -alliance-management-function-in-the-biopharma-industry.

12. G. Hamel, "Collaborate with Your Competitors and Win," *Harvard Business Review*, January–February 1989, https://hbr.org/1989/01/collaborate -with-your-competitors-and-win.

13. Deloitte, *Strategic Alliances in Life Sciences* (Zurich: Deloitte, 2014), https://www2.deloitte.com/ch/en/pages/life-sciences-and-healthcare/articles /strategic-alliances-in-life-science.html.

## Chapter 10

1. We borrow the phrase from a Deloitte report: J. Bourke, "The Diversity and Inclusion Revolution: Eight Powerful Truths," *Deloitte Review*, no. 22,

January 22, 2018, https://www2.deloitte.com/us/en/insights/deloitte-review/issue
-22/diversity-and-inclusion-at-work-eight-powerful-truths.html.

2. R. Lorenzo et al., "How Diverse Leadership Teams Boost Innovation,"
Boston Consulting Group, January 23, 2018, https://www.bcg.com/en-us
/publications/2018/how-diverse-leadership-teams-boost-innovation; T. Kochan
et al., "The Effects of Diversity on Business Performance: Report of the Diversity Research Network," *Human Resource Management* 42, no. 1 (2003):
3–21; "Why Diversity and Inclusion Matter: Financial Performance," Catalyst,
June 24, 2020, https://www.catalyst.org/research/why-diversity-and-inclusion
-matter/.

3. V. Hunt, D. Layton, and S. Prince, "Why Diversity Matters," McKinsey &
Company, January 1, 2015, https://www.mckinsey.com/~/media/mckinsey/business
%20functions/people%20and%20organizational%20performance/our%20
insights/why%20diversity%20matters/diversity%20matters.pdf.

4. E. Mannix and M. A. Neale, "What Differences Make a Difference? The
Promise and Reality of Diverse Teams in Organizations," *Psychological Science
in the Public Interest* 6, no. 2 (2005): 31–55.

5. G. A. Maxwell, S. Blair, and M. McDougall, "Edging towards Managing
Diversity in Practice," *Employee Relations* 23, no. 5 (2001): 468–482.

6. C. N. Collier and T. Raney, "Understanding Sexism and Sexual Harass-
ment in Politics: A Comparison of Westminster Parliaments in Australia, the
United Kingdom, and Canada," *Social Politics: International Studies in Gender,
State and Society* 25, no. 3 (2018): 432–455.

7. Lest you assume that this phenomenon is attributable to certain kinds
of interrupters—for example, members of Parliament who are less educated or
less accomplished—consider this: the same pattern happens in the US Supreme
Court, which ostensibly has some of the best-educated and best-equipped
justices in the country. And it doesn't stop there: the same behavior appears in
German Parliament proceedings. See M. Och, "Manterrupting in the German
Bundestag: Gendered Opposition to Female Members of Parliament?," *Politics
and Gender* 16, no. 2 (2020): 388–408; and Collier and Raney, "Understanding
Sexism."

8. In these analyses, we used hours billed (and paid by the client) as a proxy
for value. The results are more extreme when we use amount billed, because
women's hourly rates were lower on average. We did not find a gender discrep-
ancy in the number of billed versus paid hours. In other words, the clients did
not, on average, perceive less value in the women's contributions.

9. See Chapter 12 for more on the downsides of this kind of work pattern.

10. Research interview with authors; permission granted for publication. For
further information, see S. Turban, L. Freeman, and B. Waber, "A Study Used
Sensors to Show That Men and Women Are Treated Differently at Work," hbr
.org, October 23, 2017, https://hbsp.harvard.edu/product/H03YZL-PDF-ENG.

11. We especially thank Cai Kjaer and Lawrence Lock Lee at SWOOP (https://
www.swoopanalytics.com/).

12. Remember, though, that compared with the demographics of the popula-
tion, women were disproportionally relying on other women.

13. D. B. Wilkins and G. M. Gulati, "Why Are There So Few Black Lawyers in Corporate Law Firms? An Institutional Analysis," *California Law Review* 84, no. 3 (1996): 493–625. See also S. K. Johnson, D. R. Hekman, and E. T. Chan, "If There's Only One Woman in Your Candidate Pool, There's Statistically No Chance She'll Be Hired," hbr.org, April 26, 2016, https://hbr.org/2016/04/if-theres-only-one-woman-in-your-candidate-pool-theres-statistically-no-chance-shell-be-hired.

14. L. M. Roberts, A. J. Mayo, and D. A. Thomas, *Race, Work, and Leadership: New Perspectives on the Black Experience* (Boston: Harvard Business Review Press, 2019); P. F. Hewlin, "Wearing the Cloak: Antecedents and Consequences of Creating Facades of Conformity," *Journal of Applied Psychology* 94, no. 3 (2009): 727.

15. R. J. Ely and D. A. Thomas, "Getting Serious about Diversity," *Harvard Business Review*, November–December 2020, 114–122.

16. See S. Chilazi and I. Bohnet, "How to Best Use Data to Meet Your DE&I Goals," hbr.org, December 3, 2020, https://hbr.org/2020/12/how-to-best-use-data-to-meet-your-dei-goals.

17. L. Romansky et al., "How to Measure Inclusion in the Workplace," hbr.org, May 27, 2021, https://hbr.org/2021/05/how-to-measure-inclusion-in-the-workplace.

18. R. J. Ely and D. A. Thomas, "Cultural Diversity at Work: The Effects of Diversity Perspectives on Work Group Processes and Outcomes," *Administrative Science Quarterly* 46, no. 2 (2001): 229–273.

19. J. Y. J. Cheng and B. Groysberg, "Research: What Inclusive Companies Have in Common," hbr.org, June 18, 2021, https://hbr.org/2021/06/research-what-inclusive-companies-have-in-common.

20. Cheng and Groysberg, "Research."

21. A. Ignatius, "Cultivate Curiosity," *Harvard Business Review*, September–October 2018, https://hbr.org/2018/09/cultivate-curiosity.

22. Accenture, *Enabling Change: Getting to Equal 2020: Disability Inclusion* (Accenture Research, 2020), https://www.accenture.com/_acnmedia/PDF-142/Accenture-Enabling-Change-Getting-Equal-2020-Disability-Inclusion-Report.pdf.

23. J. Steimle, "Reverse Mentoring: Investing in Tomorrow's Business Strategy," *Forbes*, May 5, 2015, https://www.forbes.com/sites/joshsteimle/2015/05/05/reverse-mentoring-investing-in-tomorrows-business-strategy/?sh=80cc0da67695.

24. Bank of New York Mellon Corporation and Jennifer Brown Consulting, *Reversing the Generation Equation: Mentoring in the New Age of Work* (Jersey City, NJ: Bank of New York Mellon Corporation and Jennifer Brown Consulting, 2018), https://information.pershing.com/rs/651-GHF-471/images/per-reversing-the-generation-equation.pdf. For more information about successful reverse mentoring, see J. Jordan and M. Sorell, "Why Reverse Mentoring Works and How to Do It Right," hbr.org, October 3, 2019, https://hbr.org/2019/10/why-reverse-mentoring-works-and-how-to-do-it-right.

25. Jordan and Sorell, "Why Reverse Mentoring Works."

## Chapter 11

1. In 2019, for example, Raytheon ranked second in US foreign military sales: $15.1 billion out of a total of $68 billion. See *Defense Daily's* summary: V. Machi, "Lockheed Martin, Raytheon Lead in FY '19 Foreign Military Sales," *Defense Daily*, October 7, 2019, https://www.defensedaily.com/lockheed-raytheon -lead-fy-19-foreign-military-sales/business-financial/. Per Statista, this represented about half of all of Raytheon's revenue for that year. See "Revenue of Arms Company Raytheon from 1999 to 2019," Statista, February 2020, https://www.statista.com/statistics/262815/revenue-of-raytheon/.

2. H. K. Gardner, "Coming through When It Matters Most," *Harvard Business Review*, April 2012, 82–91.

3. B. M. Staw, L. E. Sandelands, and J. E. Dutton, "Threat Rigidity Effects in Organizational Behavior: A Multilevel Analysis," *Administrative Science Quarterly* 26, no. 4 (1981): 501–524.

4. I. L. Janis, *Victims of Groupthink: A Psychological Study of Foreign-Policy Decisions and Fiascoes* (Boston: Houghton Mifflin, 1972).

5. J. S. Mueller, S. Melwani, and J. A. Goncalo, "The Bias against Creativity: Why People Desire but Reject Creative Ideas," *Psychological Science* 23, no. 1 (2012): 13–17.

6. See H. K. Gardner and R. S. Peterson, "Executives and Boards, Avoid These Missteps in a Crisis," hbr.org, April 24, 2020, https://hbr.org/2020/04 /executives-and-boards-avoid-these-missteps-in-a-crisis.

7. See, for example, E. Carlson, "How Loneliness Could Be Changing Your Brain and Your Body," CNET, June 15, 2020, https://www.cnet.com/news/how -loneliness-could-be-changing-your-brain-and-body/; and C. N. Hadley and M. Mortensen, "Are Your Team Members Lonely?," *MIT Sloan Management Review*, December 8, 2020.

8. M. W. McCall Jr. and M. M. Lombardo, *Off the Track: Why and How Successful Executives Get Derailed*, Technical Report No. 21 (Greensboro, NC: Center for Creative Leadership, 1983).

9. See, for example, two McKinsey & Company white papers on related topics: K. Ellingrud et al., "Diverse Employees Are Struggling the Most during COVID-19—Here's How Companies Can Respond," McKinsey & Company, November 17, 2020, https://www.mckinsey.com/featured-insights/diversity-and -inclusion/diverse-employees-are-struggling-the-most-during-covid-19-heres-how -companies-can-respond; and S. Coury et al., "Women in the Workplace 2020," McKinsey & Company, 2020, https://www.mckinsey.com/featured-insights /diversity-and-inclusion/women-in-the-workplace.

10. See A. C. Edmondson, *The Fearless Organization: Creating Psychological Safety in the Workplace for Learning, Innovation, and Growth* (Hoboken, NJ: Wiley, 2018).

11. N. van Dam and E. van der Helm, "The Organizational Cost of Insufficient Sleep," McKinsey & Company, February 1, 2016, https://www.mckinsey .com/business-functions/organization/our-insights/the-organizational-cost-of -insufficient-sleep.

12. N. Goel et al., "Neurocognitive Consequences of Sleep Deprivation," *Seminars in Neurology* 29, no. 4 (2009): 320–339; I. M. Verweij et al., "Sleep Deprivation Leads to a Loss of Functional Connectivity in Frontal Brain Regions," *BMC Neuroscience* 15, no. 1 (2014): 1–10.

13. E. van der Helm, N. Gujar, and M. P. Walker, "Sleep Deprivation Impairs the Accurate Recognition of Human Emotions," *Sleep* 33, no. 3 (2010): 335–342; E. L. McGlinchey et al., "The Effect of Sleep Deprivation on Vocal Expression of Emotion in Adolescents and Adults," *Sleep* 34, no. 9 (2011): 1233–1241.

14. W. H. Macey and B. Schneider, "The Meaning of Employee Engagement," *Industrial and Organizational Psychology* 1, no. 1 (2008): 3–30; S. A. Stumpf, W. G. Tymon Jr., and N. H. van Dam, "Felt and Behavioral Engagement in Workgroups of Professionals," *Journal of Vocational Behavior* 83, no. 3 (2013): 255–264.

15. See Edmondson, *Fearless Organization*.

16. H. K. Gardner, *Smart Collaboration for In-House Legal Teams* (Surrey, UK: Globe Law and Business, 2020), 94.

17. Gardner, *Smart Collaboration*, 95.

18. "State Department Announces Resolution of Raytheon Company Arms Export Control Enforcement," media note, Office of the Spokesperson, April 30, 2013, https://2009-2017.state.gov/r/pa/prs/ps/2013/04/208655.htm. Half of the fine would be suspended if those funds were directed by the company into compliance-related measures.

## Chapter 12

1. BioNext engaged a team from Gardner & Collaborators to conduct a process similar to the one outlined in Chapter 3, but the trigger this time was overcommitment rather than a lack of collaboration. Both are failures to engage in smarter collaboration.

2. This chapter draws, in part, on M. Mortensen and H. K. Gardner, "The Overcommitted Organization," *Harvard Business Review*, September–October 2017; and H. K. Gardner and M. Mortensen, "How to Stay Focused If You're Assigned to Multiple Projects at Once," hbr.org, November 7, 2017, https://hbr.org/2017/11/how-to-stay-focused-if-youre-assigned-to-multiple-projects-at-once.

3. B. M. Staw, "Knee-Deep in the Big Muddy: A Study of Escalating Commitment to a Chosen Course of Action," *Organizational Behavior and Human Performance* 16, no. 1 (1976): 27–44; C. Heath, "Escalation and De-escalation of Commitment in Response to Sunk Costs: The Role of Budgeting in Mental Accounting," *Organizational Behavior and Human Decision Processes* 62, no. 1 (1995): 38–54; M. H. Bazerman, T. Giuliano, and A. Appelman, "Escalation of Commitment in Individual and Group Decision Making," *Organizational Behavior and Human Performance* 33, no. 2 (1984): 141–152.

4. Behavioral economics explains this problem as the "sunk cost fallacy," which is akin to social psychology's term *escalation of commitment*. See, for

example, H.R. Arkes and C. Blumer, "The Psychology of Sunk Cost," *Organizational Behavior and Human Decision Processes* 35, no. 1 (1985): 124–140; and B. M. Staw, "The Escalation of Commitment: An Update and Appraisal," in *Organizational Decision Making*, ed. Zur Shapira (New York: Cambridge University Press, 1996), 191–215.

5. Research communications with author.

6. S. Leroy, "Why Is It So Hard to Do My Work? The Challenge of Attention Residue When Switching between Work Tasks," *Organizational Behavior and Human Decision Processes* 109, no. 2 (2009): 168–181.

7. Stated briefly, the project office stepped in to inject rigor into the reprioritization and reallocate resources aligned to the priorities—steps that the team managers weren't taking on their own.

## Chapter 13

1. See the press release describing OceanX's founding: "Announcing the Launch of OceanX, a Bold New Mission to Explore the Ocean and Bring It Back to the World," Cision, June 5, 2018, https://www.prnewswire.com/news-releases /announcing-the-launch-of-oceanx-a-bold-new-mission-to-explore-the-ocean-and -bring-it-back-to-the-world-300659943.html.

2. From the OceanX website, accessed April 29, 2022, https://oceanx.org/.

3. The Dalios had been using a converted fifty-six-meter research vessel, which was replaced by the eighty-seven-meter *OceanXplorer*.

4. Footage from one episode in the *Blue Planet II* series was repurposed for use in an exhibit at the American Museum of Natural History in New York. The exhibit was deliberately aimed at younger audiences, whom the Dalios see as the oceans' best hope for the future.

5. See "Bridgewater Capital Founder Ray Dalio on Ocean Philanthropy," Lux, 2021, https://www.lux-mag.com/oceanx-ray-mark-dalio/.

6. A group of thirty-nine such low-lying island nations have joined together in an alliance to advocate for their cause. See N. Lasky, "Rising Sea Level Threatens Very Existence of Island Nations," World War Zero, August 14, 2021, https:// worldwarzero.com/magazine/2021/08/rising-sea-level-threatens-existence-of -island-nations/.

7. Kristina Hill made her comments in an interview with the *Guardian*, summarized in L. Rosenberg, "By 2025, Some of the Florida Keys Could Be Submerged Due to Rising Sea Levels," Green Matters, October 22, 2021, https://www.greenmatters.com/p/florida-keys-underwater.

8. Southeast Florida Regional Climate Change Compact, homepage, accessed April 29, 2022, https://southeastfloridaclimatecompact.org/. Monroe County has a particular stake in fighting the effects of climate change. It is, according to the landing page of its website, the "home of the fabulous Florida Keys." Monroe County, Florida, official website, accessed April 29, 2022, https://www .monroecounty-fl.gov/.

9. "12th Annual Southeast Florida Regional Climate Leadership Summit," Southeast Florida Regional Climate Change Compact, October 13, 2020,

https://southeastfloridaclimatecompact.org/event/virtual-climate-leadership
-summit-2020/.

10. *Nature-Based Coastal Defenses in Southeast Florida* (Big Pine Key, FL: Nature Conservancy, n.d.), https://www.nature.org/media/florida/natural
-defenses-in-southeast-florida.pdf.

11. *Nature-Based Coastal Defenses.*

12. *Nature-Based Coastal Defenses.*

13. "Coral Restoration," Florida Reef Resilience Program, accessed April 29, 2022, http://frrp.org/coral-restoration/.

14. "Social Equity," Southeast Florida Regional Climate Change Compact, accessed April 29, 2022, https://southeastfloridaclimatecompact.org/recommend
ation-category/eq/.

15. S. J. Leischow and B. Milstein, "Systems Thinking and Modeling for Public Health Practice," *American Journal of Public Health* 96, no. 3 (2006): 403–405.

16. "This Is Broad," Broad Institute, accessed April 29, 2022, https://www
.broadinstitute.org/about-us.

17. "Partner Institutions and Community," Broad Institute, accessed April 29, 2022, https://www.broadinstitute.org/about-us/partner-institutions-and
-community#top.

18. "Building Communities," Broad Institute, accessed April 29, 2022, https://www.broadinstitute.org/building-communities/global-alliance-for
-genomics-and-health.

19. See Topcoder, "Advancing DNA Sequencing with Marek.Cygan ‖ Topcoder Member Case Study," YouTube, April 5, 2019, video, 2:32, https://www.youtube
.com/watch?v=n4rO-xqPgsU.

20. "Harvard and the Broad Institute Deliver Precision Medicine Advancement through Crowdsourcing," Topcoder, June 11, 2016, https://www.topcoder.com
/blog/harvard-and-the-broad-institute-deliver-precision-medicine-advancement
-through-crowdsourcing/.

21. "This Is Broad."

22. L. B. Jeppesen and K. R. Lakhani, "Marginality and Problem-Solving Effectiveness in Broadcast Search," *Organization Science* 21, no. 5 (2010): 1016–1033.

23. Rare Genomes Project homepage, accessed April 29, 2022, https://
raregenomes.org/.

24. P. Satterstrom and M. Kerrissey, "The Changing Nature of Social Hierarchy and Voice," *Academy of Management Proceedings* 2017, no. 1 (2017): 17385.

25. "Meet the Martians," Mars Exploration Program, NASA Science, accessed April 29, 2022, https://mars.nasa.gov/people/?category=helicopter.

26. "Taking Flight on Another World," Mars Helicopter Tech Demo, NASA Science, accessed April 29, 2022, https://mars.nasa.gov/technology/helicopter
/#Overview.

27. M. Rees, "Nasa's Webb Telescope Is a Joy. But It's the Private Ventures That Push at Limits," *Guardian*, January 2, 2022, https://www.theguardian.com

/commentisfree/2022/jan/02/james-webb-space-telescope-thrilling-future-for
-mankind.

28. H. J. Wilson and P. R. Daugherty, "Collaborative Intelligence: Humans
and AI Are Joining Forces," *Harvard Business Review*, July–August 2018,
https://hbr.org/2018/07/collaborative-intelligence-humans-and-ai-are-joining
-forces.

# INDEX

# ABOUT THE AUTHORS

**HEIDI K. GARDNER** is the author of the best-selling book *Smart Collaboration: How Professionals and Their Firms Succeed by Breaking Down Silos*. A Distinguished Fellow at Harvard Law School, she was previously a professor at Harvard Business School and a consultant at McKinsey & Co. With Ivan Matviak, she co-founded the research and advisory firm Gardner & Collaborators.

Named by Thinkers 50 as a Next Generation Business Guru, Dr. Gardner is a sought-after advisor, keynote speaker, and facilitator for organizations across a wide range of industries globally. Altogether, she has authored (or coauthored) more than eighty books, chapters, case studies, and articles. Her research received the Academy of Management's prize for Outstanding Practical Implications for Management, and has been selected multiple times for *Harvard Business Review*'s "best of" collections. Her research has been featured in major media outlets around the globe.

Dr. Gardner has lived and worked on four continents. She was a Fulbright Fellow and started her career at Procter & Gamble. She earned her BA in Japanese from the University of Pennsylvania (Phi Beta Kappa, summa cum laude), a master's degree from the London School of Economics, and a second master's and PhD from London Business School.

**IVAN A. MATVIAK** has more than twenty-five years' experience transforming complex global businesses through disciplined strategy, product innovation, operations optimization, and cross-silo collaboration.

Currently, Ivan is an executive vice president at Clearwater Analytics, a publicly traded fintech company. He worked as a senior advisor to Boston Consulting Group and the private equity firm Warburg Pincus LLC. Ivan was previously an EVP at State Street Bank, serving as chairman and president of multiple fintech subsidiaries and Head of Americas for the bank's data and analytics business.

Earlier in his career Ivan worked in Edinburgh, Johannesburg, London, New York, and Paris at the Bank of Scotland, Bain & Company, Walt Disney Company, and Procter & Gamble. Over his career Ivan launched and led multiple global businesses in consumer products, technology and finance. Presently Ivan is a board member for Boston Partners in Education and Historic Newton.

Ivan has coauthored several publications on collaboration and professional service firm strategy. He co-founded Gardner & Co. and co-developed its suite of technology-based collaboration tools including the Smart Collaboration Accelerator.

Ivan holds an MA from the University of Pennsylvania, an MBA and master's in International Affairs from the Wharton Business School, and is a fellow at the Joseph H. Lauder Institute for International Studies.